WORKER'S COMPENSATION

A Field Guide For Employers

BY **ED PRIZ**

CO-AUTHOR SCOTT PRIZ

ISBN: 1439270597
ISBN-13: 9781439270592

Table of Contents

Workers' Compensation: A Field Guide for Employers & Others

Preface

Since my last book on Workers' Compensation (published in 2005), there have been some significant developments in the field. So in order to provide employers with an updated resource, this *Field Guide* has been developed. It builds on my earlier book, *The Ultimate Guide to Workers' Compensation Insurance*, just as that work built on my first book, *CompControl.*

Since 2005, the largest insurance company in the world, AIG, has been essentially nationalized. Other major insurers have seen their stock prices and financial ratings affected by the economic crisis that is now in full-tsunami mod. And some states have made significant adjustments to their Workers' Compensation insurance systems.

Additionally, my co-author (my son and business partner, Scott Priz) and I have had the benefit of working on a number of additional cases, some of which have revealed new and interesting things for employers to watch out for in the field of Workers' Compensation insurance. So this new book is more than just an update of my prior books on Workers' Compensation insurance. It also includes new information and new subjects that weren't covered in those earlier books.

For those who haven't read those earlier books, let me introduce myself. I've worked as a consultant on Workers' Compensation insurance costs since 1983. Before that, I was an insurance producer (that is to say, an insurance agent) handling commercial insurance, including Workers' Compensation. As a consultant, I've specialized in finding and correcting premium overcharges in Workers' Compensation insurance. And I've found a lot of them over the years—something in excess of $20 million dollars of over-charges, at this writing.

Six years ago, my son Scott joined me in my consulting practice, and in that time he's not only learned all of my techniques for un-covering Workers' Comp overcharges, he's found one or two new ones as well. So in this latest book, I wanted to make sure he was involved as co-author so readers can get the additional benefit of his experience in this specialized field.

Even though there have been significant changes over the past few years, some things haven't changed. We still find that employ-ers are often overcharged on Workers' Compensation insurance premiums. This results partly from the complexity of the rules that govern Workers' Comp premiums, and partly from the fact that employers are often at a disadvantage when disputing how premi-ums have been computed. Insurance company auditors and rating bureau employees can often cite arcane rules and regulations to justify higher premium charges—rules with which most business owners and managers just don't have much expertise. In that envi-ronment, it's very difficult for employers to know when the insur-ance people have gotten things right, and when they have gotten things wrong.

This book, like its predecessors, is meant to level that playing field. It's meant to help non-insurance industry people—the peo-ple who have to pay those Workers' Compensation premiums—understand better how premiums are supposed to be calculated, what can sometimes go wrong in the process, and how to correct mistakes that often occur.

I often like to cite Ronald Reagan's suggestion, "Trust, but verify." President Reagan was using it in the context of dealing with the Soviet Union, but the maxim is worth remembering when dealing with insurance companies also. The problem is that, in order to verify, one needs to understand the ground rules that apply. That's where this book comes into play.

Employers need to understand that premium overcharges are far from uncommon, even with the assistance of good insurance agents and brokers. It's not the result of a conspiracy by the insurance industry. My experience has been that most insurance professionals are ethical and conscientious. But the system that governs Workers' Compensation insurance premiums is complicated, and the regulatory framework is fragmented and limited.

Insurance companies tend to be pretty vigilant about identifying and correcting any mistakes that cost them money—that is, serves to lower premiums. Insurers devote a fair amount of resources to uncover frauds by workers and employers that either drive up claims or improperly lower premiums. But the insurance industry just doesn't devote anything near the same effort to catching mistakes that increase premiums. And state insurance regulators just don't have the time and resources to do that either.

That's why I ended up working in this field, providing a private enterprise solution to that unmet need. Since 1983, I've made my living finding and correcting mistakes by the insurance industry that increase Workers' Compensation insurance premiums for employers. I've found over the years that overcharges happen to all kinds of employers, all over the country. I've found overcharges happening to small machine shops and to multi-state, Fortune 500- type employers. I've found overcharges hurting manufacturers, contractors, hospitals, and even an NFL team.

And it hasn't mattered much whether those employers were using a small insurance agency down the block, or a big national broker. The problem of overcharges is endemic.

So that's where this *Field Guide* is helpful. Our aim is to give employers of all types and sizes the ammunition they need to spot overcharges when they occur, and provide information about how such overcharges can be successfully reversed. We provide information about different types of insurance policies, different types of insurance companies, different types of agents and brokers, and the different ways your company might be overcharged. We also try to explain how employers can sort out fact from fiction when it comes to Workers' Compensation insurance and the way this necessary coverage is priced, sold, and serviced.

For most employers in the U.S., Workers' Compensation insurance is something of a necessary evil. It is often expensive for employers, but mandated by their state statutes. It can also be a source of great frustration, and occasionally even threaten to put an employer out of business. Our hope is that this *Field Guide* will help employers to make sure the system functions properly and insures their workplace exposures at a fair and proper cost, without nasty surprises and shocks.

One last note: we've tried hard to make sure the information in this new book is accurate and up-to-date as of 2010. However, changes can and do occur with some regularity in this field, so keep in mind that what might have been accurate in 2010 may have changed by 2011, or later. We'll try to post updates on our website, www.cutcomp.com, so you may want to check periodically there for the very latest information.

CHAPTER 1

THE BIG PICTURE

Workers' Compensation is, primarily, an obligation imposed upon employers by state statutes. It was a development of the early 20th Century, starting in 1911, when one state after another enacted legislation that crafted an historic compromise. The compromise established that the liability of an employer towards workers who were injured or made ill on the job was essentially no-fault, but in turn, provided some important limitations on those liabilities.

Prior to this, injured workers had to take legal action against their employers to receive compensation for their medical costs and lost wages. This created a system where workers found it difficult, costly, and time-consuming to get compensation for the costs of workplace injury and illness, while employers were exposed to un-predictable and potentially devastating liabilities under the tort system. The great compromise enacted by states tried to address both these shortcomings.

Some writers on the subject have suggested that the concept of Workers' Compensation may have originated with the code of Caribbean pirates: injured buccaneers would be compensated with shares of booty taken by their able-bodied comrades. As much as I enjoy the idea of a swashbuckling origin for the mundane subject of my life's work, Workers' Compensation in the U.S. mainly origi-nated from more prosaic roots. And as soon as those new state statues began to spring up, insurance companies stood ready to insure employers for those new liabilities. A fair premium charge would be required, understandably, but nonetheless Workman's Compensation insurance (as it was originally known) in short order grew to be a very large and important line of business for American insurers.

The idea is straightforward: an employer pays a certain premium to an insurance company, and in return, the insurance company takes responsibility for workers who are injured, sickened, or killed in the course of their employment. And in most states, insurance is essentially the only available method of handling the Workers' Compensation liabilities imposed by law, at least for all but the largest employers. There are some notable exceptions to this, which will be covered in detail later in this *Field Guide*. But for most employers, Workers' Compensation is synonymous with insurance.

And for most employers, Workers' Compensation is also synonymous with significant expense and aggravation.

Employers small and large, from California to New Hampshire, find Workers' Compensation insurance to be one of their greatest costs of doing business. Employers nowadays don't find that the promised benefits of the Workers' Compensation compromise always materialize for them, as costs seem high and sometimes very unpredictable.

Workers similarly often find the compromise to be chaffing, especially as some reforms to the benefits statutes have been felt to be unfair to workers with serious injuries. As with many compromises, both parties often feel that they're getting the short end of the stick. But in the Workers' Compensation field, there is another important player: insurance companies.

Insurers essentially stand in the middle between employers and workers. Insurers accept legal responsibility to pay the claims of insured employers, in return for premiums. So in theory, employers trade off unpredictable claims costs for more predictable premium charges. The problem, as I have observed it over the years, is that those premium charges themselves can be unpredictable, sometimes unfair, and often excessive even under the terms of the rules of the insurers themselves.

Today, every state establishes fairly comprehensive and specific benefits for workers who are injured or made ill (or worse, maimed or killed) in the course of employment. Benefits include medical expenses, death benefits, compensation for lost wages, and vocational rehabilitation. And almost every state requires employers to satisfy these statutory liabilities by means of certain specific mechanisms. Employers generally must have in place acceptable Workers' Compensation insurance, or be approved by the state as a qualified self-insurer. States can and do impose penalties on employers that fail to meet these statutory requirements.

In the U.S., most Workers' Compensation obligations are imposed upon employers by the various states, but there are also some specific federal statutes that can apply to certain kinds of work. There are federal Workers' Compensation statutes that apply to longshore workers and harbor workers, and to workers on defense installations, among others. But most employers deal primarily with regulations created by the various state jurisdictions, including Washington D.C. and Puerto Rico. This causes the Workers' Compensation system in the U.S. to have a kind of patchwork quality. There are great similarities among all these state regulatory systems, but also significant differences that employers need to keep in mind.

Monopoly State Funds

A few U.S. jurisdictions do not allow private insurance for Workers' Compensation. In these jurisdictions, you must obtain coverage from a government-administered fund. These jurisdictions are often called "Monopoly States" for Workers' Compensation, and currently are: North Dakota, Ohio, Puerto Rico, the U.S. Virgin Islands, Washington (state, not D.C.), and Wyoming.

Different States, Different Approaches

In most U.S. states or territories, employers can meet their Workers' Compensation obligations by buying an insurance policy from an approved insurer. However, a few jurisdictions require employers to get this coverage only via a government-operated fund. So in these states, you can't buy an insurance policy that covers your Workers' Comp obligations for those jurisdictions. If you do business in one of these jurisdictions, you have to obtain coverage from the particular fund for that jurisdiction.

A few other states operate state Workers' Compensation funds that compete with private insurance companies.

Option States

In these jurisdictions, employers can choose between private insurance and a government-operated fund: California, Colorado, Idaho, Maryland, Montana, New York, Oklahoma, Oregon, Pennsylvania, and Utah.

In recent years, a couple of notable states that used to operate state funds have discontinued this practice. Nevada had utilized a monopoly state fund until just a few years ago, but has now shifted over to a private insurance system. So too has West Virginia, with that state's former monopoly fund morphing into an insurance company that now competes with other insurance companies. Similarly, Arizona and Michigan, in recent years, have changed their former state funds (that used to compete with private insurers) into mutual insurance companies.

In theory, an employer also has the option of qualifying as an approved self-insurer, but the requirements for this vary significantly from one state to another. Generally, this option is only available for larger employers, and even when allowed, it applies only to the employers operations in that particular state. So if an employer is qualified as a self-insurer in Illinois, say, if the employer operates in other states (e.g., Missouri or Indiana) the employer would either have to separately be approved by those states for self-insurance or purchase insurance for those states' exposures.

A third option available in many states is group self-insurance. In this option, an organization is approved to offer Workers' Compensation self-insurance to members within a state. In such group trusts, the individual participants do not have to meet the state's requirements for self-insurance, as the group has already met state requirements. However, there can be problems with such group self-insurance programs. Many smaller employers have entered into such arrangements without fully appreciating the unique liabilities inherent in them. In recent years, some group self-insurance trusts have failed in a number of states. In these cases, premiums collected have proven to be inadequate to pay the claims of the groups. And in those situations, member have discovered one important drawback to these group self-insurance trusts: individual members can be held liable for their pro-rata share of the claims costs of the entire group, even years after the employer may have left the group.

The State-By-State Mosaic

One problem with trying to deal with the "big picture" in Workers' Compensation insurance is that, once you start to examine it, you see that it's kind of like a mosaic. Since Workers' Compensation is primarily governed by individual states and territories, there is no single unified set of rules for employers. There are many similarities across the various states and territories of the U.S., but also very significant differences. Benefits, coverage, and rules governing premiums can change significantly once you cross a state border. If your business expands to a new state, you may find yourself governed by rules that are very different from the rules to which you've been accustomed.

The closest thing that the Workers' Compensation insurance system has to a uniform rulemaking body is the National Council on Compensation Insurance (or NCCI, as it is commonly known).

This organization creates the insurance policies used in most states, writes the rules that govern premium computation in those states, and gathers data from insurance companies used to develop Workers' Compensation insurance rates.

NCCI isn't used by all states—but it is used by most states that allow private insurance. Even among states that do use the NCCI system, there can be some significant differences in rules from one state to the next. When it comes to Workers' Compensation insurance, the devil is very much in the details.

In the following state-by-state notes, we describe a number of them as being "an NCCI state." This means that the NCCI manuals have been approved in that state, and thus the NCCI classification system and the NCCI formula for experience modification factors are used there. However, keep in mind that there can still be some significant differences between one NCCI state and another. We explain that in more detail later in the book.

In the following state-by-state notes, we've tried to note any unique features of that state's requirements for employers regarding Workers' Compensation insurance, including the minimum size of employers required to purchase insurance and any noteworthy rules that affect Workers' Compensation premiums there. We've also tried to note the rating bureau used in the state (independent bureau or NCCI) and the state agencies responsible for handling disputed Workers' Compensation claims and the state agencies responsible for handling insurance disputes (almost always separate agencies). Claims disputes are usually handled by a different agency than the agency that handles disputes over insurance coverage or insurance premiums.

ALABAMA

This is an NCCI state. Employers must either purchase a Workers' Compensation insurance policy from an approved insurance company or be approved to self-insure (realistic only for larger employers). Employers with **more than four employees** (full- or part-time) **must** have Workers' Compensation insurance (or obtain coverage via another approved method). In Alabama, employers can meet their Workers' Compensation obligations by either purchasing insurance, becoming a member of a group self-insurance trust, or by being approved as a self-insurer. One other option is to obtain coverage by means of a PEO (Professional Employer Organization)—otherwise known as employee leasing. This option is covered in more detail later in this book.

If a company is incorporated or an LLC, the officers and members are counted as employees. And all employers with more than four employees are required by law to carry workers' compensation insurance. However, an officer may elect to be exempt by filing a form WC15 (Officer Exemption Notice) to the Department of Industrial Relations, Workers' Compensation Division and the employer's insurance carrier.

At the end of any calendar year, an exempted corporate officer may revoke the exemption by filing written notice thereof with the Department of Insurance and the employer's insurance carrier. If the corporate officer elects to be exempt from coverage, the election shall not relieve the corporation from continuing coverage for all other eligible employees who may have been covered prior to the election or who may subsequently be employed.

Sole proprietors and partners are excluded from Workers' Compensation requirements unless they choose to file an election to accept the provisions of the Alabama Workers' Compensation Law. To accept the provisions of the Workers' Compensation law and be covered by a Workers' Compensation policy, sole proprietors/partners must complete a form WC14 Part I and file it with the Department of Insurance. Once filed, the WC14 stays in effect until it is withdrawn by the sole proprietor/partner by filing Part II of the WC14.

In Alabama, Workers' Compensation claims matters are handled by:
DEPARTMENT OF INDUSTRIAL RELATIONS
WORKERS' COMPENSATION DIVISION
649 MONROE STREET
MONTGOMERY, AL 36131
(334) 242-2868
1-800-528-5166
Website: http://dir.alabama.gov/wc

This body also regulates individual self-insurers and group self-insurance programs.

Disputes about Workers' Compensation insurance (including premiums) are the province of the Alabama Department of Insurance. Contact information for this body is as follows.

Regular U.S. Mail Address:
Alabama Department of Insurance
PO Box 303351
Montgomery, AL 36130-3351

Overnight Address:
Alabama Department of Insurance
201 Monroe Street
Suite 1700
Montgomery, AL 36104
Phone Numbers, Fax Numbers, & Email Addresses
Phone: (334) 269-3550; Fax: (334) 241-4192;
Email: Insdept@insurance.alabama.gov; Website: www.aldoi.org

ALASKA
This is an NCCI state. Alaska requires all employers with more than one employee to obtain Workers' Compensation insurance (unless the employer is approved as a self-insurer. Alaska does not allow group self-insurance pools. Some exceptions to the requirement

to obtain insurance are that sole proprietors don't have to insure themselves (but they would have to provide insurance if they have an employee); general partners in a partnership also don't have to insure themselves, but again have to get insurance if they have employees; executive officers in a nonprofit corporation aren't required to get insurance for themselves; and the same is true for members in a member-managed limited liability company, part-time baby-sitters, cleaning persons (non-commercial), harvest help and similar part-time/transient help, sports officials for amateur events, contract entertainers, commercial fishers, taxicab drivers whose compensation is by contractual arrangement, a participant in the Alaska temporary assistance program, and professional hockey team players and coaches if those persons are covered under a health care insurance plan. In addition, executive officers in a for-profit corporation may exempt themselves by filing an Executive Officer Waiver with the Alaska Department of Labor and Workers' Compensation.

Alaska still maintains a Second Injury Fund (at least at the time of this writing). Second Injury Funds provide reimbursement to insurers and self-insured employers for claims of workers where it can be documented that the workers had pre-existing conditions that contributed to the claim.

Alaska also maintains a separate Fishermen's Fund covers licensed commercial fishermen for injuries while fishing onshore or offshore.

In Alaska, claims matters are under the jurisdiction of:
The Alaska Department of Labor and Workforce Development, Division of Workers' Compensation
<u>Contact Information:</u>
PO Box 115512
Juneau, AK 99811
Phone: (907) 465-2790; Fax: (907) 465-2797
Website: http://labor.state.ak.us/wc/

Insurance disputes **(such as those over premium charges) would be under the jurisdiction of:**
The Alaska Division of Insurance **(part of the Department of Community and Economic Development)**

Contact Information:
9th Floor State Office Bldg.
333 Willoughby Avenue 99801
PO Box 110805 Juneau, AK 99811-0805
Phone: (907) 465-2515; Fax (907) 465-3422; TDD (907) 465-5437
Email: insurance@alaska.gov
Robert B. Atwood Building
550 W. 7th Avenue, Suite 1560
Anchorage, AK 99501-3567
Phone: (907) 269-7900; Fax (907) 269-7910; TDD (907) 465-5437
Email: insurance@alaska.gov Website: http://www.dced.state.ak.us/insurance/

ARIZONA

This is an NCCI state. **Employers must meet their Workers' Compensation obligations by purchasing insurance from a private insurance company or be authorized to self-insure. Arizona formerly maintained a competitive state fund, but as has happened in other states in recent years, what used to be the state fund has been transformed into a non-profit mutual insurance company that is no longer part of state government. This mutual insurer, SCF Arizona, currently writes about 70 percent of the Workers' Compensation insurance in Arizona, but has to compete with other insurance companies in the state.**

Arizona requires all employers with one or more employees to maintain valid Workers' Compensation insurance (or be approved for self-insurance).

The state agency with jurisdiction over claims, and over employer compliance with Workers' Compensation insurance requirements, is the Industrial Commission of Arizona**.**

Industrial Commission Contact Information:
Phoenix Office:
800 W. Washington Street
Phoenix, AZ 85007
Phone: (602) 542-4653
Website: http://www.ica.state.az.us/index.html
Tucson Office:
2675 E. Broadway
Tucson, AZ 85716

Insurance disputes (such as disputes over proper Workers' Compensation insurance premiums) are the jurisdiction of:
Arizona Department of Insurance
2910 N. 44th St. Suite 210
Phoenix, AZ 85018-7269
Phone: Phoenix Area: (602) 364-4457; Statewide: (877) 660-0964
Website: http://www.id.state.az.us/

An interesting aspect of Arizona Workers' Compensation statutes is that an independent contractor that performs work different from the client's normal work and who is not supervised by clients during execution of that work are considered true independent contractors, not employees of the client for purposes of Workers' Compensation. This is a significant difference between Arizona rules and those of many other states. The Arizona statute also requires there be a written agreement signed by both parties.

ARKANSAS
This is an NCCI **state. In Arkansas, employers must meet their Workers' Compensation obligations by either purchasing an insurance policy from an approved insurer or by being approved to be self-insured. Most employers with three or more employees must**

purchase Workers' Compensation insurance. For employers in the building trades, the threshold is two or more employees. Where a subcontractor is used, the threshold is one employee. Sole proprietors or partners who devote full time to the business are covered unless they elect to be exempted. (This is different from many other states, where sole proprietors and partners are not automatically eligible, and must elect to be covered.) Executive officers of a corporation may choose to exclude themselves (but must cover employees).

In Arkansas, if a sole proprietor or partner elects not to obtain Workers' Compensation coverage for him or herself, a primary contractor that utilizes their services is not liable for the Workers' Compensation liability (this is different from the way this issue is treated in many other states). However, a prime contractor is still liable for uninsured workers of a subcontractor if those workers are not the sole proprietor or a partner.

The government agency in Arkansas that has jurisdiction over claims and over enforcing employer compliance with Workers'

Compensation coverage is:
The Arkansas Workers' Compensation Commission
324 Spring Street
PO Box 950
Little Rock, AR 72203-0950
Phone (501) 682-3930 or (800) 622-4472
Website: http://www.awcc.state.ar.us/

The government agency in Arkansas that has jurisdiction over disputes regarding Workers' Compensation insurance premiums between employers and their insurance company is:
Arkansas Insurance Department
1200 West Third Street
Little Rock, AR 72201
Phone: (501) 371-2600 or (800) 282-9134; Fax: (501) 371-2618
Website: http://insurance.arkansas.gov/

CALIFORNIA

This is not an NCCI state. Instead, California, which is the largest single state market for Workers' Compensation insurance, has its own separate rating bureau, the Workers' Compensation Insurance Rating Bureau of California, or WCIRB. This means that all the rules and regulations that govern Workers' Compensation insurance classifications, premium computation, and experience rating are set out in manuals from WCIRB, not NCCI. And thus, the details about what kinds of work are assigned to which particular classification codes can be different in California. Additionally, some of the fine details regarding how experience modification factors are calculated are different. Contact information for the WCIRB is:

Workers' Compensation Insurance Rating Bureau of California
525 Market Street, Suite 800
San Francisco, CA 94105-2767
Phone: (888) CA-WCIRB (888-229-2472); Fax: (415)778-7272
E-mail: customerservice@wcirbonline.org; Website: https://wcirbonline.org

Employers in California can choose between private insurance companies or the state-administered Workers' Compensation fund, known as the State Compensation Insurance Fund, or SCIF. An employer in California can also elect to self-insure for Workers' Compensation, but this is typically feasible only for larger employers.

In California, as soon as an employer has a single employee, the employer must have Workers' Compensation coverage (either from an approved insurance company, SCIF, or be approved for self-insurance. A roofing company is required to have Workers' Compensation insurance even if it has no employees. And unlike many other states, a real estate broker is required to cover its agents, even if they are independent contractors.

In California, unlike most other states, one can go back only one year into the past when correcting an error in classification code on Workers' Compensation policies. Most states will generally allow an employer to go back at least as far as three years prior to the current policy.

Workers' Compensation claims are the jurisdiction of:
The California Department of Industrial Relations, Division of Workers' Compensation
(The DWC maintains a number of offices throughout California. Their headquarters address is:
1515 Clay Street
17th floor
Oakland, CA 94612-140
Phone: (510) 286-7100
Website: http://www.dir.ca.gov/dwc/

Workers' Compensation insurance (including disputes over premiums) is the jurisdiction of the California Department of Insurance.

Contact information for the division that handles premium disputes is:
California Department of Insurance
Consumer Services Division
300 South Spring Street, South Tower
Los Angeles, CA 90013
Phone: (800) 927-HELP (4357) or 213-897-8921
(Calling from within CA) (Outside CA)
Website: http://www.insurance.ca.gov

COLORADO

This is an **NCCI** state. Colorado is another state that used to have a competitive state fund, but that state fund is now Pinnacol Assurance, a public/private hybrid that looks like an insurance company but still is connected to the state. In Colorado, all public and private employers with one or more full or part-time workers must either purchase Workers' Compensation insurance or be approved for self-insurance (which, as in most states, is only feasible for larger employers). There are exceptions to this, including:

- Certain casual maintenance or repair work performed for a business for under $2,000 per calendar year
- Certain domestic work, maintenance or repair work for a private homeowner that is not done full time
- Licensed real estate agents and brokers working on commission
- Independent contractors who perform specific for-hire transportation jobs
- Drivers under a lease agreement with a common or contract carrier
- Any person who volunteers time or services for a ski area operator
- Persons who provide host home services as part of residential services and supports
- Federal employees (covered under federal laws) and railroad employees (covered under federal laws)

A corporate officer of a corporation or a member of a limited liability company may elect to reject the requirement to carry workers' compensation insurance. The election to reject coverage is completed by providing written notice on a form available from the Division of Workers' Compensation (part of the Department of Labor & Employment).

A corporate officer is defined as the chairperson of the board, president, vice-president, secretary, or treasurer who is an owner of at least ten percent of the stock of the corporation and who controls, supervises, or manages the business affairs of the corporation. A member is defined as an owner of at least ten percent of the membership interest of the limited liability company at all times and who controls, supervises, or manages the business affairs of the limited liability company.

Independent contractors are not considered to be employees of a business that hires them, as long as the independent contractor is free from the business' control and direction over how the service is performed, and the individual is customarily engaged in an independent business related to the service being performed. These are the two key principles of independent contracting in Colorado. A written contract may be helpful in proving independent contractor status. *However, the actual facts of the work relationship are the most important evidence.*

Sole proprietors and partners in a business are not required to carry Workers' Compensation insurance on themselves (but would be required to carry insurance as soon as they have any employees).

The state agency responsible for resolving disputes over Workers' Compensation insurance premiums is:

Colorado Division of Insurance
1560 Broadway, Suite 850
Denver, CO 80202
Phone: (303) 894-7499
Website: http://www.dora.state.co.us/Insurance/

The state agency responsible for enforcing employer compliance with WC obligations and with resolving disputes involving benefits is:

Colorado Division of Workers' Compensation
633 17th Street, Suite 400
Denver, CO 80202-3626
Phone: (303) 318-8700
Website: http://www.coworkforce.com/dwc/

CONNECTICUT

This is an NCCI state. All employers are required either to carry insurance from an approved insurer or to be approved as a self-insurer by the CT Workers' Compensation Commission.

Workers' Compensation Commission
Capitol Place
21 Oak Street
Hartford, CT 06106
Phone: (860) 493-1500; Fax: (860) 247-1361
Website: http://wcc.state.ct.us/

Disputes over Workers' Compensation insurance premiums are handled by the Connecticut Insurance Department.
Connecticut Insurance Department
153 Market St.
Hartford, CT 06103
Mailing Address:
PO Box 816
Hartford, CT 06142-0816
Phone: (860) 297-3800 or (800) 203-3447; Fax: (860) 566-7410
Website: http://www.ct.gov/cid

DELAWARE

This is **not** an NCCI state. Instead, Delaware and Pennsylvania share their own unique rating bureau that administers a separate and distinct set of manual rules, including a separate classification system. This classification system does not match up on a one to one basis with the NCCI classification system, or with classification systems used in other states. The classification system used in Delaware and Pennsylvania uses a three-digit code system, rather than the four-digit code system used everywhere else.

Unlike every other state, Delaware **does not allow** the **premium portion of overtime to be deducted** from payroll that is used to compute Workers' Compensation insurance premiums.

In Delaware, every employer with one or more workers must obtain valid insurance or be licensed as a self-insurer.

The **Rating Bureau** for Delaware is:

Delaware Compensation Rating Bureau, Inc.

United Plaza Building - Suite 1500

30 South 17th Street

Philadelphia, PA 19103-4007

Phone: (302) 654-1435

Website: http://www.dcrb.com

Insurance, including Workers' Compensation, is regulated by:

Commissioner of Insurance of the State of Delaware

Main Office

841 Silver Lake Blvd.

Dover, DE 19904

Phone: (302) 674-7300

Wilmington Office

Carvel State Office Building, 5th Floor

820 N. French St.

Wilmington, DE 19801

Website: http://www.delawareinsurance.gov

Workers' Compensation benefits and self-insurance authorization handled by:

The Office of Workers' Compensation

4425 North Market Street

Wilmington, DE 19802

Phone: (302) 761-8200 (New Castle) or (302) 422-1134 (Kent & Sussex)

Website: http://www.delawareworks.com/industrialaffairs/services/ workerscomp.shtml

DISTRICT OF COLUMBIA (WASHINGTON, D.C.)

This is an NCCI jurisdiction, with Workers' Compensation coverage written by private insurance companies. The District does not maintain any state fund for Workers' Compensation. The District does operate a special/second injury fund, which reimburses insurers and self-insured employers for claims arising from pre-existing disabilities or for claims against uninsured employers.

Claims and Benefits matters are overseen by:
DC Department of Employment Services
Labor Standards Bureau
Office of Workers' Compensation
64 New York Avenue, NE, 2nd floor
Washington, DC 20002
Phone: (202) 671-1000
Website: http://does.dc.gov

Insurance (including Workers' Compensation insurance) is regulated by:
Department of Insurance, Securities and Banking
810 First Street, NE, Suite 701
Washington, DC 20002
Phone: (202) 727-8000
Website: http://disr.washingtondc.gov

FLORIDA

This is also an NCCI state. Insurance, including Workers' Compensation insurance, is regulated by:

Florida Department of Financial Services, Division of Workers' Compensation
200 East Gaines St.
Tallahassee, FL 32399-4220
Phone: (850) 413-1601
Email: **Workers.CompService@fldfs.com; Website: http://www. myfloridacfo.com/WC/**

In Florida, there are some unique rules and regulations of which employers should be aware. In general, Florida treats employers in construction-related industries differently than non-construction employers.

Employers in **construction** industries must get Workers' Compensation coverage when they employ one or more part-time or full-time workers. Sole proprietors, partners, and corporate officers are considered employees. However, corporate officers of members of an LLC who meet certain statutory requirements (mainly owning at least 10 percent of the company) can obtain an exemption from the state for Workers' Compensation. This means that if someone hires an exempt worker as an independent contractor or subcontractor, they do not acquire Workers' Compensation liability for that exempted worker.

For employers in **non-construction** industries, Workers' Compensation coverage must be obtained when they have four or more part-time or full-time workers. Corporate officers are considered employees unless they elect to be exempt. Sole proprietors and partners of non-construction companies are not considered employees unless they elect to be employees.

For employers in the **agricultural** industry, Workers' Compensation coverage is required once they have five or more regular employees and/or twelve or more seasonal employees, who work for more than thirty days.

In Florida, employers can meet their statutory obligations for Workers' Compensation by buying a Workers' Compensation insurance policy from an approved insurance company, by being approved to self-insure, or by joining a commercial self-insurance fund that has been approved.

If an employer can't get an insurance company willing to underwrite Workers' Compensation coverage through the voluntary market, there is an assigned risk program administered by the Florida Workers' Compensation Joint Underwriting Association

(FWCJUA) that can be reached at (941) 378-7400 or through their website at www.fwcjua.com.

Another way to obtain valid Workers' Compensation coverage in Florida is through an employee leasing arrangement, often known as a PEO arrangement. This book addresses PEO arrangements in detail in subsequent chapters.

Florida also has a unique rule regarding changes of classification. In Florida, unlike most other states, if an insurance company moves all payroll from one classification to another classification that were both originally on the policy, this is considered to be the same as adding a new classification. Under NCCI rules in almost every state, an insurance company is prohibited from adding a more expensive classification late in the policy term. In Florida, this is expanded so that moving all payroll from one class to another class is considered the same as adding a new classification. If all payroll is moved from a less expensive class to a more expensive class late in the policy term, it is prohibited unless there has been a change in the insured's operation or the insured has deceived the insurer about the nature of the insured's operations.

GEORGIA

This is an NCCI state. Workers' Compensation is provided by private insurance companies. Companies employing three or more workers either full- or part-time must obtain valid Workers' Compensation coverage. Although corporate officers of an LLC can exempt themselves, such exempt workers do not reduce the threshold number at which coverage is required. Partners or sole proprietors are not considered employees in Georgia. Employers must either obtain valid Workers' Compensation insurance or qualify as a self-insurer with the state.

Georgia is the one other state that, although an NCCI state, has a special state rule like Florida in that if an insurance company moves all payroll from one classification to another classification, leaving no payroll in the original class, it is considered a change in classification.

Insurance, including Workers' Compensation insurance, is regulated by:
Office of Insurance and Safety Fire Commissioner
Two Martin Luther King, Jr. Drive
West Tower, Suite 704
Atlanta, GA 30334
Phone: (404) 656-2070 or (800) 656-2298; Fax: (404) 657-8542
Website: http://www.gainsurance.org

The state agency that adjudicates disputed Workers' Compensation claims, and also is in charge of authorizing employers for self-insurance, is:
The State Board of Workers' Compensation
270 Peachtree Street, NW
Atlanta, GA 30303-1299
Phone: (404) 656-2048
Website: http://sbwc.georgia.gov/

HAWAII

This is an NCCI state. Workers' Compensation insurance is provided by private insurance companies that follow NCCI manual rules and regulations. Every employer with one or more employees is obligated to meet the state's Workers; Compensation requirements by obtaining insurance or becoming approved as a self-insurer. The state also allows group self-insurance for Workers' Compensation. Real estate agents and brokers who earn only commissions, however, are exempted from the requirement to be covered.

Insurance, including Workers' Compensation insurance, is regulated by:
Insurance Division
Department of Commerce and Consumer Affairs

Mailing Address
Insurance Division
PO Box 3614
Honolulu, HI 96811

Office Location
Insurance Division
King Kalakaua Building
335 Merchant Street, Rm. 213
Honolulu, HI 96813
Phone: (808) 586-2790 or (808) 586-2799; Fax: (808) 586-2806
Website: http://hawaii.gov/dcca

The state agency that adjudicates Workers' Compensation claims and approves employers to be self-insured:
Hawaii Department of Labor and Industrial Relations
830 Punchbowl St., Room 209
Honolulu, HI 96813
Phone: (808) 586-9166
Website: http://hawaii.gov/labor

Mailing address:
PO Box 3769
Honolulu, HI 96812-3769

IDAHO

This is an NCCI state. Idaho is also one of the states that operate a state fund for Workers' Compensation coverage that competes with private insurance companies.

Some family members working for a sole proprietorship in Idaho are exempt from Workers" Compensation coverage. To determine specific details, one should check with the Idaho Industrial Commission, which has jurisdiction over Workers' Compensation claims. Owners, corporate officers, and board members are exempt from Workers" Compensation coverage in Idaho, but may elect to be covered.

Employers with one or more full-time, part-time, seasonal, or occasional employees are required to maintain a workers' compensation policy unless specifically exempt from the law. Workers' Compensation is required to be in place when the first employee is hired. Employment that **may be exempt** from required coverage includes:

- Household domestic service
- Employment of family members living in the employer's household (applies only to sole proprietorships)
- Employment in a business that is not carried on by the employer for the sake of pecuniary gain (an example would be a homeowner who is building his own home and who hires workers to assist in building the home)
- The owner of a sole proprietorship, working members of a partnership or limited liability company, or individuals who are corporate officers and who own at least 10 percent of the stock and who are directors (if the corporation has directors)
- Employment covered under Federal Workers' Compensation Laws
- Pilots of agricultural spraying or dusting planes (under certain conditions)
- Associate real estate brokers and real estate salespersons when paid solely by commission
- Volunteer ski patrollers
- Officials of athletic contests in secondary schools only (grades 7 to 12 inclusive or any combination thereof)
- Casual employment or work which occurs occasionally or at irregular times and which is not related to the type of business conducted by the employer
- Employment as an outworker (defined as a person to whom materials are furnished to be treated in any way at a location not under the control of the employer—an example would be a worker who receives mass mailing

materials from the employer and assembles them at home)

- Certain family member employees of a sole proprietor employer who do not reside in the same household as the employer may file an election for exemption with the Industrial Commission

Workers' Compensation insurance is regulated by:
Idaho Department of Insurance
700 West State Street
PO Box 83720
Boise, ID 83720-0043
Phone: (208) 334-4250; Fax: (208) 334-4398
Website: http://www.doi.state.id.us

The state agency that adjudicates Workers' Compensation claims and authorizes employers to be self-insured within the state:
Idaho Industrial Commission
PO Box 83720
Boise, ID 83720-0041
Phone: (208) 334-6000
Fax: (208) 334-2321
Website: http://www.iic.idaho.gov

ILLINOIS

This is an NCCI state. Illinois does not have a state fund, so employers must obtain insurance, qualify for self-insurance, or become members of a group self-insurance trust. Although there is no state fund, there is an Assigned Risk program so that employers who cannot get an insurance company to underwrite their workers' compensation insurance voluntarily can still get coverage. The Assigned Risk program in Illinois is operated by the NCCI, but employers can access the assigned risk program through licensed insurance agents in Illinois. The Assigned Risk program in Illinois is a pooling mechanism administered by NCCI, but the actual Workers' Compensation insurance policy that an employer obtains will be from a private insurance company. (The pooling mechanism operates behind the scenes.) Assigned Risk coverage in Illinois is usually much more expensive than coverage through the voluntary market, so employers are encouraged to try to find coverage through the voluntary market.

In Illinois, essentially every employer with any employees must either get a valid Workers' Compensation insurance policy, be approved as a qualified self-insurer in Illinois, or be a member of a valid group Workers' Compensation trust. Some reference works mistakenly state that Illinois requires Workers' Compensation insurance only for employers in "extra-hazardous" kinds of employment. This is technically true, but the statute defines extra-hazardous so broadly that it covers virtually all kinds of employment in the state.

The Illinois Workers' Compensation Act exempts real estate brokers, broker-salespersons, and salespersons who work solely on commission. Sole proprietors, partners, and members of an LLC are not required to cover themselves, but may elect to do so. However, once an insurance policy is purchased, sole proprietors, partners, LLC members, and corporate officers are automatically covered unless they specifically exempt themselves on an individual basis. And thanks to recent court decisions, such exemptions must be made in writing, on an individual basis, and on two separate forms (one to exclude the individual from the policy another to exclude them from the Workers Comp Act itself.

Illinois has a couple of unique statutory features that can benefit employers. The first is a statute that requires insurance companies to refund overcharges that occur under Workers' Compensation insurance policies due to errors in classification, an experience modifier, or any other kind of rating program. This law became effective in 1984, so it is theoretically possible for an employer to obtain a refund for overcharges as far back as 1984, if it can be documented (and if the insurance company is still in business).

The second unique statutory feature in Illinois applies only to renewal policies. It prohibits insurance companies from making any change on a renewal policy that increases premiums by 30 percent or more unless the insurer provides a sixty-day notice to the policyholder. (This applies only if there has been no change in the insured's operations, however.)

Workers' Compensation insurance is regulated by:
Illinois Department of Insurance
 320 W. Washington Street
Springfield, IL 62767-0001
Phone: (217) 782-4515; Fax: 217/558-2083 (Consumer Complaints)
Website: http://www.insurance.illinois.gov/

Workers' Compensation claims are adjudicated, and employer's requests to be approved as a self-insurer are regulated, by:
Illinois Workers' Compensation Commission
100 W. Randolph
Chicago, IL 60601
Phone: (312) 814-6611
Website: http://www.iwcc.il.gov/

INDIANA

This is not technically an NCCI state, although many people (even those in the insurance business) think that it is. Indiana maintains its own independent Workers' Compensation rating bureau, the Indiana Compensation Rating Bureau, or ICRB. The ICRB uses NCCI for ratemaking and uses the NCCI classification system, but does not always follow NCCI classification interpretations. For some classifications, the ICRB interpretation can differ significantly from the NCCI interpretation. For specific and detailed classification information in Indiana, it's wise to consult the ICRB directly.

ICRB
5920 Castleway West Drive or PO Box 50400
Indianapolis, IN 46250
Phone: (317) 842-2800; Fax: (317) 842-3717
Website: http://www.icrb.net/

In Indiana, essentially all employments are covered by the Workers' Compensation Act, so employers with any workers, full- or part-time, need to either purchase valid Workers Compensation insurance or be approved as a qualified self-insurer. Indiana exempts "casual labor" from the Workers' Compensation Act, but the burden of proof is on the employer to show that the work meets the statutory definition of "casual." Sole proprietors, partners, and members of an LLC are exempt, but may elect to cover themselves.

Indiana also allows independent contractors working in the construction trades to exempt themselves from Workers Compensation requirements by filing for a Certificate of Exemption from the Indiana Workers Compensation Board. Such a certificate means that the independent contractor has chosen to be exempt from Workers Compensation benefits, and thus any company that uses their services would not acquire Workers Compensation liability from the use of such workers. However, this exemption is not available to independent contractors who are a corporation, except as a Limited Liability Corporation.

Owner/operators of trucks are exempt, as are real estate professionals who are paid based on sales volume, are licensed, and who have a written agreement specifying they are not employees for tax purposes. There are other exemptions to the Indiana act as well for municipal police and fire employees, federal and railroad workers, and some other specific categories.

Insurance, including Workers Compensation insurance, regulated by:
Indiana Department of Insurance
311 West Washington Street, Suite 300,

Indianapolis, IN, 46204
Phone: (317) 232-2395
Website: http://www.in.gov/idoi

Workers Compensation claims and self-insurance approval for employers are the responsibility of:
Workers' Compensation Board of Indiana
402 West Washington Street Room W-196
Indianapolis, IN 46204
Phone: (800) 824-COMP
Website: http://www.in.gov/wcb/

IOWA

This is an NCCI state. Iowa has no state fund to compete with private insurance companies. Most employers are required to either purchase valid workers' compensation insurance or be approved as a self-insurer in the state. Limited exemptions apply when employment is in the home, involves relatives, or is casual. Sole proprietors, partners, and members of an LLC are exempt, but may elect to be covered.

Insurance, including Workers Compensation insurance, is regulated by:
Iowa Insurance Division Phone: Des Moines Area: (515) 281-5705
330 Maple St. Toll Free (within Iowa): (877) 955-1212 Des Moines, IA 50319-0065 Fax: (515) 281-3059 Website: http://www.iid.state.ia.us/

Workers Compensation claims and approval for employers to be self-insured are handled by:
Division of Workers' Compensation Phone: (515) 281-5387 or (800) JOB-IOWA
1000 East Grand Avenue
Des Moines, IA 50319-0209 Website: http://www.iowaworkforce.org/wc

KANSAS

This is an NCCI state, with private insurance companies who write Workers Compensation insurance following NCCI manual rules and regulations. Most employers need to purchase a Workers Compensation insurance policy from an approved insurer, be approved to self-insure, or become a member of a group self-insurance pool. All employers (except agricultural) are subject to the Workers' Compensation Act, except those whose total annual payroll is less than $20,000.00 Real estate professionals who are primarily paid based on sales are exempt, as are owner/operators in the trucking field.

Insurance, including Workers Compensation insurance, is regulated by:
Kansas Insurance Department Phone: (785) 296-3071 or (800) 432-2484 (in Kansas only)
420 SW 9th Street Fax: (785) 296-2283
Topeka, KS 66612 Website: http://www.ksinsurance.org

Workers Compensation claims and approval for an employer to self-insure are handled by:
Kansas Department of Labor Phone: (785) 296-2996
Division of Workers' Compensation
800 SW Jackson, Suite 600 Website: http://www.dol.ks.gov/wc/html/wc_ALL.html
Topeka, KS 66612-1227

KENTUCKY

Kentucky is also an NCCI state, which means that Workers Compensation insurance by private insurance companies follows the manual rules and regulations of the NCCI. Every employer with one or more workers must have Workers Compensation insurance, be approved to be self-insured, or be a member of an approved group self-insurance pool. Sole proprietors and partners are not required to cover themselves, but may elect to cover themselves. Members of an LLC also are not required to cover themselves, as long as they participate in the profit or loss of the LLC. Corporate officers are covered, but may elect to exempt themselves. The other statutory exceptions to the Workers Compensation requirement are:

(1) Domestic servants working in a private home of an employer who has less than two employees each regularly employed forty or more hours a week in domestic servant employment.

(2) Any person employed by a homeowner to do residential maintenance, remodeling or repair lasting no more than twenty consecutive workdays.

(3) Individuals performing services for aid or nourishment only from religious or charitable organizations.

(4) Employees protected by federal law including railroad and maritime workers.

(5) Persons employed in agriculture (farm laborers).

(6) Any person who would otherwise be covered but who elects not to be covered in accordance with administrative regulations.

(7) Any person participating as a driver or passenger in a voluntary vanpool or carpool program while that person is on the way to or from his place of employment.

(8) Members of an established religious sect with a conscientious objection to receiving benefits of any public or private insurance.

One interesting aspect of Kentucky Workers Compensation insurance is that the Assigned Risk program in this state is not more expensive than coverage through the voluntary market, which is different than in many other states.

Insurance, including Workers Compensation insurance, is regulated by:
Kentucky Department of Insurance Phone: (502) 564-3630
215 W. Main St.
Frankfort, Kentucky 40601 Website: http://doi.ppr.ky.gov/kentucky

Workers Compensation claims and approval for employers to be self-insured are governed by:

Kentucky Labor Cabinet Phone: (502) 564-5550 ext. 4532

Division of Workers' Claims Fax: (502) 564-9533

657 Chamberlin Avenue

Frankfort, KY 40601 Website: http://www.labor.ky.gov/workersclaims/

LOUISIANA

Louisiana is also an NCCI state, so private insurance companies that write Workers Compensation insurance must follow NCCI manual rules and regulations. All employers in Louisiana are required to either purchase valid Workers Compensation insurance, be approved to self-insure, or join a group self-insurance pool. The assigned risk plan in Louisiana is a separate Louisiana Workers Compensation Corporation, which operates as a non-profit insurance company and not a state fund. Coverage from LWCC is sold through insurance agents in Louisiana. Sole proprietors, partners, corporate officers, and members of LLCs are not required to cover themselves, as long as they own at least 10 percent of the company. Domestic workers and farm workers are also exempted, as are musicians performing under a performance contract.

Louisiana Workers Compensation Corporation Phone: (225) 924-7788

2237 South Acadian Thruway

Baton Rouge, LA 70808 Website: http://www.lwcc.com

Insurance, including Workers Compensation insurance, is regulated by:

Louisiana Department of Insurance Phone: (225) 342-5900 or (225) 342-0895

1702 N. 3rd Street or PO Box 94214

Baton Rouge, LA 70802 Website: http://www.ldi.louisiana.gov

Workers Compensation claims and approval for employers to be self-insured is handled by:
Louisiana Workforce Commission Phone: (225) 342-7555
1001 N. 23rd Street
Baton Rouge, LA 70802 Website: http://www.laworks.net

MAINE

Maine is also an NCCI state, so private insurance companies must follow NCCI manual rules and regulations. All employers must get Workers Compensation insurance, be approved as a self-insurer, or be a member of a group self-insurance pool. The exceptions to this requirement in Maine are for domestic service, certain agricultural workers, and casual laborers.

Insurance, including Workers Compensation insurance, is regulated by:
Maine Department of Professional and Financial Regulation
Bureau of Insurance Phone: (207) 624-8475
#34 State House Station
Augusta, ME 04333-0034 Website: http://www.maine.gov/pfr/insurance

This state agency also regulates and approves employers who wish to be self-insured.

The state agency that has authority to help resolve disputed claims and enforce employer compliance with Workers Compensation requirements is:
Maine Workers' Compensation Board Phone: (207) 287-3751
7 State House Station Fax: (207) 287-7198
Augusta, ME 04333-0027 Website: http://www.state.me.us/wcb

MARYLAND

Maryland is another NCCI state, which means that private insurance companies that write Workers Compensation insurance follow manual rules and regulations developed by NCCI. Employers are subject to the state's Workers Compensation statute as soon as they have one employee. Owner-operators of commercial trucks are not considered employees in Maryland. Real estate agents/brokers who work solely on commission also are not considered employees. Sole proprietors and partners are not subject to the statute, but may elect to bring themselves under the Act. Casual employees also are not considered subject to the statute.

Employers with one or more employees must obtain Workers Compensation insurance from an approved insurance company or from the Injured Workers' Insurance Fund (IWIF), which is the state's Workers Compensation fund that competes with insurance companies. Employers who meet the state's requirements can also be approved to self-insure Workers Compensation in Maryland.

Insurance, including Workers Compensation insurance, is regulated by:
Maryland Insurance Administrator
525 St. Paul Place
Baltimore, MD 21202-2272 Phone: (410) 468-2000 Website: www.mdinsurance.state.md.us

The state agency in charge of adjudicating Workers Compensation claims and for approving self-insurance for employers is:
Maryland Workers Compensation Commission
10 East Baltimore Street
Baltimore, MD 21202-1641 Phone: (410) 864-5100 Website: http://www.wcc.state.md.us/

The Maryland Workers Compensation Fund (which competes with private insurance companies):
Injured Workers Insurance Fund
8722 Loch Raven Boulevard Phone: (410) 494-2000 Website: http://www.iwif.com
Towson, MD 21286-2235

MASSACHUSETTS

This is **not** an NCCI state, but instead has its own independent rating bureau, the Workers Compensation Rating and Inspection Bureau (WCRIB) with manual rules and regulations that can differ from those of NCCI in some ways. Workers Compensation insurance is still written by private insurance companies, but they have to follow WCRIB manual rules rather than those of NCCI.

All private sector employers must purchase either Workers Compensation insurance or be approved to self-insure within the state as soon as they have one or more employees. Independent contractors are not eligible for benefits from companies that retain their services, but by statute independent contractor status if tightly defined. The work done by the independent contractor has to be different from the usual business of the employer, and the independent contractor has to be free of control by the employer. The independent contractor also has to be customarily engaged in an independently established trade or business. Sole proprietors, partners, and members of LLCs are not subject to the Workers Compensation Act, but may elect to bring themselves under the Act.

The Workers Compensation rating bureau for Massachusetts is:
Workers' Compensation Rating and Insurance Bureau
101 Arch Street Phone: (617) 439-9030
Boston, MA 02110 Website: www.wcribma.org

Insurance, including Workers Compensation insurance, is regulated by a division of the Office of Consumer Affairs and Business Regulation:
Division of Insurance
One South Station, 5th Floor Phone: (617) 521-7794 Consumer Line: (617) 521-7777
Boston, MA 02110 Fax: (617) 521-7575 Website: www.mass.gov/doi

The state agency that adjudicates Workers Compensation claims and approves employers to be self-insured is a division of the Executive Office of Labor and Workforce Development:
Department of Industrial Accidents
600 Washington Street; 7th Floor Phone: (617) 727-4900
Boston, MA 02111
Website: http://www.mass.gov/?pageID=elwdhomepage&L=1&L0=Home&sid=Elwd

MICHIGAN

Michigan is another state that is **not** part of the NCCI system. Michigan maintains its own separate Workers Compensation rating bureau, the Compensation Advisory Organization of Michigan (CAOM). But, there is an important distinction that applies in Michigan—CAOM doesn't really mandate that insurance companies follow its manual rules and regulations. Insurance companies are free to file their own manuals of rules with Michigan regulators if they wish, so CAOM's manual rules are only compulsory for assigned risk coverage, which CAOM administers through the Michigan Workers' Compensation Placement Facility.

Employers with three or more employees (or one employee who works more than thirty-five hours a week) are subject to the requirement of having Workers Compensation insurance or being approved to be a self-insurer within Michigan. Group self-insurance is also allowed in Michigan for approved group plans.

An interesting point about Michigan is that it is one of only a few states that do not integrate with NCCI for experience rating. Thus, an employer that operates in Michigan and also in other states would have a separate and stand-alone Michigan experience modification factor and then a distinct and separate experience modifier for other states.

The state agency that is responsible for adjudicating Workers Compensation claims and for approving employers to be self-

insured within Michigan is part of the Department of Energy, Labor, and Economic Growth:
Workers' Compensation Agency Mailing address: Workers' Compensation Agency,
 7150 Harris Drive, 1st Floor, B-Wing, PO Box 30016
Dimondale, MI 48821 Lansing, MI 48909
Phone: (888) 396-5041 Website: http://www.michigan.gov/wca

The Michigan Workers Compensation Rating Bureau is:
Compensation Advisory Organization of Michigan Phone: (734) 462-9600
17197 N. Laurel Park Drive, Suite 311 Website: http://www.caom.com
Livonia, MI 48152

Insurance, including Workers Compensation insurance, is regulated by a department of the Department of Energy, Labor, and Economic Growth:
Office of Financial and Insurance Regulation
PO Box 30220 Phone: (517) 373-0220
Lansing, MI 48909 Website: http://www.michigan.gov/dleg

MINNESOTA

This is **not** an NCCI state. Instead, Minnesota has the Minnesota Workers' Compensation Insurers Association, or MWCIA. The MWCIA develops the manual rules and regulations that govern how insurance companies calculate Workers Compensation insurance premiums in the state. MWCIA also calculates experience modification factors for use in Minnesota Workers Compensation policies. Unlike Michigan, however, Minnesota integrates modifier data with NCCI when an employer operates in multiple states, so the Minnesota modifier is not a stand-alone modifier. If an employer operates in Minnesota and also in NCCI states, the data will be combined to produce a single modifier used both in Minnesota and in the other states.

In Minnesota, every employer with employees is required to carry Workers Compensation insurance or to be approved as a self-insurer within Minnesota. Sole proprietors, partners, members of LLCs, and executive officers of a closely held corporation that own at least 25 percent of the corporation are exempt from the requirement to be insured or to self-insure—as long as they don't have any employees who aren't partners, members of the LLC, or exempt executive officers. But such exempted business owners can elect to cover themselves. Family farms also are exempt, with some limitations. And casual employees are excluded—"casual" meaning they aren't working in the usual trade or business of the employer and the work is one-time or infrequent.

Minnesota has a new law, effective in 2009, regarding independent contractors and Workers Compensation coverage. The new law requires individuals (not corporations, partnerships, or LLCs) who work as independent contractors in the building construction industry to obtain an exemption certification from the Department of Labor and Industry. This exempts these individuals from Workers Compensation coverage of those who hire them, along with exempting them from unemployment, wage and hour, and occupational and safety and health laws. Applicants for such an exemption must pass a nine-point test to qualify as an independent contractor.

The Minnesota Workers Compensation rating bureau is:
Minnesota Workers' Compensation Insurers Association, Inc
7701 France Avenue South, Suite 450 Phone: (952) 897-1737
Minneapolis, MN 55435-3200 Website: www.mwcia.org

The agency that has responsibility for mediating disputed Workers Compensation claims and for approving employers to be self-insured in Minnesota is:
Minnesota Department of Labor and Industry Phone: (651) 284-5005
443 Lafayette Road N. Website: http://www.doli.state.mn.us
St. Paul, MN 55155-4307

Insurance, including Workers Compensation insurance, is regulated by:

Minnesota Department of Commerce Phone: (651) 296-2488

Office of Insurance Commissioner Website: www.state.mn.us/portal/jsp/home.do?agency=Insurance

85 7th Place East, Suite 500

St. Paul, MN 55101

MISSISSIPPI

Mississippi is an NCCI state, meaning that insurance companies writing Workers Compensation insurance here are governed by NCCI manual rules and regulations. In Mississippi, employers that have five or more employees regularly employed are required to purchase Workers Compensation insurance or to be approved to self-insure in the state. (Employers with fewer than five employees may elect to purchase insurance, but are not required to do so.) Group self-insurance is also allowed in the state. Domestic and farm labor and employees of non-profit fraternal, charitable, religious, or cultural organizations are not covered under the law unless coverage is provided voluntarily by the employer. Independent contractors are ordinarily excluded from coverage although special protection is given to employees of subcontractors.

Insurance, including Workers Compensation insurance, is regulated by:

Mississippi Department of Insurance Phone: (601) 359-3569

1001 Woolfolk State Office Building Website: http://www.mid.state.ms.us/

501 N. West St.

Jackson, MS 39201

The state agency responsible for adjudicating Workers Compensation claims and for approving employers to self-insure in Mississippi is:

Mississippi Workers Compensation Commission

428 Lakeland Drive Phone: (866) 473-6922
Jackson, MS 39216 Website: http://www.mwcc.state.ms.us

MISSOURI

This is an NCCI state, with Workers Compensation insurance provided by private insurance companies that follow NCCI manual rules and regulations. In Missouri, employers with five or more employees must obtain valid Workers Compensation insurance, or be approved to self-insure within the state. But employers in the construction industry who erect, demolish, alter, or repair improvements must insure or be approved as self-insurers once they have one employee. Sole proprietors and partners are not required to insure themselves for Workers Compensation, but may elect to do so. Members of an LLC may elect to reject Workers Compensation coverage for themselves. Independent contractors or subcontractors are considered employees of those who retain their services (unless the I.C. or sub have their own coverage); however, the owner of premises being worked on by an independent contractor is not the employer for Workers Compensation purposes. A for-hire motor carrier is not considered an employer of a lessor or of a driver of a lessor.

Domestic servants, farm labor, and qualified real estate agents and direct sellers also are not considered employees for purposes of Workers Compensation insurance in Missouri.

Insurance, including Workers Compensation insurance, is regulated by:
Missouri Department of Insurance, Financial Institutions, and Professional Regulation,
301 West High Street, Room 530 mailing address: PO Box 690
Jefferson City, MO 65101 Jefferson City, MO 65102-0690
Phone: (573) 751-4126 Website: http://www.insurance.mo.gov

The state agency that adjudicates Workers Compensation claims and approves employers to self-insure in Missouri is:
Missouri Department of Labor and Industrial Relations
Division of Workers Compensation

421 East Dunklin Street Phone: (573) 751-9691
PO Box 504 Website: http://www.dolir.mo.gov/wc/
Jefferson City, MO 65102-0504

MONTANA

This is an NCCI state, so insurance companies that write Workers Compensation insurance follow NCCI manual rules and regulations. In Montana, every business that has an employee must either purchase valid Workers Compensation insurance or be approved to self-insure in the state. Group self-insurance is also allowed in Montana. In addition to private insurance, Montana operates a State Fund for Workers Compensation that competes with insurance companies. Independent contractors in Montana can obtain an exemption certification that exempts them from the state's Workers Compensation Act, and thus companies that hire such independent contractors would not acquire Workers Compensation liability for them.

Sole proprietors, partners, and members of an LLC are not required to insure themselves, but may elect to do so.

Insurance, including Workers Compensation insurance, is regulated by:
State Auditor's Office, Division of Insurance
840 Helena Ave. Phone: (406) 444-2040
Helena, MT 59601 Website: http://sao.mt.gov/insurance

The Montana State Fund contact information is:
Montana State Fund Phone: (406) 444-6500
PO Box 4759 Website: http://www.montanastatefund.com
Helena , MT 59604-4759

The Montana state agency that adjudicates Workers Compensation claims is:
Montana Workers Compensation Court mailing address: PO Box 537

1625 11ᵗʰ Ave. Helena, MT 59624-0537
Helena, MT
Phone: (406) 444-7794 Website: http://wcc.dli.mt.gov

NEBRASKA

Nebraska is another NCCI state, so private insurance companies here follow NCCI manual rules and regulations. Nebraska does not operate a State Fund, so employers must either purchase a valid Workers Compensation insurance policy, be approved to self-insure in the state, or join a group self-insurance program. Employers with one or more employees are subject to the Workers Compensation Act in Nebraska.

Sole proprietors, partners, and members of LLCs are not required to insure themselves, but may elect to do so. Executive officers of a corporation are considered employees unless they own 25 percent or more of the corporation. For a non-profit corporation, executive officers are considered employees unless they are paid less than $1,000 per year.

Unlike many other NCCI states, the Assigned Risk plan in Nebraska is not administered by NCCI, but instead is administered by Travelers Insurance Company through a program delegated by the Nebraska Department of Insurance.

Insurance, including Workers Compensation insurance, is regulated by:
Department of Insurance
941 O Street, Suite 400 Phone: (402) 471-2201
Lincoln, NE 68508-3639 Website: http://www.doi.ne.gov

The state agency that adjudicates Workers Compensation claims and approves employers to self-insure is:
Nebraska Workers Compensation Court
PO Box 98908 Phone: (402) 471-6468
Lincoln NE 68509-8908 Website: http://www.wcc.ne.gov

NEVADA

Nevada is now an NCCI state, with private insurance companies writing Workers Compensation insurance governed by NCCI manual rules and regulations. Until 1999, however, Nevada had been a state with a monopoly state fund. That state fund has been reconstituted as a competitive mutual insurance company.

Employers must obtain valid Workers Compensation insurance or be approved to self-insure as soon as they have one employee. Group self-insurance is also allowed. Sole proprietors are not required to insure themselves, unless they are contractors.

Nevada does not impose Workers Compensation liability on a company that uses an independent contractor, as long as that independent contractor is not in the same business, trade, or occupation, and the independent contractor operates an independent enterprise. But this important exception does not apply to contractors—they have liability for any uninsured subcontractors or independent contractors they hire.

Insurance, including Workers Compensation insurance, is regulated by a division of the Department of Business & Industry:
Division of Insurance Phone: (775) 687-4270
788 Fairview Dr., Suite 300 Website: http://www.doi.state.nv.us
Carson City, NV 89701

The Division of Insurance is also responsible for approving employers to self-insure for Workers Compensation.

Workers Compensation claims disputes are the responsibility of:
Department of Administration, Hearing Officer
1050 E. William Street, Suite 400
Carson City, NV

NEW HAMPSHIRE

New Hampshire is also an NCCI state, meaning that private insurance companies that write Workers Compensation insurance follow the manual rules and regulations of the NCCI. Every business with one or more employees must obtain valid Workers Compensation insurance. Sole proprietors, partners, and self-employed persons are not required to insure themselves, but may elect to do so. Corporations and LLCs with fewer than three executive officers or members (and no other workers) are not required to insure those officers or members, but may elect to do so. Once a corporation or LLC has four executive officers or members, all are considered employees; however, they may elect to exclude three such officers or members. Independent contractors are not considered employees if they meet a number of strict criteria set forth in statutes, such as having their own FEIN. Real estate agents and brokers working on commission also are not employees for purposes of Workers Compensation in New Hampshire.

Insurance, including Workers Compensation insurance, is regulated by:
New Hampshire Department of Insurance Phone: (603) 271-2261
21 South Fruit Street, Suite 14 Website: http://www.nh.gov/insurance/
Concord, NH 03301

Workers Compensation claims, and employers who wish to self-insure, are overseen by a division of the New Hampshire Department of Labor:
Workers' Compensation Division Phone: (603) 271-3176
NH Department of Labor Website: http://www.labor.state.nh.us/workers_compensation.asp
95 Pleasant Street
Concord, NH 03301

NEW JERSEY

This is **not** an NCCI state, but instead has its own rating bureau, the New Jersey Compensation Rating and Inspection Bureau, which is part of the New Jersey Department of Banking and Insurance. This bureau has responsibility for creating manuals and rules of classification and experience rating for New Jersey employers. In New Jersey, all employers (save those that have only Federal WC exposure) must obtain valid Workers Compensation insurance or be approved to self-insure in the state. Sole proprietors, partners, and members of LLCs are not considered employees under the Workers Compensation statutes, but may elect to cover themselves. Executive officers of a corporation are considered employees, and the statute does not give them the option to opt out of coverage. The only exceptions to the definition of employee are those who are eligible for coverage under the federal Longshore and Harbor Workers Act, and casual employees.

Unlike some states, the rating bureau in New Jersey establishes manual rates that are used by all insurance companies in New Jersey. Therefore, different insurers would use the same manual rates for New Jersey exposures.

The manual rules for premiums, experience rating, manual rates, and classifications are developed by:
New Jersey Compensation Rating & Inspection Bureau
60 Park Place Phone: (973) 622-6014
Newark, NJ 07102 Website: http://www.njcrib.com

The NJCRIB also administers the state's Assigned Risk program, called the New Jersey Workers Compensation Plan.

The state agency with responsibility over Workers Compensation claims matters and approving employers to self-insure within the state is:
Division of Workers' Compensation
Department of Labor and Workforce Development
1 John Fitch Plaza mailing address: PO Box 110

Trenton, NH 08625 Trenton, NJ 08625-0110
Phone: (609) 292-2515 Website: http://lwd.state.nj.us/labor/wc/
wc_index.html

And insurance, including Workers Compensation insurance, is
regulated by:
Department of Banking and Insurance
Division of Insurance
20 West State Street Mailing Address: PO Box 325
 Trenton, NJ 08625 Trenton, NJ 08625
Phone: (609)-292-7272 Website: http://www.state.nj.us/dobi/
division_insurance/index.htm

NEW MEXICO

This is an NCCI state. All employers with three or more employees (including part-time employees) must purchase insurance or
be approved to self-insure (but for employers in the construction
fields, all employers must have coverage). Group self-insurance also
is allowed in this state. Also, under New Mexico rules, if someone
owns more than one business, the employees of all the separate
businesses are counted to determine if the employer is required
to purchase insurance. Also, out-of-state employees are counted to
determine if a New Mexico employer must purchase insurance. If
the number of employees is normally three, but sometimes drops
down below this, the employer must still keep insurance coverage in place. Coverage is not required for domestic servants, real
estate salespersons, or farm or ranch workers (but non-farm work
done on a farm, such as packing or processing of farm products,
is not exempted).

Generally, every worker used by a business in New Mexico is considered an employee except for casual labor not for the purpose of the
employer's trade or business. Sole proprietors are not required to
insure themselves (or their spouses), but must insure any employees once they hit the thresholds detailed above. When determining if the employee has reached the threshold (three employees

for non-construction business) the sole proprietor and/or spouse would not be counted. However, for a partnership, LLC, or corporation, the partners, LLC members, or corporate officers would be counted in determining if the business must insure, even though partners, LLC members owning at least 10 percent, and corporate officers owning at least 10 percent of the company can exclude themselves from coverage.

Workers Compensation insurance is provided by private insurance companies, and an Assigned Risk program for those who cannot get an insurance company to underwrite their business is operated by the Insurance Division of the New Mexico Public Regulation Commission. Costs in the assigned risk program here are more expensive than insurance costs would be if coverage were obtained in the "voluntary market" (through a private insurance company voluntarily underwriting the business). The assigned risk plan in New Mexico can be accessed through insurance agents in the state.

There is no state fund for Workers Compensation in New Mexico. The state did establish, in 1991, a mutual insurance company named New Mexico Mutual Casualty Company, but this is not a state fund. It operates the same as other insurance companies authorized to write Workers Compensation insurance in the state and its rates are not subsidized.

The state agency with jurisdiction over Workers Compensation claims (and approval of employers to self-insure) is:
New Mexico Workers' Compensation Administration
2410 Centre Avenue SE Mailing Address: PO Box 27198
Albuquerque, NM 87125 Albuquerque, NM 87125-7198
Phone: (505) 841-6000 Website: http://workerscomp.state.nm.us/

Workers Compensation insurance coverage (and disputes over premium) would be the jurisdiction of:
Insurance Division
Public Regulation Commission

Physical Address: Mailing Address
P.E.R.A. Bldg., 4th Floor PO Box 1269
1120 Paseo de Peralta Santa Fe, NM 87504-1269
Santa Fe, NM 87501
Phone: (505) 827-4601 Website: http://www.nmprc.state.nm.us/
id.htm

NEW YORK

This is **not** an NCCI state, but instead has its own independent rating bureau, the New York Compensation Insurance Rating Board (generally known as CIRB). CIRB develops its own manuals of rules that govern classifications, premium computation, and experience modification factors. Employers that operate only with New York would have experience modification factors calculated by CIRB, but for employers that operate in New York as well as other states, an interstate experience modifier would be calculated by NCCI that incorporates New York rating data with that of other states. In other words, the New York experience modifier is not a stand-alone modifier for employers operating in multiple states.

Just about all employers in New York State must provide workers' compensation coverage for their employees. An employer can obtain coverage through an approved insurance company or through the New York State Fund. Large employers can also be approved to self-insure for Workers Compensation in the state. Group self-insurance is also allowed.

The requirement to obtain valid coverage covers not only for-profit operations, but also all employments conducted for-profit. Part-time employees, borrowed employees, leased employees, family members, and volunteers working for a for-profit business also must be covered. State law also requires coverage for domestic workers employed forty or more hours per week by the same employer, including full-time sitters or companions, and live-in domestic worker, as well as farm workers whose employer paid

$1,200 or more for farm labor in the preceding calendar year. Coverage is also required for all corporate officers if the corporation has more than two officers and/or two stockholders and for officers of one- or two-person corporations if there are other individuals in employment. But these officers may choose to exclude themselves from coverage. Most workers compensated by a nonprofit organization also are required to be covered.

New York law exempts from coverage requirements certain kinds of workers:

1. Individuals who volunteer their services for nonprofit organizations and receive no compensation
2. Clergy and members of religious orders that are performing religious duties
3. Members of supervised amateur athletic activities operated on a nonprofit basis, provided that such members are not otherwise engaged or employed by any person, firm, or corporation participating in such athletic activity
4. People engaged in a teaching capacity in or for a nonprofit religious, charitable, or educational institution
5. People engaged in a non-manual capacity in or for a nonprofit religious, charitable, or educational institution— manual labor includes, but is not limited to such tasks as filing; carrying materials such as pamphlets, binders, or books; cleaning such as dusting or vacuuming; playing musical instruments; moving furniture; shoveling snow; mowing lawns; and construction of any sort
6. Persons receiving charitable aid from a religious or charitable institution who perform work in return for such aid and who are not under any express contract of hire, and certain persons receiving rehabilitation services in a sheltered workshop
7. People who are covered for specific types of employment under another workers' compensation system such as those employed in certain maritime trades, interstate railroad employees, federal government employees and others covered under federal workers' compensation laws

8. The spouse and minor children (under eighteen years old) of an employer who is a farmer as long as they are not under an express contract of hire
9. Certain employees of foreign governments and Native American nations
10. New York City police officers, firefighters, and sanitation workers who are covered under provisions of the New York State General Municipal Law—uniformed police officers and firefighters in other municipalities may also be excluded
11. People, including minors, doing yard work or casual chores in and about a one-family, owner-occupied residence or the premises of a nonprofit, noncommercial organization—casual means occasionally, without regularity, without foresight, plan or method—coverage is required if the minor handles power-driven machinery, including a power lawnmower.
12. Real estate salespersons who sign a contract with a broker stating that they are independent contractors
13. Media sales representatives who sign a contract stating that they are independent contractors
14. Insurance agents or brokers who sign a contract stating that they are independent contractors
15. Sole proprietors, partners, and certain one/two person corporate officers with no other individuals providing services integral to the business (although they may elect to cover themselves)

LLC members are not required to cover themselves, but most cover any employees they hire. If an LLC obtains a Workers Compensation policy for employees, the members are excluded unless they choose to include themselves. But if the LLC has no employees and purchases coverage, members are automatically included. Partners of New York partnerships are not required to cover themselves, but must obtain coverage for any employees. If a partnership with employees does choose to obtain coverage, partners are not automatically covered, but may elect to add coverage for themselves. For a partnership with no employees, partners would be automatically covered if the partnership purchases coverage.

Limousine drivers that meet certain criteria are covered by New York Black Car Operators' Injury Compensation Fund, Inc., which obtains coverage through the New York State Fund.

In New York, if an employer uses the services of a PEO (Professional Employer Organization) to obtain Workers Compensation coverage, the PEO must provide a separate Workers Compensation policy for each client employer.

Effective September 9, 2007, all out-of-state employers with employees working in New York state are required to carry a full, statutory New York state Workers Compensation policy. An employer has a full, statutory New York state workers' compensation insurance policy when New York is listed in Item 3A on the Information Page of the employer's workers' compensation insurance policy.

In New York, certain kinds of construction work are subject to payroll maximums. That is, there is a maximum amount of a worker's payroll that can be used to calculate premium charges. For such construction work, there are also territorial differentials—differentials in rates that reflect where in the state the work is being done. The maximum weekly wage of contractors is $825 per week. However, this is balanced by the Territory Premium Differential that is added to all contractors in New York state that due work on the construction of one or two-family residential housing. Depending on where the work is being done, the premium differential adds a surcharge to most construction premiums. If a contractor does not keep track of weekly wages of employees, they are unable to take advantage of the payroll limitation rule, and their premium will still be raised by the Territory Premium Differential.

The rating bureau that writes the manuals governing classifi-
cations, premium computation, and experience modification
factors is:
New York Compensation Insurance Rating Board
200 E. 42nd St.
New York, NY 10017
Phone: (212)697-3535
Website: http://www.nycirb.org/

The state agency with jurisdiction over Workers Compensation
claims and with approving employers to self-insure is:
New York State Workers' Compensation Board
20 Park Street
Albany, NY 12207
Phone: (877) 632-4996
Website: http://www.wcb.state.ny.us

The New York Workers' Compensation Fund that competes with
insurance companies is:
New York State Insurance Fund
They have offices in various locations across New York State.
Website: http://ww3.nysif.com

Workers Compensation coverage and premium disputes are under
the jurisdiction of:
New York State Department of Insurance
This agency also has offices scattered across the state.
Phone: (800) 342-3736
Website: http://www.ins.state.ny.us

NORTH CAROLINA

This is **not** an NCCI state, but instead has its own independent rating bureau, the North Carolina Rate Bureau. However, this independent rating bureau follows NCCI manual rules fairly closely.
The North Carolina Rate Bureau also administers the assigned
risk plan in North Carolina. Employers must obtain Workers

Compensation coverage once they have three employees. For sole proprietors, partnerships, or LLCs, the three employees must be in addition to the sole proprietors, partners, and members of the LLC. For corporations, the executive officers count in the head-count of employees. All employees, including part-time, seasonal, or family members are counted.

Employers must either obtain valid Workers Compensation insurance from an approved insurance company, be approved by the Department of Insurance to self-insure, be a member of an approved group self-insurance trust, or get coverage through the assigned risk plan.

The North Carolina Rate Bureau develops manuals that govern classifications, premium calculations, and experience modification factors in the state. The bureau calculates experience modifiers for employers doing business only within North Carolina, but also reports rating data to NCCI for calculation of an interstate modification factor for employers operating in North Carolina and also in other NCCI jurisdictions. The North Carolina modifier is not a stand-alone modifier, so an employer operating in N.C. and in NCCI states would have an interstate modifier calculated by NCCI that would apply both in NCCI states and in North Carolina.

North Carolina Rate Bureau
5401 Six Forks Road
Raleigh, NC 27609
Phone: (919) 582-1056
Website: http://www.ncrb.org/ncrb

Workers Compensation claims are under the jurisdiction of:
Workers' Compensation Industrial Commission
4340 Mail Service Center
 Raleigh, NC 27699-4340
Phone: (919) 807-2500
Website: http://www.ic.nc.gov/

Workers Compensation insurance coverage and premium disputes are under the jurisdiction of:
North Carolina Department of Insurance
430 N. Salisbury St.
Raleigh, NC 27603-5926
Phone: (919) 807-6750
Website: http://www.ncdoi.com

NORTH DAKOTA

This state maintains a monopoly state fund for Workers Compensation insurance. This means that employers must use this fund for their Workers Compensation coverage in the state and that private insurance is not available for Workers Compensation in North Dakota. Legislation was introduced in early 2009 to allow private insurance for Workers Compensation in the state, but as of this writing, this change has not yet been approved. So for now, all things Workers Compensation in North Dakota are the jurisdiction of:
North Dakota Workforce Safety & Insurance
1600 East Century Avenue, Suite 1
 Bismarck ND 58503–0644
Phone: (701) 328–3800
Website: http://www.workforcesafety.com

OHIO

This is another one of the handful of states that operate a monopoly state fund. Their state fund is the only game in the state for Workers Compensation coverage if an employer is not big enough to qualify to self-insure. However, the Ohio Bureau of Workers' Compensation (BWC) has shifted over to using the NCCI classification system, rather than its own classification system. However, the BWC retains the authority to decide how to interpret and assign those NCCI classification codes, although there are appeals systems to their (sometimes questionable) decisions regarding classifications. Disputed claims fall under the jurisdiction of another state agency, the Ohio Industrial Commission.

Employers with one or more employees are required to obtain Workers Compensation coverage. Executive officers of a corporation are considered employees. Coverage is elective for sole proprietors, partners, individuals incorporated as a corporation (with no employees), ministers, and officers of a family farm corporation.

Ohio does not remove the premium portion of overtime pay from payroll used to compute Workers Compensation charges, in contrast to most other states.

A controversial feature exists in the Ohio Workers' Compensation system—group rating. Members of certain approved groups can get *very* substantial discounts (on the order of 75 percent or more) on the rates charged by the BWC. This means that employers that can't qualify for membership in such groups pay much, much higher rates for their Workers Compensation coverage from BWC. The Ohio system also has been wracked with scandals in recent years over how the funds collected by BWC are invested. Some observers suspect the monopoly fund in Ohio will not last too much longer, as pressure is building to allow insurance companies to come in and compete with the fund. There has also been legal pressure brought to bear to end or modify the group rating system.

Bureau of Workers' Compensation
30 W. Spring St.
Columbus, OH 43215-2256
Phone: (800) 644-6292
Website: http://www.ohiobwc.com

The Industrial Commission of Ohio
30 W. Spring St.
Columbus, OH 43215
Phone: (614) 466-6136
Website: https://www.ohioic.com

OKLAHOMA

This is an NCCI state, so the manual rules about classifications, premium computation, and experience modification factors are developed by NCCI. Employers in Oklahoma with one or more employees must either obtain coverage from an approved private insurance company, be approved to self-insure, become covered by a group self-insurance plan, or obtain coverage from CompSource Oklahoma. CompSource Oklahoma is part of state government but operates as an insurance company, albeit one that does not pay premium taxes and is not subject to rate approval by the Property Casualty Rate Board. It is the former state fund that was transformed in 1993 into an insurance company, but with unique features. CompSource Oklahoma functions as the assigned risk plan for the state.

Oklahoma does exempt certain employments: domestic servants or casual workers in a household who earn less than $10,000 annually; workers covered by federal Workers Compensation statutes; agricultural employers with less than $100,000 in annual payroll; licensed real estate professionals paid on commission; employers with five or fewer employees, all of whom are related by blood; and public employees. Sole proprietors, partners, members of LLCs who own at least 10 percent of the company, and stockholder-employees of corporations who own at least 10 percent of the company are not employees, but may elect to be covered. If such exempt owners of a business do not elect to cover themselves, when they act as subcontractors, they do not create Workers Compensation liability for the contractor retaining their services. Owner-operators of trucks are also not employees if the owner-operator actually operates the truck and if the person contracting with the owner-operator is not the lessor of the truck.

Enforcement of employer compliance with Workers Compensation requirements is handled by:
Workers Compensation Enforcement Unit
Oklahoma Department of Labor
4001 N. Lincoln Blvd.

Oklahoma City, OK 73105
Phone: (405) 528-1500
Website: http://www.ok.gov/odol/Workers_Compensation_
Enforcement/index.html

Workers Compensation insurance is regulated by:
Oklahoma Insurance Department Mailing Address:
2401 N.W. 23rd Street, Suite 28 PO Box 53408
Oklahoma City, OK 73107 Oklahoma City, OK 73152-3408
Phone: (405) 521-2828
Website: http://www.ok.gov/oid

For information about coverage through the former competitive
state fund:
CompSource Oklahoma
PO Box 53505
Oklahoma City, OK 73152-3505
Phone: (405) 232-7663
Website: http://www.compsourceok.com

OREGON

This is an NCCI state. Employers with one or more employees must
purchase Workers Compensation insurance from an approved private insurer or be approved to self-insure. Oregon exempts domestic workers, gardeners, or maintenance people working at a private
home, casual employees (not in the same trade or business as the
employer), workers subject to federal Workers Compensation provisions, and police and fire fighters of municipalities with popula-
tion over two hundred thousand that have their own compensation
and disability programs.

Sole proprietors, partners, and members of LLCs are not considered employees of their own company, unless the company
is engaged in construction work. Executive officers of a corporation are not considered employees (but there are statutory
exceptions and limitations that apply to timber companies).

Newspaper delivery people over nineteen are not considered employees, and neither are caddies. Independent contractors who meet specific criteria and are registered with the state do not create Workers Compensation liability for companies that retain their services.

Oregon's assigned risk plan is funded by the state, which utilizes the services of two insurers that also operate in the voluntary market in the state. This assigned risk program can be accessed through insurance agents in the state.

Workers Compensation claims and employer compliance are regulated by:
Workers' Compensation Division
350 Winter St. NE
PO Box 14480
Salem, OR 97309-0405
Phone: (503) 947-7810
Website: http://www.cbs.state.or.us/external/wcd/index.html

Workers Compensation insurance is regulated by:
Insurance Division Mailing Address:
350 Winter St NE
Salem, OR 97301-3883
PO Box 14480
Salem, OR 97309-0405
Phone: (503) 947-7980
Website: http://www.cbs.state.or.us/external/ins/index.html

PENNSYLVANIA

This is **not** an NCCI state, instead it uses a distinctive Workers Compensation classification system that it shares with the state of Delaware. Rules for classification, premium computation, and experience rating are the responsibility of the Pennsylvania Compensation Rating Bureau, a non-government agency licensed and regulated by the Pennsylvania Insurance Department. As in

Delaware, the premium portion of overtime pay is not excluded from computation of Workers Compensation premiums, in contrast to other states. The PCRB classification system uses a three-digit code (as opposed to the four-digit code system used by NCCI). So, while the NCCI classification code for clerical work is 8810, in Pennsylvania it is 953. There are only about 350 classification codes used in the Pennsylvania system, as opposed to over five hundred in the NCCI system, but insurance companies are allowed to develop "subclassifications" to supplement the PCRB classes, if they so choose. Such subclassifications have to be filed with and approved by state insurance regulators before an insurer can use them. But in theory, at least this does give insurance companies the option of using more classifications than just the PCRB's classes.

Pennsylvania Compensation Rating Bureau
United Plaza Building - Suite 1500 Phone: (215) 568-2371
30 South 17th Street Website: www.dcrb.com
Philadelphia, PA 19103-4007

Workers Compensation insurance in Pennsylvania is regulated by:
Pennsylvania Insurance Department
Harrisburg regional Office Phone: (717) 787-2317
1209 Strawberry Square Website: http://www.ins.state.pa.us/ins
Harrisburg, PA 17120

PUERTO RICO
This state requires all employers to participate in their monopoly state fund for Workers Compensation

The Puerto Rico State Insurance Fund is known as CFSE or Corporacion Del Fondo Seguro del Estado.

Website: http://www.cfse.gov.pr/wps/portal

RHODE ISLAND

This is also an NCCI state, so insurance companies writing Workers Compensation follow NCCI manual rules regarding classifications, premiums, and experience rating.

Employers with one or more employee must carry workers' compensation insurance coverage (or be approved to self-insure or be part of an approved group self-insurance program) or be subject to fines, penalties and/or criminal prosecution. Sole proprietors and partners are not required to insure themselves. Corporate officers are usually included as employees unless they file a waiver form with the Department of Labor & Training. If corporate officers exempt themselves from Workers Compensation coverage, they are not covered for workplace injuries or illness through their health insurance.

In Rhode Island, an independent contractor is not eligible to file for Workers Compensation benefits from a party that hires that contractor, but the independent contractor must file a Notice of Designation as Independent Contractor Form with the Department of Labor & Training.

Workers Compensation insurance rates and premiums are regulated by:
Rhode Island Department of Business Regulation
1511 Pontiac Avenue
Cranston, RI 02920
Website: http://www.dbr.ri.gov/   Phone: 401-462-9500

The Rhode Island Department of Labor & Training, Division of Workers Compensation, monitors employer compliance with Workers Compensation coverage compliance, approves employers for self-insurance, and that makes sure that claims are properly paid by insurers.

Rhode Island Department of Labor and Training
Division of Workers Compensation

1511 Pontiac Avenue, Building 71-1, First Floor, PO Box 20190, Cranston RI 02920-0942
Website: http://www.dlt.ri.gov/wc/   Phone: 401-462-8100

Workers Compensation claims disputes are adjudicated by:
The Workers Compensation Court
One Dorrance PlazaProvidence, RI 02903
Website: http://www.courts.ri.gov/workers/defaultnew-workers.
htm Phone: 401-458-5000

Rhode Island used to have a state fund that would compete with private insurance companies, but this has been changed into a mutual insurance company, Beacon Mutual Insurance.   This insurer serves as the Assigned Risk plan for Rhode Island, and also has dominated Workers Compensation insurance there. The company has been plagued by serious scandal in recent years involving corruption, political favoritism, and crony underwriting.

SOUTH CAROLINA
South Carolina uses the NCCI system of rules governing classifications, experience modifiers, and premium computation. Workers Compensation insurance is required of any employer who regularly employs four or more full- or part-time workers. There are some exceptions, including agricultural employees, railroads and railway express companies and their employees, and employers who had a total annual payroll during the previous year of less than $3,000, regardless of the number of workers employed during that period. Also exempt are Textile Hall Corporation and certain commission paid real estate agents. Uninsured subcontractors or independent contractors create Workers Compensation exposure for those who hire them. Sole proprietors and partners do not have to cover themselves, but may elect to do so. But once corporate form is chosen, all workers, including owners, must be covered. Employers that qualify may self-insure; group self-insurance is also allowed.

Workers Compensation insurance is regulated by
South Carolina Department of Insurance
1201 Main Street, Suite 1000   Phone: (803) 737-6160
Columbia, SC 29201
Website: http://www.doi.sc.gov

Workers Compensation claims (and approving employers to self-insure) are overseen by:
South Carolina Workers' Compensation Commission
1612 Marion Street Phone: (803) 737-5700
Columbia, SC 29202-1715 Website: http://www.sc.gov

SOUTH DAKOTA

This is another NCCI state, so the NCCI system is used for classifications, experience modifiers, and other rules that govern Workers Compensation premiums. Workers Compensation coverage is required for all employers, with only a few exceptions: domestic servants (unless working for an employer more than twenty hours in any calendar week and for more than six weeks in any thirteen-week period); farm or agricultural labor; one whose employment is not in the usual course of trade, business, occupation or profession of the employer (independent contractors, including real estate agents and owner-operators of trucks certified as independent contractors by the Department of Labor; certain elected officials of the state or any subdivision of government; and Workfare participants. Workers covered by federal Workers Compensation programs are also exempt.

Workers Compensation insurance is regulated by:
South Dakota Department of Revenue and Regulation
Division of Insurance Phone: (605) 773-3563
445 East Capitol Avenue Website: http://www.state.sd.us/drr2/reg/insurance
Pierre, SD 57501

Workers Compensation claims are overseen by:
South Dakota Department of Labor
700 Governors Drive Phone: (605) 773-3101
Pierre, SD 57501-2291 Website: http://dol.sd.gov/workerscomp/
default.aspx

TENNESSEE

This is another NCCI state. Workers Compensation coverage
is required for all employers with five or more full- or part-time
workers, but for employers engaged in the mining or production
of coal, the threshold is one or more workers. For employers in
the construction industry, the threshold is also one or more workers. Coverage is not required for agricultural workers (but may be
obtained voluntarily). Domestic workers also are not required to
be covered, but may be covered voluntarily.

Workers Compensation insurance is regulated by
Department of Commerce and Insurance
Insurance Division Phone: (615) 741-2241
500 James Robertson Parkway Website: http://www.state.tn.us/
commerce
Nashville, TN 37243

Workers Compensation claims are overseen by:
Department of Labor and Workforce Development
220 French Landing Drive Phone: (615) 741-6642
Nashville, TN 37243 Website: http://www.state.tn.us/labor-wfd/
wcomp.html

TEXAS

Texas has gone through some wild and wooly times in regards
Workers Compensation in the state. Back in the early 1990s, there
was a collapse of their system (private insurance essentially disappeared) and that led to a number of reforms. Texas is currently

essentially the only state that gives employers the option to "go bare." That is, not to carry Workers Compensation insurance legally. It isn't advised, as this exposes employers to very significant liabilities, but it isn't illegal. Texas also allows employers to negotiate the experience modification factor used by their insurers (if the insurer is willing to accommodate). Texas is **not** an NCCI state, but instead their Texas Department of Insurance (known as the TDI) operates as the Workers Compensation rating bureau for Texas. The TDI develops its own manuals of rules and regulations, though these rely on NCCI manuals as a starting point. Workers Compensation insurance is provided through private insurance companies. Employers can now self-insure for Workers Compensation in Texas (in the past this was not allowed). Group self-insurance is also allowed.

Workers Compensation insurance in Texas is regulated by:
Texas Department of Insurance
Division of Workers' Compensation Phone: (800) 372-7713
333 Guadalupe Website: http://www.tdi.state.tx.us/wc
Austin, TX 78701

Workers Compensation claims are also overseen by the Division of Worker Compensation.

U.S. VIRGIN ISLANDS

All employers with one or more workers must obtain coverage from the Government Insurance Fund of the Virgin Islands, a monopoly state fund. Private insurance for Workers Compensation is not permitted here.

Workers Compensation Administration
3012 Vitraco Mall, Golden Rock Phone: (809) 692-9390
Christiansted
St. Croix, Virgin Islands 00820-4666
Website: http://www.vidol.gov/Units/Workers_Compensation/Workers_Comp.htm

UTAH

This is an NCCI state. All employers are required to carry workers' compensation insurance except for the following: some employers of agricultural laborers, casual or domestic workers, real estate brokers, sole proprietors, and partners. Directors or officers of a corporation are considered employees, but can choose to exclude themselves. Sole proprietors and partners can elect to cover themselves, but are not required to do so. Utah maintains a state fund for Workers Compensation that competes with private insurance companies. Employers can qualify to be self-insured for Workers Compensation, but Utah does not allow group self-insurance. Uninsured subcontractors or independent contractors create Workers Compensation exposure for those that hire them.

Workers Compensation insurance is regulated by:
Utah Insurance Department
State Office Building, Room 3110 Phone: (801) 538-3800
Salt Lake City, UT 84114-6901 Website: http://www.insurance.utah.gov

Workers Compensation claims are overseen by:
Utah Labor Commission
Division of Industrial Accidents Phone: (801) 530-6800
Mail Address: PO Box 146610, Salt Lake City, UT, 84114-6610
Street Address: 160 East 300 South, 3rd Floor, Salt Lake City, UT 84111
Website: http://www.laborcommission.utah.gov/Industrial Accidents/index.html

The contact information for the Utah Workers Compensation Fund is:
Customer Service Phone # Website: https://www.wcfgroup.com
(801) 288-8000
(800) 446-2667

VERMONT

This is another NCCI state. Workers Compensation coverage here is provided through private insurance companies. (There is no state fund.) Workers Compensation coverage is required for employers with one or more workers. Sole proprietors and partners are not required to insure themselves, but may elect to do so. Corporate officers can elect to remove themselves from coverage. In addition, the following people are not required to be covered by workers' compensation insurance: casual workers—workers not for the purpose of the employers trade or business; a person engaged in amateur sports, even if an employer contributes to the support of such sports; a person engaged in agriculture or farm employment for an employer whose aggregate payroll is less than $2,000 in a calendar year, unless the employer chooses to provide coverage; certain elected officials; and volunteers.

In Vermont, those who use the services of an uninsured independent contractor or subcontractor will have Workers Compensation liability for them. Employers can also qualify to self-insure their Workers Compensation liabilities in Vermont.

Workers Compensation insurance is regulated by:
Department of Banking, Insurance, Securities and Health Care Administration (BISHCA)
89 Main Street Phone: (802) 828-3301
Montpelier, VT 05620-3101 Website: http://www.bishca.state.vt.us

Workers Compensation claims are overseen by:
5 Green Mountain Drive Phone: (802) 828-4000
PO Box 488 Website: http://labor.vermont.gov/
Montpelier, VT 05601-0488

VIRGINIA

This is another NCCI state. Workers Compensation insurance is provided by private insurance companies. There is no state fund. Virginia requires every employer who regularly employs three or more full or part time workers to carry Workers Compensation insurance, to qualify as a self-insurer, or become a member of a group self-insurance plan.

Sole proprietors and partners are considered owners of businesses and are not required to cover themselves. However, they may elect to obtain coverage for workers' compensation liability by purchasing insurance.

Members of limited liability companies (LLC) are considered to be owners of a company and are not covered by workers' compensation unless specifically covered by an insurance policy or either elected or appointed as a manager. The manager of an LLC is treated as a corporate officer under the Act.

A corporation's officers may choose to reject workers' compensation coverage for accidents, but not for occupational diseases. To do so, officers must file a "Notice of Rejection" with the insurer and with the Workers' Compensation Commission. If the officers are paid regularly, they are nevertheless counted as employees to determine jurisdiction under the Act.

In Virginia, the following are generally not considered employees:
- Individuals who are properly classified as independent contractors under Virginia law (unless they specifically and formally choose to be included in their own workers' compensation insurance policy)
- Elected state and local officials (unless coverage is extended to them by the governing board of the governmental entity through a duly adopted ordinance)
- Taxi cab and executive sedan drivers if they are excluded from taxation under the Federal Unemployment Tax Act
- Licensed real estate people who are contractually identified as independent contractors, who earn substantially all their income from commissions, and who are not treated as employees for federal income tax purposes

- Casual workers, domestic workers, and farm workers, unless the employer regularly has more than two full-time employees
- Railroad workers working for common carriers involved in interstate or foreign commerce
- Non-compensated employees, officers, and directors of non-profit corporations
- Employees of federal instrumentalities
- Employees of businesses that regularly employ fewer than three employees.

Workers Compensation insurance is regulated by:
Bureau of Insurance
PO Box 1157
Richmond, VA 23218
Phone: (804) 371-9741
BOI Street Address: Website: http://www.scc.virginia.gov/division/boi/#pcmarketreg
1300 East Main Street
Richmond, VA 23219

Workers Compensation claims are overseen by:
Virginia Workers' Compensation Commission
1000 DMV Drive Phone: (877) 664-2566
Richmond, VA 23220 Website: http://www.vwc.state.va.us

WASHINGTON

The state of Washington maintains a monopoly state fund for Workers Compensation. This means that private insurance is not allowed for Workers Compensation. Contact informativon for the fund is:
Department of Labor and Industries
PO Box 4400 Phone: (800) 547-8367
Olympia, WA 98504 Website: http://www.lni.wa.gov

WASHINGTON D.C.

See earlier entry under District of Columbia.

WEST VIRGINIA

West Virginia used to maintain a monopoly state fund, but this has changed in recent years. The former state fund was morphed into an insurance company, Brick Street Mutual. At first, Brick Street had a monopoly on writing Workers Compensation insurance in the state, Effective July 1, 2008, other insurance companies could compete with Brick Street for Workers Compensation business. Brick Street and other insurers operating in West Virginia use the NCCI system for classifications, experience modifiers, and premium computation. Generally, every business with employees in West Virginia is required to have valid Workers Compensation insurance or to be approved to self-insure. The exceptions are for:

- Employers of five or fewer full-time employees in agricultural services
- An employer who is a casual employer
- An employer who is a church
- An employer who is engaged in organized professional sports activities, including an employer of trainers and jockeys engaged in thoroughbred horse racing—*provided*, that the employer must carry coverage for its employees who are not participating in the organized professional sports activities. (For example, an employer of jockeys and trainers engaged in thoroughbred horseracing may exempt such jockeys and trainers, but if the same employer also employs a driver to transport horses and equipment, the driver must be provided coverage.)
- A volunteer rescue squad or volunteer police auxiliary unit organized under the auspices of a county commission, municipality, or other government entity or political subdivision, or a volunteer organization created or sponsored by a government entity, political subdivisions, or an area or regional emergency medical service

board of directors in furtherance of the purposes of the emergency medical services act—*provided,* that if any such employers have paid employees, they must provide West Virginia workers' compensation for such paid employees

- An employer of employees who is provided coverage for benefits under the Federal Longshore and Harbor Workers' Compensation Act is exempt from having to carry West Virginia workers' compensation coverage for such employees, but must provide West Virginia Workers Compensation coverage for employees who are not provided coverage for benefits under the Federal Longshore and Harbor Workers' Compensation Act.

Workers Compensation insurance in West Virginia is regulated by:
Office of the Insurance Commissioner
Mailing Address Physical Address
PO Box 50540 1124 Smith St.
Charleston, WV 25305-0540 Charleston, WV 2530
Phone: (304) 558-3386 Website: http://www.wvinsurance.gov

Workers Compensation claims are also overseen by the Office of the Insurance Commissioner.

WISCONSIN

This is not an NCCI state. Wisconsin maintains its own non-NCCI rating bureau for determining classifications, experience modifiers, and premium computation rules. Wisconsin integrates experience rating data for experience modifiers with NCCI, however, when an employer operates both in Wisconsin and in other, NCCI states. In Wisconsin, employers must obtain valid Workers Compensation insurance or be approved to self-insure when they:

- employ three or more full-time or part-time employees;
- employ one or more full-time or part-time employees to whom you have paid combined gross wages of $500 or

more in any calendar quarter for work done at one or more locations in Wisconsin;

- as farmers, employ six or more workers on the same day for any twenty days during the calendar year; or
- are out-of-state employers with Wisconsin workers— they must have worker's compensation insurance with an insurance company licensed to write in Wisconsin and endorsed to name Wisconsin as a covered state in section 3A of the policy

Sole proprietors and partners are not required to cover themselves, but must cover any employees. They can elect to cover themselves if they choose. Members of LLCs are treated as partners for this purpose. If a closely held corporation has no more than two corporate officers and has no other employees, a worker's compensation policy is not required if both officers elect not to be subject to the Worker's Compensation Act. A closely held corporation is defined as a corporation with not more than ten stockholders.

A corporation with more than two corporate officers or any other employees is not eligible to file a Corporate Officer Option Notice and must obtain and/or maintain a worker's compensation insurance policy. All worker's compensation policies covering corporations include corporate officers, however, a closely held corporation may exclude up to two corporate officers from coverage on their policy.

The Wisconsin rating bureau contact information is:
Wisconsin Compensation Rating Bureau
Mailing Address: Street Address:
P O BOX 3080 20700 Swenson Drive, #100
MILWAUKEE, WI, 53201-3080 Waukesha, WI 53186
Phone: (262) 796-4540 Website: https://www.waip.org/WCRB/wcrbhome.htm

Workers Compensation insurance is regulated by:
Office of the Commissioner of Insurance
125 South Webster Street Phone: (608) 266-3585
Madison, WI 53703-3474 Website: http://oci.wi.gov/

Workers Compensation claims are overseen by:
Wisconsin Department of Workforce Development
Room C100 Phone: (608) 266-1340
201 E. Washington Ave. Website: http://www.dwd.state.wi.us/wc
Madison, WI 53703

WYOMING

Wyoming maintains a monopoly state fund for Workers Compensation and does not allow private insurance for this exposure. Workers Compensation is administered by:
Department of Employment
Workers' Safety & Compensation Division Phone: (307) 777-6763
1510 East Pershing Blvd. Website: http://wydoe.state.wy.us
Cheyenne, WY 82002

So there you have it—a detailed guide to the mosaic of Workers Compensation systems in the United States. As you can see from the preceding, it can vary significantly from one state to another as to which kinds of employers have to purchase Workers Compensation insurance, whether you can buy it from a private insurance company or have to deal with a state agency, and even which organization writes the rules that govern how the charges for Workers Compensation will be computed.

Most states use the NCCI system, but there are significant and notable exceptions to that. And even within the NCCI system, there can be significant variations in rules that govern classifications, experience modifiers, and other fine details. The rest of this book will try to provide some guidance for employers on how to make sure the various Workers Compensation systems, particularly the ones that utilize private insurance, don't overcharge you. With Workers Compensation insurance, the devil is always in the details.

CHAPTER 2

UNDERSTANDING YOUR POLICY

A standard Workers' Compensation insurance policy is a unique contract in many respects. Unlike other liability insurance policies, it doesn't have a maximum dollar amount limit to its primary coverage. Your auto insurance policy, for instance, has certain specified maximum amounts the policy covers per accident. If the cost of a particular accident exceeds that limit, you'll need to look elsewhere for those additional dollars (either from your own pocket, an excess policy, or from an umbrella liability policy). Workers' compensation insurance policies have a dollar limit also, but only for Part Two of the coverage, employers' liability. But Part One of the policy, the section that responds to an employer's statutory liability, has no set limits. Once the policy is in force, the insurance company is responsible for all employer claims that arise for workers' compensation benefits in the states covered in the policy.

That's the really beneficial aspect of workers' compensation from the employer's point of view. It's impossible to know in advance how great an employer's liabilities may be in a given year due to workers' compensation obligations and, thus, impossible to budget ahead of time with any certainty. A company might run several months with almost no claims and then be hit with a claim that ultimately costs hundreds of thousands of dollars. But an insurance policy has a predictable cost for which a company can plan and budget—at least in theory. This isn't always the case in practice, however. (But more on this later.)

Part One of the standard workers' compensation insurance policy transfers liability for statutory workers' compensation benefits of an employer to the insurance company, whether that liability turns out to be small, medium, or crushing. If a state increases benefit levels during the term of the policy, the policy automatically makes it the responsibility of the insurance company to pay all claims due for workers' compensation insurance for the named employer in the states covered in the policy.

Of course, as with all insurance, the devil can be in the details. And there are a few details that are very important for an employer to make sure are handled properly on a workers' compensation policy. The two most important are who is named as an insured under the policy, and what states are covered by the policy.

Check your Policy Information Page

I'm always a little amazed at how many business-people don't really look over their workers' compensation policy. The fine print of the policy can be a little daunting to the average person, but I'm talking about the basic items that almost anyone can find and understand on the policy.

For example, the "Information Pages" of the policy are normally among the first few pages and those pages show a lot of important information. (Look at figure 2-1 to see a sample Information Page.) For one thing, they show what entities are the *named insureds* under the policy. (This is shown in Item 1 of the Information Page.)

FIGURE 2-1 A TYPICAL INFORMATION PAGE OF
A WORKERS COMPENSATION POLICY

Archetypal Insurance Group Standard Workers' Compensation and
Employers' Liability Policy
INFORMATION PAGE
Policy Number From POLICY PERIOD To Coverage Provided By Agency
WC 11223344 01/01/05 01/01/05 Archetype Insurance of Virginia 99887766

ITEM Named Insured and Address Agent
1. ABC Widget Mfg. Inc. Mainstreet Insurance Agency 5533 Constitution Lane 4000
   W. Evergreen St.
   Vienna, VA 22180 Smallville, VA 22345
FEIN: 111222333 NCCI Carrier Code No. 112233
INTERSTATE ID NO. 998877
OTHER WORK PLACES NOT SHOWN ABOVE: SEE ATTACHED SCHEDULE
YOU ARE A Corporation
2. POLICY PERIOD- 01/01/05 TO 01/01/06 12:01 AM STANDARD TIME AT THE
   INSURED'S MAILING ADDRESS
               3.A PART ONE OF THIS POLICY APPLIES TO THE WORKERS'
               COMPENSATION LAW AND ANY OCCUPATIONAL DISEASE LAW OF
               EACH OF THE STATES LISTED HERE:
               MD, VA.
               3.B PART TWO OF THIS POLICY APPLIES TO EMPLOYERS' LIABILITY
               INSURANCE FOR WORK IN EACH STATE LISTED IN ITEM 3A: THE
               LIMITS OF LIABILITY ARE:
               BODILY INJURY BY ACCIDENT $100,000 EACH ACCIDENT
               BODILY INJURY BY DISEASE $500,000 POLICY LIMIT
               BODILY INJURY BY DISEASE $100,000 EACH EMPLOYEE
               3C. PART THREE OF THIS POLICY APPLIES TO OTHER STATES, IF
               ANY LISTED HERE:
               ALL STATES EXCEPT ND, OH, WA, WY AND STATES DESIGNED IN
               ITEM 3A OF THE INFORMATION PAGE
3. THE PREMIUM FOR THIS POLICY WILL BE DETERMINED BY OUR MANUAL OF
   RULES, CLASSIFICATIONS, RATES, AND RATING PLANS. ALL INFORMATION
   REQUIRED BELOW IS SUBJECT TO VERIFICATION AND CHANGE BY AUDIT.
   ADJUSTMENT OF PREMIUM SHALL BE MADE: AT POLICY EXPIRATION
CLASSIFICATION OF OPERATIONS EST ANNUAL PREMIUM
SEE ATTACHED $93,502
PREMIUM DISCOUNT 8,800-
EXPENSE CONSTANT 160
MINIMUM PREMIUM $750 TOTAL ESTIMATED ANNUAL PREMIUM $84,862
TERRORISM RISK INS ACT 924
TOTAL ESTIMATED COST $85,786
DATE OF ISSUE 02/15/05
POLICY ISSUING OFFICE: RICHMOND
COUNTERSIGNED_____ BY:_____
DATE AUTHORIZED AGENT

FIGURE 2-1 (continued)

Schedule of Operations

State: MD

LOC CLASS CLASSIFICATION OF OPERATIONS EST TOTAL RATE PER EST
ANNUAL CODE ANN REMUN $100 REMUN PREMIUM

01 3632 MACHINE SHOP NOC 1,098,381 6.78 74,470
  8742 SALESPERSONS, COLLECTORS OR 122,879 .38 467
  MESSENGERS–OUTSIDE
  8810 CLERICAL OFFICE EMPLOYEES NOC IF ANY .27 0
  SUBTOTAL FOR LOCATION 01 74,937

State: VA

02 3632 MACHINE SHOP NOC 750,000 5.43 40,725
  8810 CLERICAL OFFICE EMPLOYEES NOC 825,000 .29 2,396
TOTAL ESTIMATED MANUAL PREMIUM 118,058
  EXPERIENCE MODIFICATION FACTOR .88
  SCHEDULE CREDIT (10%) .90
TOTAL ESTIMATED STANDARD PREMIUM 93.502
  PREMIUM DISCOUNT (8,800)
  EXPENSE CONSTANT 160
  TERRORISM RISK INS ACT 1,848,381 .050 924
TOTAL ESTIMATED PREMIUM 85,786

DATE OF ISSUE: 02/15/05
POLICY ISSUING OFFICE: RICHMOND

The questions a policyholder should ask while looking at the Information Page are

- Is the named insured shown on your policy correct, accurate, and complete?
- Is your company's name shown completely?
- If you operate as a sole proprietorship or a partnership, is that shown correctly?
- Are there additional entities that should be listed, but are not?

(For example, sometimes a company leases real estate from a separate but related entity—for example, a real estate trust. If those separate entities are related to the primary employer, and it is in the interests of the employer to cover them, then those separate legal entities should be named on the policy, either on the Information Page or on a separate endorsement to the policy.

Consider a hypothetical situation. The Happy Inn Restaurant purchases Workers Compensation insurance that insures "Happy Inn, Inc." But the Happy Inn leases the building from one of the corporate owners, Bernice Benson, who owns the building individually. Bernice hires someone to do roofing work on the building and that unfortunate individual falls off the roof and is seriously injured. That individual did not carry Workers Compensation coverage on himself. He (or his family if he ultimately dies of his injuries) can and probably will sue Bernice for Workers Compensation benefits (at least, in many states he can).

The policy only shows "Happy Inn, Inc." as the named insured. So Bernice as an individual isn't insured, even though it would be the intention of Happy Inn Inc. and Bernice for her to be covered. The time to address such matters is before the claim happens, not afterwards.

Before the claim, it's simple to add Bernice Benson as an additional insured to the policy. After the claim, it may well be difficult.

While you're looking at your policy, also review carefully the list of states that the policy covers to ensure that it includes all the states you need. The policy may not necessarily list every state you do business in, as a few states do not allow private insurance. North Dakota, Ohio, Washington, and Wyoming currently require workers' compensation coverage for their jurisdictions to be provided through their "monopoly" state funds. Other than these four states, make sure that your policy lists all states in which you have employees (or uninsured independent contractors and subcontractors). This is shown in Item 3A of the Information Page.

In addition, you want to make sure that the policy provides coverage for other states where you might have an incidental exposure. Even though you may not have employees working in other states, it's conceivable someone might seek to make a claim for benefits under a particular state's benefits because a worker was traveling through the state on business or was there on a temporary basis. Other states coverage used to be provided by a separate endorsement, but it's part of the basic policy language (Part Three of the standard policy). However, you have to make sure that the policy clearly states which other states are covered for such incidental exposures. This is shown in Item 3C of the Information Page. If this is left blank, then you have no coverage for states other than those listed in Item 3A.

The best and most comprehensive approach is to have Item 3C show a broad coverage statement such as "All states and U.S. territories except North Dakota, Ohio, Washington, Wyoming, Puerto Rico, the U.S. Virgin

Islands, and those states designated in Item 3A of the Information Page."

What about employees who are working outside the U.S.? Most states provide that workers who are hired within those states, but who are injured outside those states, are entitled to benefits. But if you have U.S. employees who are working in foreign countries, you may well want to endorse your policy with a *voluntary compensation endorsement* for those employees working temporarily outside the U.S. and a *foreign voluntary compensation endorsement* for those who are located in foreign countries for longer-term projects.

A foreign voluntary compensation endorsement is not a standardized form, but it typically would provide not only statutory benefits on a voluntary basis but also coverage for endemic disease and the expense of repatriating injured or ill workers. The costs of transporting those workers back to the U.S. can be substantial, so it can be important to obtain the repatriation expense coverage if you have employees travelling internationally on business.

FEDERAL WORKERS' COMPENSATION EXPOSURES

Although the individual states' Workers Compensation statues are the primary focus of most employers' insurance, there are some federal acts that can also impose liability on an employer. The 1992 revision of the standard workers' compensation policy specifically excluded coverage for federal legislation such as the Longshore and Harbor Workers' Compensation Act, the Nonappropriated Fund Instrumentalities Act, the Outer Continental Shelf Lands Act, the Defense Base Act, the Federal Coal Mine Health and Safety Act, and the Federal Employers' Liability Act. Coverage for these laws can be added to your workers' compensation policy by endorsement, as needed. Here's a brief rundown on who might need these endorsements:

- **Longshore and Harbor Workers' Compensation Act (LHWCA).** This act provides benefits to employees (other than Masters or crew members of a vessel) who are injured in maritime employment. If you have employees loading, unloading, repairing, or building a vessel, you need this coverage endorsed onto your policy. Maritime coverage for Masters or members of a crew of a vessel is available with a maritime coverage endorsement.

- **Outer Continental Shelf Lands Act.** This act provides LHWCA benefits to employees (again, other than masters or crew members of a vessel) working on a continental shelf, such as on an offshore oil rig.

- **Defense Base Act.** This act covers civilian workers on military bases, such as if you contract to provide janitorial services to a military facility.

- **Nonapproriated Fund Instrumentalities Act.** This act extends LHWCA benefits to civilian employees of the U.S. military, like PX workers.

- **Federal Coal Mine Health and Safety Act.** This act provides workers' compensation benefits to coal miners who contract black lung disease.

- **Federal Employers' Liability Act.** This act covers employees of interstate railroad, who can be covered by a Federal Employers' liability Act coverage endorsement.

- **Migrant and Seasonal Agricultural Workers' Protection Act.** This act protects seasonal agricultural workers and establishes a private right of action against employers and contractors who violate housing and safety requirements. Coverage can be obtained through a Migrant and Seasonal Agricultural Worker Protection Act endorsement.

EMPLOYERS' LIABILITY COVERAGE

We've already made reference to Part One and Part Three of the coverage provided by the workers' compensation insurance policy. But we haven't yet talked about Part Two—employers' liability coverage. Most workers' compensation claims come under Part One of the coverage—the statutory state benefits for injured or ill workers. But don't ignore Part Two, as it can be very important to make sure this sometimes overlooked area of the policy is set up correctly.

Unlike Part One off the policy (coverage for statutory obligations), Part Two *does* have a set dollar limit. But employers' liability coverage is not always well understood by employers (or even by some insurance people). Employers' liability insures the employer for liability to employees for work-related bodily injury or illnesses that aren't subject to the statutory benefits imposed by state or federal regulations.

For example, many states exclude certain employees from the statutory benefits covered by Part One or Part Three of the policy. Employers' liability coverage would insure the employer for liability to such employees (as long the particular state where the injury or illness occurs is shown in Item 3A or Item 3C)

Employers' liability also insures an employer in cases such as "third-party over" lawsuits, where an injured worker then seeks to hold the employer responsible. For example, an employee injured by a piece of machinery at the workplace might file suit against the manufacturer of the machinery. The manufacturer might claim that the employer modified the machinery or used it improperly and is thus responsible for the liability.

But since employers' liability has a set limit, it is vital that this limit be correctly coordinated with the excess or umbrella liability coverage that is purchased separately. If the amount of employers' liability coverage on the workers' compensation policy is lower than the amount that the umbrella or excess coverage requires for the underlying coverage, there can be an insured gap. So it is vital to make sure that the employers' liability limit on the workers' compensation policy matches what is shown on the umbrella or excess liability coverage that sits on top of the primary workers' compensation policy.

DIFFERENT KINDS OF WORKERS' COMPENSATION POLICIES

All legitimate workers' compensation insurance policies provide the same coverage. There is no difference between the coverage provided by one insurer's policy and the coverage provided by the policy of a different insurance company. The policy language has been standardized, reviewed, and approved by regulators, so the only real difference among workers' compensation policies is in how the premium is computed. Even in this regard, there is a high degree of standardization, but developments over the course of the last decade or so have eroded some of that standardization in how premiums are computed. More than ever, employers need to understand the details of how insurance companies calculate premiums, as regulation of workers' compensation pricing is not as vigilant as it once was.

Guaranteed-Cost Policy

The most basic and most common type of workers' compensation policy is known as a *guaranteed-cost* policy. Bear in mind, though, that insurance terminology can sometimes be misleading to those outside the insurance industry. "Guaranteed Cost" does not mean that the premium for the policy is a fixed dollar amount. It means that, instead, the premium will be computed as a rate times hundred dollars of payroll, computed according to some fairly complicated rules that aren't all spelled out in the policy itself. But the rate that will be multiplied by payroll is shown on the policy. So, in theory, as long as payroll costs are known, an employer should know the cost of insurance.

All workers' compensation insurance policies start out with an estimated premium, because the payroll numbers for the policy period cannot be known exactly. The actual premium will vary depending upon what the actual payrolls turns out to be for the policy period. So even a "guaranteed-cost" policy has a premium that is only an estimate at the outset—subject to adjustment once actual payroll is determined.

The premium for a guaranteed-cost policy is adjusted only based on payroll changes, not on the cost of claims incurred or paid out under the policy. Remember that the premium for even a "guaranteed-cost" policy will be subject to a payroll audit and, thus, there may be additional premium charges due after the policy expires, if the actual payroll was higher than estimated. If the estimated payrolls are significantly lower than actual, you could be in for a large bill due after the policy expires. We'll go into more detail about how these premiums are calculated in the next chapter. Now, let's take an overview of the other types of workers' compensation policies employers may encounter.

LOSS-SENSITIVE PLANS

Some types of workers' compensation policies do adjust the premium based on losses incurred or paid out under the policy. Such policies are generally known as *loss-sensitive plans*, and there are a number of types. Loss-sensitive plans still use the rate times hundred dollars of payroll to calculate premiums, but then make further adjustments based on the losses under the policy. These adjustments may lower premiums if losses are low or may raise premiums even higher than the guaranteed-cost premium would be if losses are high. Here are the common types of loss-sensitive policies.

Retrospective Rating Plans

These policies compute premiums following the same rules as guaranteed-cost policies, but then make further adjustment by using a formula that incorporates the cost of claims that occur during the policy. These adjustments can make premiums lower than they would be been under a guaranteed-cost policy (if losses are low) or higher than they would be under a guaranteed-cost policy (if losses are high).

Under these policies, the major component of the cost becomes the losses covered by the policy. Because the total cost of the claims can't really be known until after the policy has ended, the *retrospective* premium adjustments are made after the policy ends. Such adjustments usually continue for a number of subsequent years, as the cost of claims can change over time. This, retrospective rating policies can sometimes create substantial additional costs for an employer long after the policy has ended. We'll get into more detail of how these "Retro" plans work in the next chapter.

Deductible Plans

These constitute another category of loss-sensitive plans. These come in two basic types: small-deductible plans and large-deductible plans. Small-deductible plans have deductibles of relatively low dollar amounts, such as $1,000 per claim. In return for accepting responsibility for paying these deductible amounts, the employer gets a discount on the premiums. This premium is computed along the same rules as the guaranteed-cost policy, but the rates have been discounted and the employer is responsible for reimbursing the insurer for the claims costs that fall under the deductible amount.

A large-deductible plan operates in similar fashion, but the size of the deductible is much larger, typically starting at $25,000 per claim and going upward from there. Like small-deductible plans, there is a discount given on the premium charges to reflect the deductible assumed by the employer. Most states that allow large-deductible plans permit insurers to offer them to employers whose premium size is above a certain threshold amount, so that these plans are typically available only for employers paying substantial premiums. Again, we get into a little more detail about these in the next chapter.

Dividend Plans

These types of plans used to be used much more commonly, but have been largely supplanted by other types of loss-sensitive plans in recent years. Still, in particular states, employers may encounter these types of plans. A dividend plan returns some portion of the guaranteed-cost premium to the employer based on loss-experience. Decades ago, mutual insurance companies paid dividends to policyholders according to the combined company-wide loss-experience, but such plans are rare now.

Sliding-scale dividend plans are a refinement of earlier dividend plans and return dividends to the employer based on the loss-experience during the term of the policy. Thus, sliding scale dividend plans can reduce premium costs if losses are low, but typically do not hold the possibility of premiums that are higher than guaranteed-cost if losses are excessive.

COMMON COVERAGE ENDORSEMENTS

Although the standard workers' compensation policy tends to provide very broad coverage, there are some endorsements that are commonly used to provide additional coverage. Here are some important endorsements that are used to extend or restrict coverage in certain situations.

Alternative employer endorsement extends coverage for employees working at another company, for example, workers from a temporary agency. This would typically be used to extend coverage to the client company of the temp agency for workers provided by the agency.

Employers' liability coverage endorsement (stopgap) is used to provide employers' liability coverage for employees in a monopoly state. Monopoly state funds do not provide the employers' liability coverage provided by Part Two of the standard workers' compensation policy, so this endorsement extends Part Two coverage to employees covered under such monopoly fund programs.

Joint Venture insured endorsement is used when the named insured on the policy is a joint venture. It clarifies that coverage extends to the members of the joint venture, but only regarding their capacity as members of the joint venture. If you also have other business enterprises separate from the joint venture, you will need separate workers' compensation coverage.

Medical benefits exclusion endorsement is used in states that allow employers to pay medical benefits directly, instead of through a workers' compensation policy. This endorsement excludes medical benefits for specified states and makes the employer responsible for payment of these benefits.

Partners, officers, and others exclusion endorsement is used when partners and executive officers wish to exclude themselves from coverage, and thus their remuneration will be excluded from premium computation.

Sole proprietors, partners, officers, and other coverage endorsement extends coverage to sole proprietors, partners, and officers who are not required to be covered, but who choose to extend coverage on themselves.

Voluntary compensation and employers' liability coverage endorsement is used to extend coverage to certain employees who are not required to be covered for workers' compensation benefits in a state, such as domestic or farm workers and commission-only salespeople.

Foreign voluntary compensation endorsement extends coverage to employees who are working outside the country for an extended period. Importantly, this can include repatriation expense, which can be a significant expense for injured workers who are out of the country.

Waiver of right of subrogation from others endorsement means the insurance company waives its right of subrogation against third parties who may be responsible for some losses under the policy. The particular parties who are covered by this waiver should be named in the endorsement.

THE EMPLOYER'S DUTY UNDER THE POLICY

The workers' compensation policy imposes certain duties upon the policyholder in the event of a claim, including:

- duty to notify the insurer if an injury that may be covered occurs;
- duty to provide for immediate medical and other services required by the applicable workers' compensation statues;
- duty to provide the insurer the names and addresses of the injured persons and of witnesses, as well as other information needed by the insurer, and to promptly give the insurer all notices, demands, and legal papers related to the injury;
- duty to cooperate with the insurer and to assist in the investigation, settlement, or defense of the claim; and
- duty to do nothing after an injury occurs that would interfere with the insurer's right to recover from others.

Remember that if you do anything to violate these duties, the insurance company may be able to claim breach of contract and void the policy.

The workers' compensation policy also lists five conditions that apply. These conditions deal with inspections, long-term policies, the transfer of the named insured's rights, cancellation of the policy, and the sole representative on behalf of all insureds.

The inspections section gives the insurance company the right to make an inspection of the workplace at any time. Historically, these inspections were done for the purposes of loss control and safety engineering, but then some insureds took legal action against the insurers, claiming that the insurance companies had failed to notify the employers of safety matters that eventually caused serious problems. Nowadays, the insurance policy makes it clear that these inspections are not intended to be a comprehensive safety program. Insurers don't want to be held responsible for any alleged deficiencies or shortcomings in those services.

The transfer of rights section prohibits the policy holder from transferring their rights or duties to another party without written consent from the insurance company.

FEDERAL WORKERS' COMPENSATION COVERAGE

Although workers' compensation coverage is primarily a matter of obligations and rules established by the individual states, there are some federal laws that come into play in certain situations.

The United States Longshore and Harbor Compensation Act (LHWCA) was enacted in 1927 to provide benefits to employees other than seamen who worked in maritime employment. Employees working upon the navigable waters of the U.S. are generally not covered by state workers' compensation laws. The coverage of the LHWCA is pretty broad, applying to compensation for disability or death of an employee injured while working on the navigable water of the U.S., including any adjoining pier, wharf, dry dock, terminal, marine railway, or other area customarily used in loading, unloading, dismantling, or building a vessel.

However, the LHWCA does not apply to an officer or employee of the federal government or any state or local governments, or any employee injured solely due to the employee's intoxication or a fellow employees willful intention. And the definition of "employee" under the LHWCA excludes clerical, secretarial, security, or data processing. It also excludes employees of camps, restaurants, recreational facilities, or retail outlets; employees of marinas; aquaculture workers; workers who build, repair, or dismantle recreational vessels under sixty-five feet long; masters or members of a crew of a vessel; and workers loading, unloading, or repairing a vessel under eighteen tons.

The Jones Act, also known as the Merchant Marine Act of 1920, also applied to maritime employees. This Act mandates benefits for seamen injured in the course of their employment due to the negligence of their owner, master, or fellow crew members. This Act itself does not define the term "seaman," so this has been left to the courts to decide. Over the years, courts have determined through decisions that certain factors determine if a worker is a "seaman." Some of these factors are that the vessel in question must be in navigable waters, the workers must have a permanent connection the vessel, and the worker must be aboard to aid in the navigation of the vessel—that is, be part of the actual operation of the ship.

CHECKLIST TO AVOID PROBLEMS

Here are six suggestions for avoiding common problems with workers' compensation policies.
- Name all related business entities (including land trusts, if any) on the policy.
- List all states where you operate in item 3A of the information page.
- Make sure that the Other States Coverage in Item 3C of the Information Page shows all states except those in Item 3A and the monopoly states.
- Review operations to see if any federal coverage must be endorsed onto the policy.
- Verify that the employers' liability limits matches what is shown on the umbrella or excess liability policy.
- Make sure that estimated payrolls are reasonable when the policy begins to avoid a large additional premiums due after the policy ends.

STEPS TO TAKE TO EVALUATE YOUR STATE-BY-STATE WORKERS COMPENSATION EXPOSURES

1. Examine your company's possible exposures to workers' compensation claims from different states. If you have

employees who live in or who travel through or in other states, you need to make sure you are properly covered in each state. Remember, many states treat uninsured contractors or subcontractors the same as an employee of yours.

2. If you have workers in monopoly-fund states, you will need to arrange coverage through those state funds. Private insurance cannot satisfy coverage requirements for monopolistic states.

3. If you are based in a monopolistic-fund state, but have some workers elsewhere, you will need to arrange coverage for those states separate from your state fund.

4. If you are self-insured in your primary state of operations, but have some employees or uninsured subcontractors in other states, you will need to arrange coverage for those other states.

5. If you are operating in multiple states, check into possible different classification definitions that apply in different jurisdictions for your operation. Make sure you are properly classified in each state to avoid either hidden overcharges or an unpleasant audit surprise of additional premium.

6. A few states do not use the interstate experience modification factor system, but instead calculate a modifier only for use within that state, based on prior losses and payrolls within that state. These "stand-alone" states are California, Michigan, Pennsylvania, Delaware, and New Jersey. If you have operations in these states, but also operate elsewhere, make sure proper experience modifiers are used for the stand-alone states.

QUICK REVIEW

- Make sure the named insured on the workers' compensation policy includes all related entities.
- Make sure the policy lists all states where you have operations.
- Make sure the policy is endorsed with any federal workers compensation endorsements your company may

need, such as Longshore and Harbor Workers and Defense Base coverage.

- Make sure the employer liability limit on the workers compensation policy matches what is required under umbrella or excess liability policy.
- Make sure the estimated payroll on the policy is reasonable to avoid large premium adjustments at audit.

CHAPTER 3

UNDERSTANDING HOW PREMIUMS ARE CALCULATED

In Chapter 2, we touched upon why the phrase "Guaranteed Cost" can be misleading. When insurance people talk about a "Guaranteed Cost" Workers Compensation insurance policy, they mean that the policy's premium is not adjusted to reflect the cost of claims paid under the policy. However, a "Guaranteed Cost" premium is not guaranteed to stay the same as the original premium on the policy. The actual premium charges for the policy can and will be adjusted to reflect the actual payroll of the insured business, so the premium shown on the policy is not the final premium that will be ultimately due for the coverage. The original policy's premium is an estimate, subject to later revision. In my experience as an agent and consultant, I've learned that while many of those adjustments made by insurance companies are proper and according to the rules, *many others are not.*

I don't think I can stress this enough. Insurance companies make lots of mistakes in computing Workers Compensation insurance premiums. Human nature being what it is, insurers tend to catch the mistakes that would cost them money—mistakes that lower premiums. They are nowhere as vigilant about catching mistakes that increase premiums.

To avoid paying premiums charges that are not correct and are not according to the rules, businesses need to learn the basics about how Workers Compensation insurance premiums are calculated— and sometimes miscalculated.

Calculating Premiums

Not all Workers Compensation policies are "Guaranteed Cost." But all policies use the guaranteed cost premium computation formula as the starting point. Loss-sensitive policies make additional adjustments to premium; they start with the same formulas and rules that are used for guaranteed-cost policies. So understanding how guaranteed cost premiums are calculated is fundamental to understanding how all Workers Compensation insurance premiums are calculated.

Rate Times Hundred Dollars of Payroll

Rate times hundred dollars of payroll is the most fundamental calculation at the heart of Workers Compensation insurance premiums. Virtually all Workers Compensation insurance premiums are calculated by multiplying a rate times hundred dollars of payroll. (For a few kinds of work such as domestic workers, the premium is often calculated on a per capita charge.) There have been efforts in recent years to allow construction-related employers to calculate premiums on an hours-worked basis, but this has only been approved in the state of Washington so far. The idea is that payroll fluctuations roughly match up with fluctuations in workplace exposure to injury. It's also a verifiable number that insurance companies can audit without undue difficulty.

In this book (and the insurance industry generally) payroll is often described as the basis for Workers' Compensation premiums, but that's not technically accurate…it's really **remuneration** that is the basis, and remuneration can include more than just payroll. The insurance industry, in its wisdom, figured out that if it based premium charges solely on payroll, some employers would inevitably try to hold down payroll costs (and, thus, their Workers Compensation costs) and compensate employees in other ways as much as possible. Insurers feared this would distort matters and shortchange them on premium, so "remuneration" is defined pretty broadly to discourage such maneuvers. Of course, for most employers, remuneration is almost exclusively payroll, but sometimes an employer can get tripped up by not understanding what really constitutes remuneration under the terms of Workers Compensation policies. In this book, we will usually use the term "payroll" but understand that this is really shorthand for "remuneration," as defined below.

Under NCCI rules, remuneration *includes*:

wages or salaries (including retroactive wages or salaries;

total cash received by an employee for commissions and draws against commissions;

bonuses including stock bonus plans;

extra pay for overtime work (but this can be adjusted to remove the premium portion);

pay for holidays, vacations or periods of sickness;

payment by an employer of amounts that would have been withheld from employees to meet statutory obligations for insurance or pensions plans such as the Federal Social Security Act or Medicare;

payment to employees on any basis other than time worked, such as piecework, profit sharing, or incentive plans;

payment or allowances for hand tools or hand-held power tools used by employees in their work;

the rental value of an apartment or house provided to an employee based on comparable accommodations;

the value of lodging, other than an apartment or house received by an employee as part of their pay to the extent shown in the insured's records;

the value of meals received by employees as part of their pay to the extent shown in the insured's records;

the value of store certificates, merchandise, credits or any other substitute for money received by employees as part of their pay;

payments for salary reduction, employee savings plans, retirement or cafeteria plans (IRC 125) that are made through employee-authorized salary reduction from the employee's gross pay;

Davis-Bacon wages or wages from a similar prevailing wage law;

annuity plans; and

expense reimbursements to employees to the extent that an employer's records do not confirm that the expense was incurred as a valid business expense.

But NCCI manual rules also specify that certain things are *excluded* **from the definition of remuneration:**

Tips or other gratuities received by employees;

Payments by an employer to group insurance or group pension plans for employees;

Payments by an employer into third-party trusts for the Davis-Bacon Act or a similar prevailing wage law provided the pension trust is qualified under IRC Sections 401(a) and 501(a);

The value of special rewards for individual invention or discovery;

Dismissal or severance payments except for time worked or vacation accrued;

Payments for active military duty;

Employee discounts on goods purchased from the employee's employer;

Expense reimbursements to employees to the extent that an employer's records confirm that the expense was incurred as a valid business expense;

Supper money for late work;

Work uniform allowances

Sick pay paid to an employee by a third party such as an insured's group insurance carrier that is paying disability income benefits to a disabled employee

Employer-provided perks such as:

- Use of company-provided automobiles
- Airplane flights
- Incentive vacations (e.g., contest winners)
- Discounts on property or services
- Club memberships
- Tickets to entertainment events

Employer contributions to employee benefit plans such as:

- Employee savings plans
- Retirement plans

Cafeteria plans (IRC 125)

The NCCI

As mentioned earlier in Chapter 1, the National Council on Compensation Insurance is an insurance-industry organization that, among other things, writes the rules that are used in most (but not all) states that govern how Workers Compensation insurance premiums are computed. It is a private corporation, technically owned by member insurance companies. It essentially acts as a centralized organization for Workers Compensation insurance ratemaking, giving a large degree of standardization to the industry. It has historically been known as a **rating bureau**, although in more recent years regulators have adopted the term "advisory organization." We'll get into more detail about NCCI and other rating bureaus later on in this book.

NCCI writes various manuals that are filed with state insurance regulators on behalf of member insurance companies. In theory, insurance companies could develop their own manuals and file them with regulators, but they have historically rarely chosen to do so. Instead, they find it more economical to be members of NCCI (and other rating bureaus) and let those rating bureaus handle the work of developing manuals of rules, and gathering data used for ratemaking and experience modification factors.

Keep in mind, the above lists of inclusions and exclusions for remuneration are from NCCI manual rules, and NCCI rules are used in most, but not all, jurisdictions. In Pennsylvania and Delaware, for example, the rules of the separate rating bureau used there do not allow the premium portion of overtime pay to be excluded from remuneration. Ohio also does not allow the premium portion of overtime pay to be excluded when computing Workers Compensation charges in its state monopoly fund system. Some other states also do not use the NCCI manual rules, so always check carefully if the rules in your particular state vary.

Remuneration is one important element of Workers Compensation premiums—and another is the rate that gets multiplied times each hundred dollars of remuneration. So next we need to understand how those rates are developed and applied in the computation of Workers Compensation insurance premiums.

Manual Rate

The rates you may see on your company's Workers Compensation policy or audit billing statement are manual rates. Workers Compensation insurance rating systems assign different kinds of work to different classifications; each classification within a particular state carries its own rate per hundred dollars of payroll (or remuneration).

The idea is that different kinds of work have different inherent exposures to workplace injury and illness, and so should have manual rates that are commensurate with that exposure. Thus, the manual rate for clerical work is typically the least expensive classification (with a rate in the range of $ 0.30 to $ 0.50 per hundred dollars of payroll) while the manual rate for a riskier kind of work such as roofing might have a manual rate of $25 or $30 per hundred dollars of payroll.

A typical Workers Compensation insurance policy for a manufacturer might have three different classifications, each with its own manual rate, while a policy for a construction-related employer might have five or six different classifications. Some kinds of employers, such as temporary employment agencies or employee leasing companies can have dozens or even hundreds of different classifications on their policies. Each classification will be listed, with a brief written description and a code number (NCCI and most other rating bureaus use a four digit code system) and the manual rate for each.

The manual rate for a classification is the rate per hundred dollars of payroll that a particular insurance company has filed to use in a particular state. Some states require that all insurance companies use the same schedule of manual rates within their jurisdiction, but nowadays many states allow competing insurance companies to develop their own schedules of manual rates.

However, the manual rates used by a particular insurance company will be the same for all policyholders insured by that particular insurer. So if hypothetical insurer Amalgamated Insurance Giant has filed to use a rate of $0.35 for clerical work (Code 8810) in the state of Illinois, every insured of Amalgamated Insurance Giant will get that $0.35 rate for clerical work in Illinois.

In other words, the manual rate doesn't vary based on your company's past loss-experience or any other underwriting evaluation done by the insurance company (that's accomplished by subsequent rating factors). The manual rate is really a starting point for calculating premiums; the rate is then adjusted to reflect your company's particular loss history and other credits or charges made by the insurance company.

Years ago, it was standard in all states to have just one set of manual rates that had to be used by all insurers in a state. So every insurance company would use the same manual rate for clerical work, for instance. But that has changed dramatically over the course of the past two decades, as most states have introduced some form of competitive rating to Workers Compensation insurance. That means that in most states, insurance companies are encouraged to develop their own schedules of manual rates, with the idea being to foster price competition among insurance companies. So the manual rate for Code 8810 could be $0.35 from Amalgamated Insurance Giant, but $0.43 from National Mutual Insurance.

The Classification Problem
Of course, most businesses aren't exclusively clerical in their work exposures. And one key to making sure your Workers Compensation insurance premiums are correct is making sure your insurance company is using the correct classification code for your particular workplace exposures. Classification systems for Workers Compensation insurance aren't always as clear-cut and easy to administer as might be wished, so mistakes in assigning the correct classifications (and thus the correct manual rates) are far from uncommon. Sometimes the difference between qualifying for a low rated classification and a higher rated one is subtle.

One important principle of Workers Compensation classification is that, generally speaking, it is the overall business enterprise that is classified, not the particular job functions. So, for example, a janitor in a manufacturing plant is not assigned to a janitorial classification, but instead is placed in the classification for the particular kind of manufacturing involved.

We'll get into much greater detail about the classification system in Chapter 4, but at this point just keep in mind that a company's manual rates will depend upon which particular classifications are used by the insurance company. Each classification will have a particular manual rate, which is multiplied by each hundred dollars of payroll for the employees who fall into that classification. Multiplying payroll by manual rates produces *manual premium.*

Experience Rating
Manual premium gets adjusted for most employers by various other rating factors. The most widely used adjustment is "experience rating," which uses the **experience modification factor**. This is a multiplier that is calculated based on a particular company's reported past Workers Compensation losses. If your company's reported past losses are lower than average, you likely will earn a credit modifier. If your past reported losses are higher than average, you will probably get a debit modifier.

Whatever your experience modifier is calculated to be, the manual premium gets multiplied by that factor. So if manual premium is $100,000 but you have a .75 experienced modifier, your *modified premium* gets reduced to $75,000. If you experience modifier were 1.25 instead, your modified premium would be $125,000.

Most employers whose annual Workers Compensation premiums exceed $5,000 qualify to be experience rated. The particular thresholds for experience rating can vary depending on which state an employer is operating in and the thresholds also are periodically adjusted. Generally speaking, however, all but relatively small employers should qualify for experience rating. We'll get into much more detail about this in a later chapter, including how to check your experience modification factor for common errors.

Merit Rating

Some states—Alabama, Arkansas, Georgia, Oregon, South Dakota, and Vermont—have programs in place that offer credits or debits on premiums for employers too small to qualify for experience rating. These programs are known as Merit Rating. For example, in Alabama, an employer that is not experience rated and whose annual premium is less than $5,000 qualifies for merit rating as follows:

No claims in most recent year 10 percent credit
No claims in most recent two years 15 percent credit
One claim in most recent year no credit or debit
Two or more claims in most recent year 10 percent debit

Other Premium Credits or Debits

Many states also allow discretionary credits or debits by insurers. These are generally known as "schedule credits" or "schedule debits" and they work much like experience modification factors. They are percentage discounts or surcharges that further adjust the modified premium. So a 25 percent schedule credit would further reduce premium charges by 25 percent. Conversely, a 25 percent schedule debit would add a 25 percent surcharge.

These schedule credits and debits are filed by insurers with state regulators and are supposed to be used on a rational and specified basis. That is, an insurance company will file with state insurance regulators that it wants to be approved for a maximum overall limit of credit and debit charges; if regulators approve it, the insurer can then apply up to that maximum 40 percent credit or debit for a particular policyholder. Within those overall limits, insurers also file sub-limits for particular criteria they propose for these adjustments. For example, if an insured filed for a 50 percent maximum credit or debit, it might use criteria like the following:

Schedule Rating Plan Credits and Debits
Criteria Maximum Credit or Debit Percent

Premises 10 percent
Classification Peculiarities 10 percent
Medical Facilities 5 percent
Safety Devices 5 percent
Employee selection, training, supervision 10percent
Management cooperation with insurer 5 percent
Management Safety Organization 5 percent

However, in actual practice, many state regulators pay little or no attention to how closely insurers actually follow these filed criteria. Insurers, therefore, often use schedule credits and debits with complete disregard for the criteria they file with regulators. They abide by the overall maximum amounts they have filed, but often use the debits/credits as discretionary adjustments to manipulate premiums for their own purposes. Thus, when insurance markets are soft, insurers will often use schedule credits to lower premiums in order to compete for an account that they view as attractive.

When insurance markets are hard, insurers will use schedule debits to increase premiums, essentially operating on a "charge what the market will bear" philosophy. An insurance company might offer significant credits to a policyholder one year and then, just a year or two later, when the insurance market has hardened, insist on considerable debit charges for that same employer. This change in rate would not be based on any changes in the specified criteria filed with regulators—just on the fact that the insurance company wants more money, and thinks it can get away with charging more in the hard market.

Unfortunately, insurance regulators tend to allow insurance companies to get away with such behavior, so it can be difficult for employers to challenge such abuses. But I have seen instances where specific complaints to regulators about such abuses have been successful when carriers were not able to justify their changes in schedule/debit charges based on the filed criteria.

Other Premium Credits

Many states have enacted other premium credits that can apply to certain employers within their jurisdictions. A number of states have enacted **contractor premium adjustment plans,** which can give employers in construction-related fields credits if their average hourly wages are relatively high. This can give some premium relief to construction businesses that pay high hourly wages. Other states allow credits for employers that maintain drug-free workplaces or for employers that elect to utilize managed care networks. Figure 3-1 shows the different kinds of premium credit programs offered by the various states.

One thing to keep in mind about many of these premium credit programs is that insurance companies have been successful in getting many of them set up in such a way that responsibility for filing the needed forms to qualify for the credits rests with the employers. If an employer doesn't realize that a premium credit might apply, and doesn't fill out and send in the appropriate forms, the employer won't get the premium credit. This is different from experience rating, which is done automatically (if not always correctly) for employers. So it can be important for employers to understand what kinds of premium credits may be available in their jurisdictions and to complete and send in the appropriate forms on a timely basis.

Standard Premium

Once the manual premium has been adjusted by the experience modification factor and any other credits and debits that apply, the resulting adjusted premium is known as the Standard Premium. This standard premium is used as a reference point by many loss-sensitive policies, but on a Guaranteed Cost policy there is one last major adjustment that is made: the premium discount.

Premium Discount

A premium discount is a size discount that is applied to Workers Compensation insurance premiums that exceed $5,000. It's also a sliding scale discount, so that as the premium grows larger, so does the percentage of the discount. These increasing discounts are figured by brackets, much like income tax brackets. The premium discount reduces premiums both on the policy and on the audit of the policy based on the bracket in which the premium fits. If the premium on the audit is different from that originally on the policy, the percentage of premium discount can change.

Other Charges

Other, relatively small, charges can contribute to Workers Compensation premiums. An Expense Constant is often added, which is a flat charge that essentially is just a surcharge for the expense of producing the policy. There is a terrorism charge that is a rate times total payroll. Some states have introduced surcharges to fund the operation of their state Workers Compensation Commissions (agencies that adjudicate Workers Compensation claims).

Summary of Calculating Premiums for Guarantee Cost Policies

So we've now reviewed the major (and some minor) elements that determine Workers Compensation insurance premiums. Manual premium is computed by determining which classifications apply to an employer and then multiplying payrolls by the manual rates for those classifications. The resulting manual premium is then adjusted by an experience modification factor, schedule credit or debit charges, and any other credits that may apply (such as a contractors premium adjustment plan credits or drug free workplace credits). Finally, premium discount, expense constant, and terrorism charges are factored in.

The following chart shows a sample premium calculation, to illustrate how these factors are used in computing premiums.

Jurisdiction	Manuals	Drug Credits	Merit Rating	Contractor Credit	Experience Modifiers	Safety Credit	State Fund
Alabama	NCCI	Yes	Yes		1		None
Alaska	NCCI			Yes	1		None
Arizona	NCCI				1		Competitive*
Arkansas	NCCI	Yes			1		None
California	Independent				2		Competitive
Colorado	NCCI				1		Competitive*
Connecticut	NCCI			Yes	1		None
D.C.	NCCI				1		None
Delaware	Independent				2		None
Florida	NCCI	Yes		Yes	1		None
Georgia	NCCI	Yes			1		None
Hawaii	NCCI		Yes	Yes	1		None
Idaho	NCCI	Yes			1		Competitive
Illinois	NCCI			Yes	1		None
Indiana	Independent				1		None
Iowa	NCCI				1		None
Kansas	NCCI				1		None
Kentucky	NCCI				1		None
Louisiana	NCCI				1		None
Maine	NCCI				1		None
Maryland	NCCI			Yes	1		Competitive
Massachusetts	Independent				1		
Michigan	Independent				2		
Minnesota	Independent				1		
Mississippi	NCCI	yes			1		
Missouri	NCCI			yes	1		
Montana	NCCI			Yes	1		
Nebraska	NCCI			Yes	1		
Nevada	NCCI				1		

Jurisdiction	Manuals	Drug Credits	Merit Rating	Contractor Credit	Experience Modifiers	Safety Credit	State Fund
New Hampshire	NCCI				1		
New Jersey	Independent				2		
New Mexico	NCCI			Yes	1		
New York	Independent			Sort of	1		
North Carolina	Independent	yes			1		
North Dakota	Monopoly				2		
Ohio	Monopoly				2		
Oklahoma	NCCI			Yes	1		
Oregon	NCCI			Yes	1		
Pennsylvania	Independent				2		
Puerto Rico	Monopoly				2		
Rhode Island	NCCI				1		
South Carolina	NCCI				1		
South Dakota	NCCI				1		
Tennessee	NCCI	yes			1		
Texas	Independent				1		
U.S. Virgin Islands	Monopoly				2		
Utah	NCCI				1		
Vermont	NCCI				1		
Virginia	NCCI				1		
Washington	Monopoly			Yes	2		
West Virginia	NCCI				1		
Wisconsin	Independent			Yes	1		
Wyoming	Monopoly				2		

Why Guaranteed Cost Isn't

The most basic kind of Workers Compensation insurance policy is often called a "Guaranteed Cost" policy, but this insurance industry term can be misleading. That's because the initial premium on a policy, even a so-called "Guaranteed Cost" policy, is only an estimate, because the payrolls are, by necessity, estimated. Only after the policy has ended can actual payrolls for the policy period be determined; then a final audited premium for the policy can be calculated by plugging in the actual payroll numbers.

To illustrate this, take a look at the following charts. The first shows a sample Guaranteed Cost policy's initial estimated premium. The second chart shows how the premium for that same policy could change once the actual audited payrolls are determined.

Chart 1 Estimated premium on the initial policy

Classification	Code	Rate	Payroll	Premium
Clerical	8810	0.32	$100,000	$320.00
Outside Sales	8742	0.78	$75,000	$585.00
Machine Shop	3632	$6.75	$750,000	$50,625
Manual Premium				51,530
Experience Modification Factor				0.78
Modified Premium				$40,193
Schedule Credit	-25%			$30,145
Drug Free Workplace Credit	-5%			$28,638
Standard Premium				$28,638
Premium Discount	-10.30%			$25,688
Discounted Premium				$25,688

Chart 2   Billed Premium for same policy after audit

Classification	Code	Rate	Payroll	Premium
Clerical	8810	0.32	$88,567	$283
Outside Sales	8742	0.78	$76,875	$600
Machine Shop	3632	$6.75	$877,543	$59,234
Manual Premium				60,117
Experience Modification Factor				0.78
Modified Premium				46,891
Schedule Credit	-25%			$35,169
Drug Free Workplace Credit	-5%			$33,410
Standard Premium				$33,410
Premium Discount	-10.30%			$29,969
Discounted Premium				$29,969

So this employer purchased a policy that cost $25,688.00 in premium at the outset, but after the policy ended and an audit was done of payrolls, the actual cost for the policy was determined to be $29,969.00. The increase in premium was due to the changes in payroll. So this "Guaranteed Cost" policy didn't mean that the original premium of $25,688 was guaranteed to not increase—it just meant that premium would be determined by multiplying rates times payroll, without any additional adjustments based on the claims incurred during the term of the policy. There are other kinds of policies, generally known as "Loss-Sensitive" policies that make additional adjustments based on the claims that are covered under the policy. We'll discuss these in more detail later.

Assigned Risk Plans

Since Workers Compensation obligations are essentially imposed upon employers by government even though most states utilize private insurance companies as the vehicle by which most employers satisfy those obligations, the question arises: what happens when insurance companies don't want to underwrite a particular employer? After all, as private businesses, insurance companies have the right to decline to underwrite certain risks. In recognition of this possible problem, the various states have all come up with some kind of "insurer of last resort"—a vehicle by which an employer can still obtain Workers Compensation insurance even if insurance companies are not willing to insure that employer voluntarily. That vehicle is generally known as "Assigned Risk" or "the involuntary market."

Not all states call their program Assigned Risk, although most do. States that have a competitive state fund usually use that fund as the insurer of last resort. States that do not have a state fund (and most don't) utilize a pooling mechanism by which employers who can't get Workers Compensation in the "voluntary market" can still get coverage—although it's often at much higher rates.

An Assigned Risk policy usually looks pretty much the same as a voluntary market policy. Sometimes employers are not even aware that their coverage has been written through the Assigned Risk plan, because agents sometimes don't make that clear to them. The policy still shows the name of a particular insurance company—Amalgamated Insurance Group, perhaps—and it won't usually make an obvious reference to being an assigned risk policy.

But in many states, the premium charges for an assigned risk policy will be much higher than the premium charges for the same policy if written in the voluntary market. ("Voluntary market" is the insurance industry term for policies written voluntarily, that is, not in an assigned risk program.)

The assigned risk plans in many states are pooling mechanisms; claims incurred under the policies are not the responsibility of the insurance company (Amalgamated Insurance Group, in our fictitious example) shown on the policy. Claims and premiums are pooled among a number of insurers who write Workers Compensation insurance in the state. So even though Amalgamated Insurance Group is shown on the front of the policy, this insurance company doesn't get to keep the premiums, and they get to pass the claims costs along to the larger pool. Amalgamated just gets a servicing fee for producing and servicing the policy. That's probably why so many people covered by assigned risk policies complain that the service they receive from the insurance company is poor.

Premium charges for assigned risk policies are calculated pretty much the same as for voluntary market policies—with a few changes that serve to make premiums much higher. (At least, this is true in most states—a few don't add higher costs to their assigned risk programs.)

For starters, the manual rates in assigned risk plans are usually higher. If the manual rate for Code 3632 in a state is $6.23, the manual rate for Code 3632 in the assigned risk plan might well be something like $7.58.
To make matters worse, in most NCCI states, you lose the premium discount factor in the assigned risk plan. And assigned risk polices aren't eligible for any schedule credits that might be offered in the voluntary market. And then there's the *ARAP* charge. ARAP stands for Assigned Risk Adjustment Program.

The ARAP is an additional surcharge for assigned risk employers once their experience modification factor rises above 1.00. How much of a surcharge depends on how much higher than 1.00 your experience modifier is, but the surcharge can easily add another 25 percent or more to the premium. So often, premiums costs in the assigned risk plan can be double what they would be in the voluntary market, once you add up the higher rates, loss of premium discount factors, loss of schedule credits, and ARAP charges.

Massachusetts, by the way, utilizes ARAP surcharges for both Assigned Risk and voluntary market coverage when employers have high experience modifiers.
To be fair, assigned risk plans in many states have hemorrhaged money for many years, becoming a serious hidden tax on the insurance industry and their policyholders. That's because when assigned risk plans paid out more in claims than they took in as

premiums, the shortfall had to be made up by assessing insurance companies. So these higher premium charges are efforts to make the overall assigned risk plans self-funding. But it also means that if your company is in the assigned risk plan, the already-high cost of Workers Compensation insurance will likely be much, much higher.

Not all states feature these higher costs in the assigned risk plans. States that use their competitive state funds as the assigned risk mechanism may not impose higher rates and other surcharges. But for most employers with assigned risk policies, moving into the voluntary market can make a huge difference in premiums. So the first order of business for employers looking to reduce Workers Compensation costs is to see if they are in the assigned risk plan, and if so, what can be done to get out of it.

Retrospective Rating Plans
A relatively recent development with NCCI assigned risk plans in many states is the imposition of a mandatory loss-sensitive rating plan for policies over $200,000 in annual premium. It's known as LSRP, or Loss Sensitive Rating Plan, and it imposes a not-very friendly version of Retrospective Rating onto those larger assigned risk policies. Retrospective Rating can lower premiums if claims are relatively low, but it also has the potential to increase premiums if claims costs are not so low. Retrospective Rating plans (or "Retro" plans, as they're commonly known) are a form of Loss-Sensitive policies. That means that premiums are adjusted based on the losses that occur during the term of the policy. Since you can't know what those claims costs are until well after the policy has ended, these premium adjustments are made after the policy expiration. Usually, there are a series of annual adjustments made, reflecting the changing costs of the claims over time.

Retro policies use a set formula to make further adjustments to Standard Premium. The details of the formula can vary widely, but they all "look back" (hence the "Retro" terminology) to see what the claims costs of the policy were. And since those claims costs change as time goes by, the Retro adjustments are annually revised to reflect the latest calculations of those claims costs. Claims costs evolve over time because even though a particular claim occurs at a particular date, one can't know at the outset exactly how expensive that claim will eventually be. Thus, the ultimate cost of a retrospectively rated policy won't typically be known until years after the policy has ended.

Retro policies calculate these subsequent adjustments by taking the Standard Premium and the losses for that policy year and running them through a formula that has been agreed upon in advance. Usually this formula is contained in an endorsement to the policy, although sometimes insurance companies utilize separate written agreements. We'll discuss problems with the use of these separate written agreements later.

A classic Retrospective formula works like this: you begin with a **Basic** charge, which is a percentage of Standard Premium. Then you take the total of all claims incurred during the policy and multiply this amount by a Loss Conversion Factor, or LCF. (The claims costs usually include not just what's been paid out by the insurance company, but also that company's reserves for claims. Reserves are the insurers' estimate of what future payments on the claim will be.) Losses multiplied by the LCF produce **converted losses**. You then add the **Basic Premium** to the **Converted Losses** and multiply that total by a **tax factor**. (States charge taxes that are included in Guaranteed Cost policy premiums, but are broken out separately on Retro policies.)

Keep in mind that the above describes the factors of what I call a "classic" Retro—the kind that's used on the LSRP assigned risk Retro—but many insurers nowadays have added some additional factors to their Retro formulas. Other insurance companies have developed policies that mimic Retro formulas by means of written side agreements that add Retro-style adjustments to Large Deductible policies.

Let's take a look at how such a Retro plan would work. If our hypothetical policy generated $100,000 in Standard Premium (that's premium after experience modifier and other credits, but without premium discount) for policy period January 1, 2008 through January 1, 2009, and had a basic factor of 30 percent, and losses for the year totaled $45,000 with a Loss Conversion Factor of 1.15 and a Tax Factor of 1.03, the Retro premium would be calculated as follows on the first Retro adjustment. This first adjustment would be based on incurred losses as they were valued on July 1, 2009.

(a) Basic Premium $30,000 ($100,000 Standard
     Premium × .30)
(b) Converted Losses $51,750 ($45,000 in losses ×
     1.15 LCF)
(c) Sum of a + b $81,750
     Tax factor 1.03
     Retro premium $84,202.50 ($81,750 × 1.03)

So under this hypothetical Retro plan, the premium would be lower than the standard premium (which was $100,000). It's lower even than it would have been if a premium discount had been applied to the Standard Premium, as it would have been under a non-assigned risk guaranteed-cost policy.

But consider what might happen for the same policy on the subsequent retrospective adjustment, done a year later. By July 1, 2010, incurred losses for the 2008-09 policy period have changed, and are now valued at $66,000. This is because the reserves for some open claims have been increased, and incurred losses include paid losses and loss reserves. So now this subsequent Retro adjustment would work out as follows:

(a) Basic premium $30,000
(b) Converted losses $75,900 ($66,000 × 1.15 LCF)
     Sum of a + b $105,900
     Tax factor 1.03
     Retro premium $109,077

Now Retro premium is higher than the Standard Premium. And if losses increase even more on later adjustments, the premium will continue to increase—at least up to a point.

That's because Retro policies also have **Minimum** and **Maximum** premium factors. These place a floor on how low premiums can go, even if there are zero losses, and a ceiling on premiums, even if losses are extremely high. These are usually expressed as percentages of Standard Premium. So if our hypothetical Retro had a Maximum of 1.30, this would mean that the maximum premium that could be charged would be 130 percent of Standard Premium. If Standard Premium were $100,000, the maximum that could be charged would be $130,000, no matter how high losses might climb.

Conversely, if the minimum premium were .35, the lowest the premium could go would be $35,000, or 35 percent of the Standard Premium of $100,000.

If you haven't dealt much with Workers Compensation insurance, you might be asking why the claims costs would increase so much over time. (If you have dealt with Workers Comp for a while, you probably know all too well why this happens.)

There are two reasons for this. First, many claims don't get fully settled or paid out during the term of the policy. So a year later, when our second Retro adjustment was done, the cost of those claims was higher. Second, as we mentioned earlier, many Retro policies (but not all) are based on **incurred losses.** Incurred losses include not just what's actually been paid out on a claim, but also the insurance company's estimates, or reserves, for what they think the ultimate cost of the claim will be. The estimation of proper reserves on a Workers Compensation claim is as much art as science, and they often change over time.

So in our second Retro adjustment above, not only could the paid out claims for 2008-09 be now higher than a year earlier, it might well also be that the reserves set a year ago for some claims have now been revised upwards in light of changing circumstances and information.

So one drawback to Retro plans is that until all the claims for the year are settled and paid and closed out, there can be additional charges for the policy that aren't known until years later. So our hypothetical employer in our example could be paying additional premium charges for the 2008-09 policy until 2014 or later.

The Maximum premium factor can help limit these unpleasant surprises, but only to a limited degree. Still, under the 1.30 Maximum premium we discussed earlier, this would mean that under our hypothetical Retro incurred losses over $83,664 would not increase premiums further. Incurred losses of $83,664 would produce Retro premium of $130,000 under this plan. Since $130,000 is the plan maximum, losses above $83,664 could not increase premiums above the $130,000 maximum. So even though losses of $90,000 would, under the Retro formula, produce a Retro premium of $137,505, the most that could be charged would be 130 percent of the Standard Premium, or $130,000.

The other side of the coin is that, even if incurred losses were zero, the Minimum premium factor means that $35,000, or 35 percent of Standard Premium, is due.

Deductible Plans

Another common type of loss-sensitive plan involves the use of a deductible. These plans come in two varieties, small deductibles and large deductibles. Small-deductible plans are normally set by statute in various states. That is, state law dictates that insurers must provide a certain set discount in return for the employer accepting a specified deductible. Small deductibles range from $100 per claim to $1,000 per claim typically. Large deductibles can range from $25,000 per claim up to a several hundred thousand dollars per claim or even a million dollars.

In such plans, the employer agrees to reimburse the insurer for the amount of the claims that fall under the deductible limits. This is a little different from deductibles in other kinds of insurance, where the insured is responsible for paying the deductible amount outright. With Workers Compensation insurance, regulators want to make sure injured workers have their claims paid without worrying about whether the employer can afford to pay. So in Workers Compensation deductibles, the insurer is still responsible for paying the claims, but it then has a right to demand reimbursement from the employer for those claims costs that fall under the deductible limits.

In fact, what is normally done is that insurance company requires the employer to pre-fund money for payment of claims under the deductible limit, and to replenish those funds as they are paid out. The insurance companies also normally require some additional security, such as a Letter of Credit, to make sure the employer is funding claims payments under the deductible. Thus, large-deductible plans have many of the characteristics of self-insurance, in that the employer is really paying for the cost of most claims, and is just purchasing the claims handling services of the insurer.

The advantage of large-deductible policies over genuine self-insurance is that the large-deductible policy is still a valid Workers Compensation insurance policy that meets the statutory requirements of the various states. For multiple state operations, it is much less cumbersome to enter into a large-deductible policy than to set up self-insurance programs that are approved by each of the various states.

Large-deductible plans normally have both a per occurrence deductible limit and an aggregate limit. The aggregate limit sets a maximum amount for all claims covered by the policy. In return for accepting these deductibles, the employer gets a very large discount applied to the manual premium. These large-deductible discount factors are not set by statute, but are individually negotiated between the employer and the insurer. The amount of discount can vary significantly from one policy to another or even between one year's policy and the next year's policy for the same employer. In small-deductible policies, the employer receives a much smaller discount that is set by statute or regulation.

This means that under Large- Deductible policies, there are really two separate kinds of charges that an employer will have to pay the insurance company. The first is the discounted premium charge, and the second is the funding for the claims costs. In actual practice, insurers usually bundle both kinds of charges into a unified billing system for the employer.

One complicating factor with Large Deductible policies is that there inevitably have to be separate written agreements that govern how the employer will fund the claims costs (and associated claims handling charges). These agreements often are very complex, and their language can make the standard Workers Compensation insurance policy (which itself is not written in user-friendly language) look straightforward by comparison. So one problem with these kinds of programs is that even large sophisticated companies may well not fully understand the details of what they have agreed to. This can lead to unpleasant surprises down the road when these programs turn out to be more expensive than the employer anticipated.

It is not uncommon for these separate side agreements to Large Deductible programs act to create payment provisions that are different from those actually set forth in the policy. The separate side agreements may act to turn a Guaranteed Cost policy into something that operates more like a Retro policy. But the provisions contained in such side agreements are often not submitted for approval by insurance regulators, the way real Retrospective Rating programs must be, and, thus, insurers can craft rating provisions that are more favorable to themselves.

Large Deductible policies were originally approved for use only with very large employers, but over time, lower premium thresholds have been approved by many states. So where once an employer had to pay a million dollars in premium to be eligible for a Large Deductible policy, currently many states allow such plans to be offered to employers paying only several hundred thousand dollars in premium. We'll get into more detail about some of these more complicated plans later in the book and describe some of the potential benefits and pitfalls of these programs.

QUICK REVIEW

A Workers Compensation premium is almost always calculated using rates per hundred dollars of **remuneration (payroll).**

Remuneration is largely payroll, but can also include other items of value provided by an employer.

Changes in payroll can result in significant changes in premium, even for so-called **"Guaranteed Cost"** policies.

For many employers, premium is adjusted based on prior losses and payrolls, by means of the **experience modification factor**. This is calculated yearly by a rating bureau like the National Council on Compensation Insurance and then applied by the insurance company to compute the premium.

Retrospective Rating policies make a further adjustment to the premium based on losses that occur during the term of the policy.

Deductible policies discount the premiums in return for the employer accepting responsibility for claims falling under the deductible limit. Deductible policies come in two varieties: **small deductible** policies that are set by state statute and **Large Deductible** policies whose terms are negotiated between the employer and the insurer.

CHAPTER 4

WHO CREATED THE CLASSIFICATION SYSTEM?

The classifications that are assigned to a business can significantly affect how much premium the company pays every year for their Workers Compensation premium. The classification code will determine the rate that your payroll is multiplied by, and will be the most significant factor in determining your premium.

The system used in workers' compensation is a unique one, different from SIC codes. It is complicated enough that even many insurance professionals do not understand well all the nuances of the system. Most employers understand the system poorly and count on the varied expertise of their agents, which creates a situation in which mistakes will happen.

Insurance carriers are pretty good about catching mistakes that are costing them money—they are on look out for claims history that suggests that the work is more dangerous than the current classification code would suggest. However, they are much less likely to catch mistakes that are costing you money.

Various classification systems are set up throughout the country. The most widely used is the one created by the National Council on Compensation Insurance, Inc. (NCCI), whose system is used even by states that are not under NCCI's jurisdiction. A few states use systems that are very unlike the one used by NCCI, but there is a good deal that is shared among all of them. Since NCCI is the most widely used classification system, we'll be discussing it the most.

These classification code systems have been devised over time by the insurance industry, subject to oversight and approval by insurance regulators. One of the several manuals produced by NCCI is the Scopes® Manual, which is a detailed explanation of the various classifications in their system. (NCCI also produces other manuals that govern Workers Compensation insurance in the states that use the NCCI system.)

NCCI was formed in 1920 after state regulators pressured insurance carriers to standardize the rules for Workers Compensation insurance. Although NCCI may, at first glance, appear to be a governmental agency, that is not what they are. NCCI is an independent organization that works as a sort of interface between insurance companies and insurance regulators. NCCI works to develop the manuals of rules that govern the computation of workers' compensation premiums and performs a lot of statistical work used to develop rates for particular kinds of work in particular states, and they calculate the experience modifications factors that used in most, but not all, states.

The idea that NCCI is governmental agency might arise in part because some other rating bureaus are indeed government established bodies. In those states that use non-NCCI rating bureaus, some of those other rating bureaus are run by the state government.

No matter which rating bureau is used in a particular state, that rating bureau sets the rules regarding how certain business enterprises are classified for the purposes of computing premiums. The NCCI produces a manual that details what is intended to be included in each classification code: *The Scopes® of Basic Manual Classifications*—the Scopes® Manual for short.

Even though this manual largely determines how your business will be classified (for operations in NCCI states, at least), it is copyrighted material that is published and sold by NCCI. So if you want to read the details of what's in this manual, you could order a copy from NCCI. But most employers don't need to go to that expense. For one thing, you can call NCCI and get information about particular classifications at no cost. NCCI maintains customer service people who are glad to discuss the details about how particular work exposures should be classified. Just keep in mind that the customer service people have to rely on the information you provide over the phone to give accurate advice. So try to be as thorough and accurate as you can be in describing your situation.

A lot of times we get calls from people asking where online they can find the details of what's covered by certain classifications. In this day and age, it's understandable that people think any and all such information should be available on the internet somewhere. But as this is copyrighted material that NCCI sells to insurance companies, insurance agents, and consultants like me, they really can't make it available free on the internet. However, a policyholder should be able to get information about their specific classifications from their agent or broker. Our company provides a lot of information at our web site, www.cutcomp.com, but we can't provide copyrighted contents of the Scopes® Manual. We'll gladly answer questions about particular classification at our toll-free number at 800-288-9256.

Which States Use NCCI
It's actually easier to list the ones that don't. Here are the states that maintain their own independent rating bureaus, with their own sets of manual rules:

California	Delaware	Indiana	Massachusetts
Michigan	Minnesota	New Jersey	North Carolina
Pennsylvania	Texas	Wisconsin	

Keep in mind that there are also the so-called "monopoly" jurisdictions where workers' compensation can be written only through a state administered fund:

North Dakota	Ohio	Puerto Rico	U.S. Virgin Islands
Washington (state)	Wyoming		

Every other state jurisdiction uses the NCCI system of manual rules for determining classifications, computing premiums, calculating experience modifiers, and other adjustments to the premium. There still can be important differences between one NCCI state and another, because each state can and often does enact particular rules and statues that can affect premiums. NCCI states operate under a unified set of manual rules, but those rules have a many exceptions for particular states.

How Classifications Affect Premium

Each particular classification will carry a particular rate per hundred dollars of payroll. So making sure your business is classified properly is vital to making sure your premiums are calculated properly. All classification systems used, whether with NCCI or others, have some common characteristics with which you should familiarize yourself.

The Governing Classification

Even the most basic kind of company will typically have more than one classification code used on its policy. The workers' compensation classification systems generally will try to classify the overall business enterprise, rather than breaking down each different kind of work done by employees. So janitors in a manufacturing plant won't go into a janitorial class, but instead into the overall classification assigned to that manufacturing operation. The classification on a policy that has the most payroll assigned to it is known as the "governing classification." This is the classification that it used to cover the overall business enterprise.

But for almost all types of businesses, the classification systems recognize certain *standard exception,* which are kinds of work that are almost always broken out into their own classifications. Clerical work is considered a standard exception for almost all employers. So, unlike our janitor in the manufacturing plant, the office workers in that same company will have their payroll assigned to code 8810, the class for clerical work. (Janitorial work is considered a *standard inclusion* in most classification codes.) Another important standard inclusion for most classifications is for shipping and warehousing. Although there is a separate classification for warehouse operations, the warehousing operations of a manufacturer are not assigned to this class. Instead, they are treated as a standard inclusion, so the shipping and warehousing employees of a manufacturing plant would be included in whatever the governing classification for that manufacturer is.

Another standard exception is for "Outside Sales." Almost all governing classifications allow outside salespeople to have their payroll broken out into code 8742. Drivers are another common standard exception; although there are a number of governing classifications that include drivers within their descriptions, so one has to look more carefully at the governing code to determine if drivers can be broken out or not.

FIGURE 4-1 *Representative Detail from the Scopes®️ manual*

The NCCI publishes a manual, known as the Scopes ® manual, that contains detailed descriptions of what is intended to be included under each classification. Here is an excerpt from that manual, to give some idea of the kind of detail they go into in this manual.

Each NCCI classification has a unique four-digit code number. The below Scopes ® entry is for Class Code 5213, Concrete Construction NOC. The NOC designation stands for Not Otherwise Classified. This means that this classification is used when some other, more specific, classification code does not fit an employer's operations.
5213

PHRASEOLOGY CONCRETE CONSTRUCTION NOC. Includes foundations or the making, setting up or taking down of forms, scaffolds, false work or concrete distributing apparatus. Excavation, pile driving, all work in sewers, tunnels, subways, caissons or cofferdams to be separately rated. Codes 5222-Concrete Construction in Connections with Bridges and Culverts—and 5506 and 5507—Street or Road Construction—shall not be assigned as the same job or location to which Code 5213 applies.

Figure 4-1 (continued)

CROSS-REF. Cleaning or Renovating Building Exteriors (N/A MN; WI) Concrete: Construction-Private Residences-Monolithic: Guniting-Not Chimneys-All Operations-guniting on chimneys to be separately rated as Code 5232-Chimney Construction (N/A MN; WI) Hod Hoise or Construction Elevator Installation, Repair or Removal 7 Drivers (N/A MA)-the following operations will be classified as:
5213 Concrete or Concrete Encased Buildings or Structures
    5057 Iron or Steel Bui8ldings or Structures
    5022 Masonry Buildings or Structures
    6003 Piers or Wharfs
    5403 Wooden Buildings or Structures Including Those Designed for Swelling Occupancy
*Satellite Dish Installation: Applies to Ground or Roof-Mounted Installations; Installation of Concrete Mounting Pad (N/A MA) Silo Erections: Concrete; Silo Erection: Pre-Cast Concrete Staves; Wrecking: Building or Structures-Not Marine-All Operations-*includes salespersons and clerical at wrecking site. Wrecking or demolition operations shall be classified as follows:
    5403 Wooden Buildings or Structures Including Those Designed for Dwelling Occupancy
    5213 Concrete or Concrete Encased Buildings or Structures
    5057 Iron or Steel Buildings or Structures
    5022 Masonry Buildings or Structures
    6003 Piers or Wharfs
Where wrecking or demolition involves buildings or structures of more than one type of construction, the highest rated classification applies (N/A MA, WI) State Special: California-Concrete Construction NOC-including foundations or the making, setting up or taking down of forms, scaffolds, false work or concrete distributing apparatus-NPD with Code 5222-Concrete
Construction-Wood or Code 5506 or Code 5507-Bridge Building-Metal, Code 6003(3)-Bridge or Trestle Construction-Wood or Code 5506 or Code 5507-Street or Road Construction-excavation, reinforcing steel installation, pile driving and all work in connection with sewers , tunnels, subways, caissons or cofferdams shall be separately rated.

Figure 4-1 (continued)

SCOPE Code 5213 applies to all commercial types of concrete building construction, self-bearing floors, foundations, piers, culverts, silos, grain elevators, etc., and includes making and erecting forms, placing reinforcing steel and stripping forms. Code 5213 would apply to each of the aforementioned steps in the concrete construction process whether all work is performed by the principal contractor or portions of the job, such as making and erecting forms, are completed by a special subcontractor.

The term "self-bearing floors" mentioned above is used as a basis for distinguishing between self-supported concrete floors, assignable to Code 5213, and ground-supported concrete floors, assignable to Code 5221. A self-bearing floor is elevated above the ground, and, being an integral part of the concrete construction itself, is assigned to Code 5213-Concrete Construction NOC. A ground-supported floor of a building which is poured either at the beginning or end of the construction job involves the type of concrete or cement work contemplated by Code 5221.

Concrete walls that are poured in flat forms on the ground level are assigned to Coded 5221, provided that the pouring insured does not tilt up the walls and secure them in place. This operation is assigned to Code 5221 since the exposure is the same as that of pouring a ground-supported concrete floor. Code 5213 is assigned to an operation in which an insured both pours the concrete and ground level to create a wall and subsequently tilts the wall into place...

SCOPES® Manual excerpt © 1990-2005 The National Council on Compensation Insurance, Inc.

This particular Scopes® entry goes on for another entire page, but you probably get the idea. Many of the Scopes® entries are similarly detailed, with exceptions noted for particular states and lots of technical details. Fortunately, many other classification definitions in the manual are shorter and easier to follow. But this illustrates the point that when it comes to classifications, the devil really can be in the details. And remember that some states don't use the NCCI system, so in those states the details can be different for a particular kind of work than would be the case in an NCCI state.

Although most businesses are allowed to break out clerical work into its own (inexpensive) classification, some kinds of businesses are not allowed to do so. Recently, I was retained to assist a public broadcasting satellite uplink facility. It had been assigned the classification code used for broadcast television and radio stations and, under the NCCI classification rules, that kind of business is not allowed to break out clerical payroll into its own classification. The details of this prohibition were not spelled out in the policy, but are in the Scopes® Manual.

I should point out that NCCI is in the process of reviewing all of their classifications, a process that was started in 2005 and was planned to take five years. Some of these details have changed, and others may change shortly. Take a look at figure 4-1 for a representative sample of the kind of detail that the Scopes® Manual goes into. Some of the entries can cover an entire page or more of the manual, although many entries are shorter than this.

One problem with the classification system is that it's difficult to keep it current with developments in the business world. Many kinds of businesses didn't even exist ten years ago—and many have changed how they do their work in fundamental ways. The classification code system, whether it uses six hundred classes (Like NCCI) or three hundred (like Pennsylvania), is hard pressed to anticipate all the varieties of work that exist in the modern world.

So, looking at the Scopes® Manual can sometimes give you a glimpse of the history of the American workplace. You will find a few very old-fashioned sounding classification codes still in existence, such as macaroni manufacturing, but software programmers and computer chip manufacturers did not get specific separate classifications until 1992. The NCCI review of its classification system will undoubtedly update things significantly, but the workplace exposures of the real world will always be a moving target.

Classification by Analogy

There is another aspect to workers' Comp compensation classification that can create problems for employers: the limited number of classifications used. With a limited number of classifications available, it's inevitable that many kinds of work will not fit neatly and exactly into a particular code. When that happens, NCCI and other rating organizations will try to find the classification that comes closest to fitting an employer. Since that usually involves a judgment call to some extent, classification by analogy can sometimes be open to dispute.

Thus, each remaining classification tends to be used for a wider variety of businesses, increasing the classification-by-analogy approach.

Here's a quick example of how classification by analogy can be problematic for employers. A few years back, I reviewed the classification of a manufacturer of fuel and oil filters for heavy machinery. This particular operation was done in a modern, new computer assisted factory that minimized the exposure of employees in the manufacturing process. But NCCI practice is to classify all filter manufacturers, by analogy, in the classification used for the manufacturing of folding paper boxes. This means that our modern, high-tech manufacturer of filters get the same classification (and manual rates) as companies that make cardboard boxes in workplaces with much greater exposure to workplace injury. While experience rating will (theoretically) adjust those manual rates eventually (assuming the loss history of the high-tech filter manufacturer really is lower than the average of the loss-experience of the box makers), the experience rating formula doesn't remove the entire penalty from this inappropriate classification. And as the number of overall classifications is decreased in the future, such problems can only increase. With fewer classifications, each one will be broader and less precise, increasing the number of times an employer gets lumped in with other kinds of companies whose injury exposure is higher.

IMPORTANT RULES REGARDING CLASSIFICATIONS
For manufacturers and other non-construction type businesses, the *single enterprise rule* is important to keep in mind when it comes

to determining proper classification. The single enterprise rule states that it is the overall business of the employer that is classified, not necessarily each and every job function done there. (So the janitor and the shipping and warehousing people go into the company's governing classification.) But there can also be important exceptions to the single enterprise rule.

For example, if the company does a kind of work that is not contemplated by the governing classification, a second classification may be assigned (other than a standard exception) in certain circumstances. But the rules that govern how and when this may be done are specific.

Under NCCI manual rules, an employer may have additional classifications that are not standard exceptions under certain circumstances:

- when each separate legal entity insured under a policy should be assigned to the classification that describes its overall business within a state;
- when the basic classification requires (per the manual) that certain operations be broken out into a separate classification;
- when the employer does construction or erection work, farm work, or repair operations or a mercantile business; and/or
- when the employer operates more than one business in a state.

Keep in mind, the assignment of certain classifications is limited to separate and distinct business operations because, according to NCCI, "they describe an operation that frequently is an integral part of the business describes by another classification." These rules are not contained in the Scopes® Manual, but are instead in another manual published by NCCI, *The Basic Manual for Workers' Compensation and Employers' Liability Insurance.* Each non-NCCI state typically has its own manual of rules published by its respective rating bureau.

It isn't always the rules about classifying the business that can trip up employers; the rules about assigning payroll of individuals within the company can also get complicated. According to the NCCI *Basic Manual,* the payroll of an employee can be divided between approved classifications that apply to an employer, as long as payroll records are kept that record how much time the employee actually spent in the different types of work. An estimate of how much time is not an acceptable measure; neither is percentage of overall time (as in "he works 20 percent of the time painting and 80 percent as a carpenter").

In practical terms, this division of payroll for individual workers typically applies primarily to those in construction or erection work. For one thing, NCCI rules don't allow a worker's payroll to be divided between the clerical class and another, even if proper payroll records are kept. The same is true for the outside sales classification—you can't divide the payroll of an individual between this class and another.

Also, for employers that operate in tight quarters, keep in mind that NCCI rules require that clerical work be done in a "physically separate" area in order to qualify for the inexpensive clerical classification. Physically separated means separated by walls and a door.

Mercantile Risks
Under NCCI rules, each separate location of a mercantile type risk is classified separately according to the kind of work done at that location.

Important Rules for Construction Employers
The NCCI rules are different for construction type risks in one important aspect. It is common for more than one type of work to be done by the same employer. Thus, it is more likely that payroll for certain employees may have to be divided between or among more than one classification. NCCI rules now allow the payroll of any employee to be divided between classifications,

if those classifications are approved for a particular employer. Since most non-construction employers don't have more than one class on their policy (other than clerical and outside sales), it's relatively rare for payroll of non-construction employees to be divided that way. It's much more common for construction risks, because their policies often have several construction classifications approved and employees often divide their time among different kinds of construction work. Consider the following example.

A client of mine made, repaired, and installed industrial furnaces. Under NCCI rules, when a company works on furnaces on its own premises, the payroll goes into a manufacturing. But when that same company's employees work on furnaces on the client's premises, payroll goes into a millwright classification. When I got involved in reviewing things, the insurance company auditor had been deciding for several years that the payroll records did not allow him to tell when employees were working on the company's premises and when they were working offsite at a client's location. So all payroll for these employees was thrown into the expensive millwright classification.

Fortunately, by reviewing their records carefully, I was able to reconstruct when employees were actually out at clients. This left the remainder of the payroll eligible for the lower furnace manufacturing classification, for a premium reduction of about $8,000 per year. If either the insurance agent or the insurance auditor had explained all this ahead of time to the employer, payroll records could have been set up to clearly differentiate between these two kinds of work. But, as is common in workers' compensation insurance, no one bothered to explain to the employer why it would be important to keep such records. This happened even though it was clear to the insurance company from prior policies that a significant portion of payroll properly belonged in the manufacturing classification.

What a Difference a State Makes

A few years back I worked with a company that manufactured steel reinforcing bars used in concrete construction. The employees also installed these steel bars at construction sites. The owners called me after a serious problem developed.

A few years earlier, they had expanded from Arizona into California. They built a manufacturing plant there, in addition to their original plant. When they set up their California policy, they used the same classification codes as they had been using for years in Arizona.

Everything was fine the first year. Then a dispute arose regarding the proper classification for the California policy. The employer had purchased coverage through the California State Fund, a competitive state fund.

The employer began to receive monthly statements from the California fund showing a different classification- one with a significantly higher rate than the old class. He discussed it with this insurance agent and the state fund staff and was told it must just be an error. So the employer corrected the invoices by hand, replacing the higher class with the lower-rated one, and paid the premium due under the less expensive class.

But eventually the California Rating Bureau, the WCIRB, and the state fund told the client that there had not been an error after all. The higher classification was correct under California rules and the employer now owed several hundred thousand dollars in back premiums.

Arizona is an NCCI state, while California has its own independent rating bureau. The lower class was right under NCCI rules but wrong under the California definitions. To make matters worse, the California State Fund said these premiums had to be paid promptly or the California policy would be cancelled.

If someone had explained at the outset that California classifications were different from Arizona rules, he would have been able to plan differently to avoid this problem. But this employer did not learn the true cost of his California workers' compensation insurance until the year was over and so the jobs they had bid on for that policy period had not been priced with the actual cost of insurance, under-pricing their product for the entire year. When the company finally understood the true costs of the California workers' compensation coverage, my client eventually moved his operations out of California.

COMMON CLASSIFICATION CODE MISTAKES
In our consulting work with employers, we see a number of mistakes in assigning classification codes. Here are some of the more common ones:

- The employer's operations have changed over time, but the classification(s) used on the policy have not kept up.
- The insurance agent and company underwriter don't bother to think for themselves, but instead just copy what's on the prior policy.
- A recent inspection by NCCI or other rating bureau has misunderstood the nature of the employer's operations in some regard and assigned an erroneous new classification.
- The classification used is correct for other states, but not for a particular state in which the employer has workers.
- Classifications have been changed mid-policy in a state that does not allow such midterm changes.

Time and time again, as we correct classification mistakes for clients, we hear employers express surprise that these mistakes haven't been caught in the normal course of the work done by their insurance agent or the insurance company. Indeed, sometimes these mistakes are caught that way, too often they are not. The lesson employers need to learn is that no one else has as much incentive to catch mistakes that raise premiums as the one paying premiums. If you sit back and trust that everything is working the way it should in a perfect world, you may be setting up your company for serious premium overcharges.

These common classification mistakes aren't theoretical—as evidenced by the following cases from our files.

We recently worked with a client who had been manufacturing several products for decades, but whose product mix had changed. Many years ago, most of their sales were of a cloth based wrap that was applied with a hot sealant to industrial pipelines. But over time, a different product came to dominate their sales—a sort of industrial strength duct tape that was also used on pipelines—but this product wasn't applied with a hot sealant.

As you might expect, the manufacturing process for these two product were very different. But the classification on the company's policy was based on the old product, which now generated only a small minority of their sales. Correcting the classification to reflect the cold-applied technology reduced the premiums significantly (in the range of 35 percent). The classification had been right, but somehow the evolution of the product line, and the manufacturing process, had not been reflected on the policies.

Or consider this problem we fixed a couple of years ago. The client was in the business of selling home furnishings to interior decorators. Their showroom wasn't open to the public, but only to those in the decorating business. In the showroom, they displayed samples from various suppliers they represented. It turned out to be that, although the classification code used on their policy was right in most NCCI states, the particular state where this client was located had what is known as a *state special* classification for their particular type of employment—and that state special had a considerably lower rate.

That's one more tricky part to the NCCI classification system—individual states that use the NCCI system can create special rules for certain industries just in their jurisdiction. So a classification code that is right in one NCCI can be wrong in the NCCI state right next door.

The situation gets exacerbated by a trend in the insurance industry of consolidating underwriting in regional offices. Combined with other trends like downsizing and turnover, this means that many underwriters tend to be younger, less experienced, and handling more states than their predecessors of a decade or two past.

It can sometimes get even more complicated, because occasionally, *even when a class is right, it can be wrong*. That's because different state jurisdictions place different restrictions on when a classification can be changed to a more expensive class. The NCCI *Basic Manual* itself places some restrictions on how late in a policy such changes can be made, but some NCCI states place even tighter restrictions on this.   This means that an insurance company is prohibited in many jurisdictions from making a change to a more expensive classification late in the policy, even if that more expensive classification is really correct for that employer.

But insurance underwriters and auditors are often unaware of such state restrictions and operate as if they were free to make such changes at will. Thus, an insurance company will sometimes change the classification code (and thus the rate) used on a policy well after the policy has begun. But if this change is against manual rules or a state statute, it may not be allowable even if the classification code change is correct per other manual rules. Insurance companies often will unknowingly violate such limitations, but if you bring it to their attention you can often get them to reverse their actions.

Here's an example of how this can work and how different states impose different limitations in this regard. We recently worked with an employer that specialized in painting commercial aircraft in both Florida and New Mexico. The insurer had changed their classification code three months into the policy into a more expensive classification code that was, it turns out, correct for their kind of work under NCCI rules. But New Mexico has statutory limitations on the ability of an insurer to change to a more expensive class more than sixty days after the policy begins. (It allows such changes after sixty days only if there has been a change in the insured's operations.) So we were able to get the insurance company to reverse its change in New Mexico (at least for that year), but couldn't fight the change for Florida, because Florida allows such changes to be made within the first 120 days of the policy.

NCCI Basic Manual Rules
The NCCI *Basic Manual* sets forth some limitations on changes to a more expensive classification code after policy inception. A few states have tougher restrictions on this practice than are contained in the NCCI *Basic Manual*. Also, the limitations in the *Basic Manual* also have some important exceptions. The manual states that changes in classification that result in lower premiums shall be made retroactive to the inception date of the policy. But changes in classification code that result in higher premiums are subject to some limitations:

- During the first 120 days of coverage, a change can be made retroactively to policy inception.
- After 120 days, but before the final ninety days of coverage, a change can only be made pro rata as of the date the company discovers the cause for such change.
- In the final ninety days, a change in classification that results in a higher premium cannot be made to the policy, but only to the next renewal policy.

State Restrictions
But a few states place different restrictions upon the ability of an insurance company to change to a more expensive classification code.

Connecticut allows a change to a more expensive class during the first sixty days to be made retroactively back to the inception of the policy, like *New Mexico*.

Florida does not exempt those in the construction or erection businesses from these limitations (the way the *Basic Manual* rules do), but also states explicitly that any error or omission in describing the employer's operations will allow the more expensive to be added as of the effective date of the policy. Florida also considers a reallocation of payroll amongst the policies codes to be a change in classifications, as long as the reallocation meets certain criteria.

Georgia also considers reallocation of payroll to be a change in classification, as long as it meets the same criteria as Florida's.

Illinois does not allow a change to a more expensive class after the policy begins unless there has been a change in the insured's operations or if the policy was in the first year for which that particular insurance company had written coverage for that employer. Illinois does not exempt those in construction or erection from these limitations.

Kansas used to have a strict policy against more adding expensive codes the policy. However, they have changed their rules, and now follow the standard NCCI rules.

New Mexico, as discussed above, allows more expensive codes to be added to the beginning of the policy only within the first ninety days.

Oklahoma allows changes to a more expensive class only within ninety days of policy inception.

Oregon allows changes to the classification to be made anytime. It does not even allow the protections offered by the NCCI *Basic Manual.*

Wisconsin allows changes to a more expensive class within the first 120 days to be made retroactively to policy inception.

California, Massachusetts, and North Carolina follow very different rules than the rest of the states. They all link changes in classification codes, either cheaper or more expensive, to when their rating bureaus inspect the insured. For these states, higher rated codes can only be added pro-rata, while lower rated codes can only be applied for the current and any policy that started a year before the inspection. This is different from most other states, which allows lower rating codes to be applied at least three years into the past.

Reallocation of Payroll

This is an area that often leads to disputes between policyholders and insurers. Reallocation of payroll means that the insurance company decides that work that was assigned to one classification on your policy really belongs in another classification on your policy. The effect on your policy is effectively a significant change in premium, although no classification is added to the policy, and most states allow a reallocation of payroll that results in a higher premium.

Oftentimes, insurers will list several classes on a policy with payroll shown as "If Any" —so no payroll is used to compute the premium on the initial policy, but if someone at the insurer decides that payroll should be moved into this class, the insurer is able to do so.

Now that we've learned about how the workers' compensation classification code system works (and what can go wrong), let's move on to Chapter 5, where we can cover how to get mistakes in classification fixed.

QUICK REVIEW
- The rules governing classification of an employer's operations for determining workers' compensation insurance premiums are written by the rating bureaus such as the National Council on Compensation Insurance (NCCI).
- Most, but not all, states use the NCCI system. Some states operate independent rating bureaus.

- For most non-construction employers, the rating bureau will try to determine an overall classification that best fits the overall work of the employer.
- A few workplace operations are normally broken out into their own classifications: clerical, outside salespeople, and (often, but not always) drivers.
- Different states may classify employers doing the same work differently.
- Classifications need to be regularly reviewed to make sure the employer isn't being overcharged through use of an out-of-date classification.
- Some states limit the ability of an insurance company to change an employer to a more expensive classification after the policy has been in effect for a while, even if the classification is correct under manual rules.

CHAPTER 5

CORRECTING CLASSIFICATION MISTAKES

How An Employer Gets Classified

So how exactly does an insurance company decide which classifications to use for a particular employer? Understanding the various ways this is done (and what can go wrong) can be an important step in the process of correcting classification mistakes. There are different ways that errors in classification can occur, depending upon an employer's circumstances and history. Here are the common causes of such problems.

A New Business

For a brand new business that has never been insured for workers' compensation insurance, the initial step in determining classification will be with the insurance agent, who will probably help you complete an application. At this stage, it is important to make sure your agent really understands your operations and the exact nature of your business. This is true whether your business is a new venture or not, but it is particularly important when applying for your first Workers' Compensation insurance policy.

It's natural to want to rely upon the experience and expertise of your insurance agent at this stage. It's also common for many businesspeople to find insurance application forms a bit frustrating and user-unfriendly. The terminology can be unfamiliar and sometimes the questions asked don't seem to be particularly applicable to your line of work. But one mistake that can be made at this point is to leave too much of the application process to the agent.

First of all, the level of experience and expertise among insurance agents can vary greatly. Your agent may inadvertently give you the impression that he or she knows more about the process than is really true. Many insurance application forms ask only relatively cursory information or don't leave a lot of room for detailed answers. But from your point of view, it is important that you provide thorough and complete information about the nature of your work. The better the job you can do in that regard, the more you can decrease the chances of a mistake in classification that will cause problems for you down the road.

Not only do you want to give the agent and underwriters thorough and accurate information to help them do their job, you also want to document that there was no omission or misrepresentation made at this stage of the process. In Chapter 4 we saw that some states limit the ability of insurance companies to change to a more expensive class after the policy begins, as long as there has been no misrepresentation by the employer. If you do a thorough job of explaining what you do at the outset and document exactly what information you provide, you can defend yourself against any later charges that you misrepresented what you do.

For a new business, the insurance company will rely upon whatever is on the application form, along with any brochures and other information provided. So you want to double-check any information that the insurance agent has written on the application and make sure it is complete and accurate. Give the agent lots of supporting documentation, like brochures and web sites, and *keep your own file that documents exactly what you have provided.* Keep a copy of the completed application, along with copies of all brochures and other documents you provide, and keep the file with your insurance documents in case some dispute arises later.

The completed and signed application, along with supporting documents, will be sent to one or more insurance companies, where an underwriter will review them and (in theory) exercise independent judgment about the classification codes used on the application form. However, in practice, sometimes underwriters don't al invest sufficient time and effort at this stage of the game. That's how mistakes in classification can arise and why insurance companies will sometimes want to try and change classifications after the policy has begun.

This can be especially true if your policy is being written through an assigned risk plan. In many jurisdictions, insurers handle assigned risk plans as a necessary cost of doing business—something that has to be done, but that they aren't real enthusiastic about doing. So an assigned risk underwriter may not be able to take a lot of time and effort to check the classification codes the agent has put on the application. If the agent has made a mistake, it may take a while before someone at the insurance company figures it out.

In general, the employer is much better off if the classifications are right from the onset. Changes to a more expensive class can be a very costly and unpleasant surprise when they are done in midterm. You have already made your business plans, figuring on a certain cost for workers' comp, and finding out halfway through the year that your cost projections were way off can throw a real monkey wrench into your business plans.

Ask your agent if he or she has experience with other employers who have been assigned to the classification that is being used for your new business. Ask if the agent has consulted the NCCI Scopes® Manual, and ask to see the written classification description from the manual that the agent is relying upon. If the agent can't or won't provide this, it may be a warning sign of potential trouble down the road.

You can always contact NCCI yourself and discuss what the proper classification code is for your business (at 800-NCCI-123). Just keep in mind that such telephone discussions aren't binding, and that sometimes errors are made. The customer service person you may be talking with has to rely on the information provided by you over the phone, and if you inadvertently omit some key piece of information, you may get inaccurate classification advice. Getting the classification right at the outset can be very important, so it's worth expending some effort to try and get it right.

If your insurance company tries to change you to a more expensive class sometime after the policy has begun, you may be able to resist it based on the state restrictions we detailed last chapter. But you may need to show that the mistake wasn't due to misrepresentation or omission by you or the agent.

An Established Business

With a business that isn't applying for Workers' Compensation insurance for the first time, agents and underwriters pay a lot of attention to what classifications have been used on prior policies—sometimes too much attention. A normal part of the insurance underwriting process is to look at prior audits and at experience modification factor worksheets. Both of these kinds of documents show what classification codes have been used in recent past policies for your company; insurance agents and insurance company underwriters rely heavily on these to guide them about how to classify your operations. The problem, of course, is that any past classification mistakes will just get perpetuated that way.

Many times, when my consulting practice discovers a classification mistake for a client, we see that the mistake has been going on for many years. As we'll discuss later, most state allow an employer to recover such overcharges only for a few past years. So if the insurance company has been overcharging you due to a classification mistake, it will be able to keep its unwarranted premiums for all but the most recent few years. It can be vital, therefore, to be alert for such mistakes. But the tendency of so many agents and underwriters to rely on past classifications can work against uncovering long-standing classification mistakes.

The Role of the Rating Bureau

Rating bureaus like NCCI not only write the classification manual rules, but they are also supposed to assist and guide member insurance companies in applying those rules correctly. And in a perfect world, mistakes usually get caught by a system of checks and balances among insurers, rating bureaus, and insurance regulators. Guess What!! We don't live in a perfect world.

A long time ago, in an insurance industry far, far removed from the current one, rating bureaus and regulators kept insurance companies on a tighter leash. But here and now, the old checks and balances just aren't working as well. Still, rating bureaus like NCCI can and do play a role in correcting classification mistakes made by insurers.

Perhaps the most common mechanism for doing this is the inspection process. As part of its duties, NCCI performs inspections of workplaces in order to determine proper classifications. These used to be done at nominal cost to employers, but nowadays the cost of an inspection can be seven or eight hundred dollars. This is all part of a change at NCCI that began a decade or so ago, shifting away from assessments on member insurance companies to a fee-for-services model for its revenues. This has made inspections more expensive and, thus, less likely to be requested by insurance companies or employers.

An inspection can officially resolve classification disputes between insured and insurer. But since inspections have become expensive, employers want to do their homework first and make sure the results of an inspection will be positive. Additionally, they should try to negotiate for responsibility for the inspection to lie with the insurer or at least for the inspection to be done on a "loser pays" basis.

Sometimes, if an insurance company suspects that the classification used historically for an employer is too low, it will request an NCCI inspection on its own. We often find that employers have been the subject of an NCCI inspection without being aware of it. We've never quite figured out how these inspections are so often done in a kind of "stealth" mode, but perhaps when the inspector shows up, the shop personnel believe it's just an "insurance inspection" and never understand that the NCCI inspection is unique. At any rate, it can be a good idea to check with NCCI or other appropriate rating bureaus to see what inspections it may have on file for your company, as employers are often unaware of inspection reports.

If there is an inspection report on file, you definitely want to get a copy of it and check it over carefully. Sometimes, small errors in describing your operations can make a difference between a costly classification and a much less expensive class—potentially worth thousands or tens of thousands of dollars a year in premium charges.

What Can Go Wrong With Inspections

Like so much else in the insurance system, the inspection system has been going through significant changes in recent years. NCCI has been trying different methods of getting inspections done, with varying results. For many years, NCCI used only its own in-house inspectors to do this work. While not foolproof, using its own specially trained inspectors ensured that inspectors were knowledgeable and experienced in the NCCI classification system.

However, in an attempt to increase efficiency and reduce costs, NCCI moved to a system of outsourcing to third-party inspectors. This approach seemed to reduce the quality of the field inspections and NCCI has now moved to return to using its own inspectors. But this means that some inspections done in recent years may have problems due to the less expert third-party inspectors who were used for several years.

Even with well-trained inspectors, things can still go wrong with inspections. Typically, the field inspector writes a report that is then reviewed by an office-bound classification expert. So the final classification decision is made by someone who has not seen your operations firsthand, but is relying on the field inspector's description. If the field inspector misunderstands some crucial aspect of your operation or leaves out some detail from the written report, the classifier may assign an incorrect classification. So it is vital to review written inspections with the proverbial fine-tooth comb to make sure all details are correct and nothing has been left out.

The Value of Working for Third Parties

Here's an interesting example of how a part of an employer's operations can be misclassified due to a misunderstanding of a small detail. This particular employer operated a trucking company. Also covered under the workers' compensation insurance policy were mechanics who worked on these trucks. Now, normally, mechanics are classified into a much less expensive class code than the one used for trucking companies. But the NCCI had inspected and informed the employer that under NCCI rules, the mechanics went into the trucking classification, because mechanics working for a trucking company are classed into the governing classification of trucking. And this is correct.

Except that this particular trucking company operated the repair work as a separate business. The trucking company was a corporation while the repair work was done by a separate company that was a sole proprietorship and the mechanics not only worked on the trucks of my client, they also did repair work for third parties. Under these circumstances, the mechanics were eligible, under NCCI rules, to be separately rated in a much less expensive classification.

We eventually got NCCI to understand these details and to revise its decision. This lowered the client's premiums to $6,000 a year.

Figures 5-1 and 5-2 show two checklists that can be used to review inspection reports by those in manufacturing work and those in construction work.

Notice that each checklist has an entry for checking work done by either subcontractors with their own insurance or leased/temp employees who are insured on someone else's policy. This can be important, as sometimes this can make a difference in the classifications that are assigned to your company. If some particular work function is done exclusively by subcontractors or employees insured elsewhere, it can make a big difference.

The SCOPES® Manual—A Vital Tool

As we've mentioned earlier, the Scopes® Manual published by NCCI contains detailed descriptions of what each of the classification codes in the NCCI system is intended to cover. To check if the classification codes used for your business are correct, you really need to look at what the codes on your policy are intended to cover.

If you're in an NCCI state, the Scope® Manual is the bible of classifications. You can order a copy form NCCI or subscribe to an online edition, but be aware that it can be a little expensive. So you might instead want to ask your insurance agent to send you a copy of the pertinent Scopes® entries for the classes on your policy. Most insurance agents who write workers' compensation insurance will probably have access to this manual.

The only problem with relying on just some excerpts from the manual that your agent can send you is that this might limit your checking too much. Having access to the entire manual can enable you to look at other possible classifications and decide if another is really more appropriate for your operations. Remember, also, to check for state special classifications that might apply in your state. State special classifications are detailed in a separate section in the back of the Scopes® Manual.

Figure 5-1 Checklist for manufacturers to check inspection and classification reports

	ACTUAL	INSPECTION REPORT
Raw Materials		
Used		
Description of		
Operations		
Operations Conducted		
As a Separate Business		
Enterprise		
Machinery and		
Equipment Used		
Finished Products		
Any Work Done by		
Leased or Temp Workers		
Insured Elsewhere?		

Figure 5-2 Checklist for construction employers to check inspection and classification reports

	ACTUAL	INSPECTION REPORT
Work Operations Performed by Own Employees		
Work Operations Performed by Subs Or Independent Contractors with Own Insurance		
Work Operations By Subs or Independents without Own Insurance		
Permanent Yard Employees?		
Executive Supervisors?		
Usual Kinds of Worksites (Residential, Commercial, Multistory, etc.)		
Trades Employed		

Of course, the Scopes® Manual is an NCCI publication. Thus, it will not apply to every state, because some states do not use the NCCI classification system. Here's a rundown of some states where the Scopes® Manual is not going to be authoritative. To get details about the non-NCCI rating bureaus used in these states, consult the state-by-state directory at the end of Chapter 1. These states don't use the NCCI classification system, but still allow private insurance for Workers' Compensation. There are also states that don't allow private insurance for this, but instead require employers to obtain coverage through a state-administered fund. Their rules about classification of employers also will vary from the NCCI system. The following states allow private insurance, but don't follow NCCI classification rules.

California. This is the largest single state market for Workers' Compensation and it operates completely independently of NCCI. The pertinent manuals are published by the Workers' Compensation Insurance Rating Bureau of California (WCIRB). While many classes are very similar to those in the NCCI system, there can be very important differences as well. In order to find out what each classification in California is intended to cover, you need to review the manuals published by WCIRB.

Delaware and Pennsylvania. These two states share their own unique rating system. Their shared rating bureau is completely independent of NCCI and their classification system is radically different. The NCCI system has a little over five hundred national classes; the system used by Delaware and Pennsylvania has just over three hundred classifications. Even the numbering system is different for these two states—three digits, not four as in the NCCI system and elsewhere.

Indiana. Even a lot of insurance people seem to think that Indiana is an NCCI state, but this is not accurate. Indiana has an independent non-NCCI rating bureau, but it follows NCCI rules to a large extent (but there can be differences, too).

Massachusetts. This is a non-NCCI state with its own rating bureau, and, thus, its classifications can vary from NCCI standards in the Scopes® Manual.

Michigan. Michigan takes a rather unusual approach. It maintains its own rating bureau, but this bureau has real jurisdiction only over classifications used on assigned risk policies. For policies written in the voluntary market, the state doesn't enforce manual rules about classifications, so insurance companies can use their own judgment about classifications.

Minnesota. Minnesota takes the same approach as Michigan— when it comes to classifications, only assigned risk policies are subject to strict jurisdiction of a rating bureau. For voluntary market policies, insurance companies are free to exercise their own judgment about classes.

New Jersey. This state maintains its own independent rating bureau that writes the manuals and then determines proper classifications.

New York. This state has an independent non-NCCI rating bureau that publishes its own manuals regarding classifications and other rules governing workers' compensation insurance in that state.

North Carolina. This state maintains an independent rating bureau, the North Carolina Rate Bureau, which calculates experience modifiers for use in North Carolina. Although it operates independently, it uses the NCCI Scopes® Manual as the basis for classifications.

Texas. This is another non-NCCI state. Texas doesn't exactly operate its own rating bureau; the Texas Department of Insurance (TDI) has a separate workers' compensation unit that writes the manual rules that apply in Texas, including classification rules.

Wisconsin. This state maintains a non-NCCI rating bureau that writes its own manual rules for classification. The classification system is generally similar to the NCCI one, but can differ in some classification particulars, so to be sure you need to consult that rating bureau's manuals.

A Classification Case From Our Files

The client was a concrete contractor. The classification assigned—concrete contractor—seemed appropriate. But when we looked into the case, we saw there were some factors that made that classification far too expensive.

Part of the problem was caused by the insured company's name: Suncrete, Inc. (This is a fictionalized version of its actual name.) The company constructed buildings using a proprietary concrete-based formula, hence the "crete" part of its name. For years, it had been classified in the expensive concrete contractor class.

But we learned during our review that the actual work with the special concrete material was performed by subcontractors that had their own insurance. The client's own employees performed a variety of construction and carpentry operations, but did not actually work with the concrete. All the correct classifications for the work actually performed by the client's employees were much less expensive.

Fortunately, we were able to produce certificates of insurance for the subcontractors and convince the NCCI that the client's employees did not do the concrete work. The NCCI approved a number of carpentry classifications that carried about half the rate of the concrete classification. The result was a substantial reduction in premium and a refund of $60,000 for prior years when the wrong classification had been used.

Inspection or No Inspection, Classes Can Be Wrong

It may sound like a bad joke, but the truth is that there are two ways your business can be misclassified—if you haven't been inspected...or if you have. If you haven't been inspected, it means that your classifications have been determined by some insurance underwriter using his or her best judgment, based on information provided. And while insurance underwriters try to do their best, the system is complex—mistakes happen. And even if you have been inspected, the same still applies—the system is complex and even rating bureaus make mistakes.

You really can't rely upon the traditional insurance system to catch mistakes in classification reliably. Typically, the system is a lot better at catching mistakes that lower premiums than at catching mistakes that increase premiums. Insurance agents may assure you, either directly or indirectly, that they review such things for you, but in my experience the ability of insurance agents to determine if classifications are right or not varies widely. Maybe your agent really is knowledgeable about classification, but maybe not. Frankly, the odds are better than even that he or she doesn't know as much in this area as you've been led to believe.

With a little time and effort, you can do some checking on the classifications used for your business. After all, you don't need to become expert about all the classifications—just about the ones that are being used for your business or that might be used.

So dig out your policy and recent audits, make a list of the classification codes being used, and then do some research into what those classes are intended to cover. Your agent can probably be helpful in obtaining copies of the manual descriptions of what's covered by each class. If your agent can't or won't help with this, it's probably an indicator that you need to consider finding a new agent.

If what you see in the manual isn't a spot-on match for what you company does, dig further. Talk with people at NCCI or the other appropriate rating bureaus to see what they think. Although the quality of the advice available over the phone from rating bureaus isn't always as consistently good as one might wish, it can still be valuable. And talk with your competitors, if possible, to learn what classification codes are used on their policies. If you don't have competitors who are friendly enough to share this information, check with any industry-specific associations to which you belong. Often, they've already done some research and have experience in this area that they are happy to share with you.

Fixing Classification Mistakes

OK, so let's assume you've done all the above and you've found something you feel really isn't right. How do you get your insurance company to correct it?

Two keys to getting such situations fixed are patience and attention to details. Insurance company underwriters and auditors often receive communications from policyholders that are long on indignation, but short on detail. Most of these insurance folks are genuinely honest and ethical and will want to do the right thing—if only you can overcome their natural human tendency to resist admitting (even to themselves) that they've made a mistake.

Your agent can be of real assistance here, as many insurance companies can be pretty stubborn about wanting such communications to be funneled through the agent. Sometimes this isn't possible, if the agent just isn't giving you much service or if you're complaining about a prior policy that was written with a different agent. But as a general principle, you probably want to start the process of fixing a classification mistake by working through your agent.

Put in writing exactly why you feel the classification(s) used is/are wrong for your business. Be as specific and detailed as possible. Make reference to the specific descriptions in the manuals (like the NCCI Scopes® Manual) that you feel support your case. And then follow up as if your life depended on it.

Insurance agents and insurance companies are swamped with paperwork, e-mail, faxes, and pressing deadlines. So it can be very easy for something like a communication about a mistake in classification to get lost in the shuffle, even with the best of intentions. Nobody else has as much incentive as you do to make sure this gets addressed, so don't assume that agents and companies will properly review or act upon your initial communications.

Whatever their response to your initial complaint is, make sure you get it in writing. You want to set up a file and document it carefully with every letter, fax, and e-mail you receive on this subject. Keep a detailed record of all phone conversations you have about this as well, noting date, person you spoke with, and what was said or agreed to. If they commit to a deadline or timetable for action, be prepared that you may have to initiate follow-up when those key deadlines arrive.

Sometimes, even with all this effort, I have seen insurance companies just try to "make the problem go away" by responding with double-talk or just plain insisting that they're right and they're not going to reconsider their position. If you feel that they're just being stubborn and refusing to respond to your legitimate concerns, you still have options open to you.

If There Is a Rating Bureau Inspection
When your company already has been inspected by NCCI or other rating bureau, you can communicate with the rating bureau and point out the specific areas in the report that you feel are inaccurate or incomplete. I have often been successful in getting NCCI to change something in a classification report, even after the client had been told that classification decision was final, just by sending detailed information to someone higher up at NCCI who has more experience with the classification system.

So in these situations, you want to work your way up through the rating bureau bureaucracy and find someone higher up the food chain that is more experienced and knowledgeable in classification matters. Then send a detailed written communication to this person.

If this is unsuccessful, and you still feel your argument has merit, every state has some kind of appeals mechanism that employers can use to try and get classification decisions reversed. Your state's department of insurance can explain what the process is for your particular state. Normally you can appear before such bodies without having to hire an attorney.

Keep in mind that these appeals boards operate with certain restrictions. The time allotted for your presentation will probably be limited. That means you have to focus on the particular reasons you feel the classification needs to be changed. You may want to consult with an insurance agent or consultant before doing this, as I sometimes see employers whom do this on their own spend their limited time going off on a tangent away from the heart of the classification problem. Sometimes employers and managers are just too close to the situation to see that the point they most passionately want to make isn't really germane to the classification in question.

The second important thing to keep in mind is that the appeals process in most states isn't a legal hearing. This means that your testimony about your operations isn't under oath—and the people who are listening to your presentation know it. So your own verbal testimony about what your company does and how you do it may not necessarily be compelling to an appeals board. To whatever extent possible, document every important point that makes a difference to the classification. Have written documentation that backs up your testimony and have it in such a form that you can give copies to the appeals board.

It may be irritating to think that the people listening to your appeal might take your testimony about your company's operations with a grain of salt, but I have sometimes seen appeals boards discount uncorroborated testimony. So document everything you can. If a video of your operations will be enlightening about some unique aspect of your work, arrange to have a television and playback equipment at the hearing.

Keep in mind that in most states you can even make a further appeal, if you feel it is warranted. I have helped several clients successfully appeal decisions made by the Workers' Compensation Appeals Board of California. Again, talk to your state's insurance regulators to find out what the particular process is for that state.

If There Is No Inspection
If you can't make headway working with your insurance company and if the rating bureau hasn't inspected your company, you may want to consider requesting an inspection. Keep in mind that many rating bureaus like NCCI now charge significant fees for an inspection, so if at all possible you want to negotiate for the insurance company to pay for the inspection. If you fight hard enough for this, you can often get them to accept responsibility for paying for the inspection. If this can't be worked out, you should at least insist that the inspection be done on a "loser pays" basis, so that if the inspection upholds your request for a change in class, the insurance company pays the bill. Only if the inspection upholds the decision of the insurance company would you be responsible for the charges.

Once the inspection is arranged, don't be a passive participant in the process. I have seen many such inspections go awry because the employer wasn't properly prepared. Before the inspector arrives, you should review the key points you want to make sure he or she understands. Don't assume the inspector will know to ask the right questions. Do your homework ahead of time, know what the important differences are between the classifications involved in your dispute, and make sure you have available documents and key people who can verify the key elements in your assertions.

If the results of the inspection aren't favorable, be sure to carefully review a written copy and see if there are any inaccuracies or omissions. If there are, immediately send in a written correction and then follow up to make sure it is taken into account. If necessary, consider using the appeals process as detailed above.

When Inspections Go Awry

This client was a private school in Vermont. NCCI had recently inspected it at the behest of its insurance company, and the inspector changed the way a number of their employees were classified, resulting in a large premium increase that would raise premiums from that point forward.

This school ran group homes and dormitories for students, and the NCCI inspector had decided that their residential counselors were nonprofessional staff, who were classified as Code 9101 with the rate of $8.01 per hundred dollars of payroll, rather than as "Professional Employees" Code 8868, with a rate of $0.78 per hundred dollars of payroll.

This obviously had a huge impact on their premiums. The inspector was adamant in his interpretation of the classifications. The school had already asked him to reconsider, but he stuck to his guns.

However, we forwarded this matter to a more senior (and more experienced) classification expert at NCCI. We pointed out that these "Residential Counselors" were responsible for working with and supervising students, had to be certified in first aid and CPR, planned and ran recreational activities for the students, and were part of the treatment team for the students.

The more experienced classification supervisor at NCCI overruled the inspector and returned these counselors to the professional classification, and the crisis over vastly increased workers' compensation premiums was averted.

In this case, the problem wasn't so much an inaccurate description of the employees' work as it was an incorrect interpretation of rules by an inspector. But if we hadn't gotten the matter reviewed by a more experienced NCCI person, the change in classification would have stuck, resulting in severe financial problems for the school.

Remember that even if an inspector insists that he or she is right, appealing the inspection (either formally to the appeals board or informally to higher-ups at the rating bureau) can often get an unfavorable inspection overturned. The key is to look carefully at the classification definitions and then to present convincing information and documentation to support the classification change you are requesting. An inspection by a rating bureau may seem like the final word, but it doesn't have to be. If you're convinced that an inspection has assigned an incorrect classification to your operations, don't take no for an answer.

After You Win

If you are successful in getting a rating bureau to approve a new classification, through either a new inspection or an appeal, be prepared to have to do some work with your insurance company. In an ideal world, winning at the appeals board should make everything else automatic, but it often doesn't work that way. The rating bureau will typically only insist that your current insurance company correct the classification on the current policy. But if you've been misclassified for past years, you should insist that your insurance company return any premium overcharges that have occurred in the past. Many states allow you to go back only three or four years. One state, Illinois (my home state), allows refunds going all the way back to 1987, if you can document the facts of the matter. Again, the insurance regulators in your state can inform you about how far back you can go in that state.

Expect that your insurance company may attempt to avoid making such refunds even after you press your case with them. They may say, for instance, that rating bureau inspections only require classification corrections to be made from that date forward. That's technically true, but if you can document that there has been no change in your operations, you should be able to persuade state insurance regulators to support your claim to go back at least three years into the past.

The standard workers' compensation insurance policy has language in it that makes it the responsibility of the insurance company to get your classification right. Under Part Five-Premium, paragraph B, entitled "Classifications," it reads:

> Item 4 of the Information Page shows the rate and premium basis for certain business or work classifications. These classifications were assigned based on an estimate of the exposures you would have during the policy periods. *If your actual exposures are not properly described by those classifications, we will assign proper classifications, rates, and premium basis by endorsement to this policy.* (Emphasis mine.)

Notice that the policy doesn't say, "We will try to use the correct classification" or "We will use the correct classification to the best of our ability." It says, "If your actual exposures are not properly described by those classifications, we will assign proper classifications, rates, and premium basis…" The policy contains a promise by the insurance company that it *will* use the correct classifications, rates, even if different from what's on the policy. You might need to remind a recalcitrant insurer about this policy language, as sometimes underwriters and auditors haven't really read the fine print of their own policy. But if push comes to shove, this is your written guarantee that your insurance company has promised to use the correct classifications and rates for your policy. You should definitely hold it to that promise.

Temporary or Leased Employees

Earlier, we discussed how it can sometimes affect your overall classification if you use temporary or leased employees for some portions of your work. This is because such employees are usually insured under the policy of the temporary agency or the employee-leasing firm (often called a PEO, *professional employer organization*). The use of temporary workers and leased workers has grown considerably in recent years and has caused some real ripples in the workers' compensation insurance field.

Once upon a time, temporary agencies provided someone to sit in for your secretary while he or she was on vacation and not much else (or so it seemed, anyway). Do you remember the movie *Dave*, about the temp agency owner who impersonated the president of the United States? Kevin Kline played the titular character as a small-town everyman who was honest but naïve and loved finding temp work for maiden-aunt types. If you don't have occasion to use modern temporary agencies, that may be your image of the industry. But if you spend more time running your business that watching cable-TV reruns, you probably already know just how different reality is. Nowadays, so-called *alternative employers* like temp agencies and PEOs provide workers for factories, distribution centers, and construction sites on a large scale. The growth of these kinds of employers has caused significant stresses and strains in the workers' compensation arena, and one of the most significant stresses has been in the areas of classifications.

If you use such alternative employment techniques, it may seem that you have outsourced your worries about the workers' compensation for those employees. And that's certainly true to a large extent, but not entirely. The first and foremost thing to watch carefully when using such alternative employment sources is to make sure your temp agency or PEO maintains valid workers' compensation insurance. I know this sounds elementary, but not all temporary agencies or PEOs are created equal in this regard.

Earlier in this book, we talked about how insurance markets cycle between soft markets and hard markets. Alternative employers like temporary agencies and PEOs are often hit hardest by shifts to hard markets. Part of the whole business model that makes temporary agencies and PEOs feasible is that they can arrange for employee benefits and insurance with economies of scale that allow them to take care of these business expenses at a cost lower than their client companies could do on their own. When it comes to workers' compensation insurance, however, it often becomes very difficult for such alternative employers to find economies of scale when the insurance market turns hard.

A few years ago, one of the largest PEOs in the U.S. was abruptly and unexpectedly driven out of business in significant part by the sudden shifting of the workers' compensation market to hard conditions. It didn't happen all at once, of course, but rather in a horrific sort of slow-motion collapse over the course of a year. During that time, the PEO struggled and failed to obtain valid workers' compensation coverage for all those employees it had leased to client companies all over the country. And many of those client companies that were allowing those leased employees to work in their shops and offices learned to their regret that the PEO was unable to keep the promises it had made about those workers being covered by its policy. So guess where those injured workers got coverage. They were covered by the policies of those client companies, even though those companies had already paid the PEO to cover those workers. And of course, the insurance companies insisted on getting premiums for all those workers who were supposed to be covered elsewhere, but weren't. So, the client companies ended up paying for Workers' Compensation twice for those workers— once to the PEO and again to their own insurance carriers.

The other thing about temp agencies and PEOs is that they can be terribly difficult for insurance companies to classify properly for Workers' Compensation purposes. That's because the standard insurance policy was just not designed with such employers in mind. And the insurance industry hasn't tried very hard to come up with innovative solutions to the classification problems of such employers, preferring to try and shoehorn them into a policy format that was really designed for more traditional kinds of employers.

The standard workers' compensation policy was designed for employers that would have only a few classifications. A typical manufacturer has one governing classification and two or perhaps three standard exception classifications (for clerical, outside sales, and perhaps drivers). A typical contractor may have a few more, because the contractor may be performing several kinds of construction-related work at job sites that require separate classes. But a temporary agency or employee leasing company might have dozens, even hundreds of classifications on its policy or audit.

Properly classifying such alternative employers can create real problems for both the insurance company and the employer. The insurance company wants to get fair and proper premium for the real exposures of those workers who are out in all those workplaces, yet the mix of workplaces can change from year to year, even from month to month. The standard policy just doesn't have the flexibility to work very well with large numbers of classifications that can change often.

It's just as bad from the point of view of the policyholder-employer. The cost of workers' compensation insurance is a vital factor in pricing the fees charged by temp agencies and PEOs. But how do you project the actual cost of the insurance if the insurance company can radically change the classifications (and rates) for the work after the policy has expired? I have worked with temp agencies that have received audit bills for twice or three times the premium they had expected, because the insurance company had retroactively changed a lot of the classification codes used to compute the premium.

The NCCI manual rules that protect the employers from those kind of late-in-the-game class changes don't apply to temporary agencies and employee-leasing companies in many states, so these alternative employers are far more vulnerable to this tactic by insurers. And make no mistake...it can be devastating.

The Alternative Employer Trap

People who run temp agencies or PEOs may not fully realize how this trap can ensnare them. Many such employers have no recourse but to be insured through assigned risk plans. This means that not only are they probably paying much higher premiums than they might in the voluntary market, but they are probably also receiving a lower level of service in terms of underwriting and loss control. That's a pretty broad generalization and a harsh one with which some in the insurance industry might disagree. I know that insurers don't like to think they are really shortchanging assigned risk policyholders, but I can only tell what I've seen over the years in the field. Because insurers aren't really playing with their own money on assigned risk plans, they have a reasonable tendency to hold down expenses on policies that aren't making them much money and where they aren't really on the hook for the claims.

That oversimplifies things a bit, I know, because ultimately insurers will be assessed to make up shortfalls in the assigned risk pools. So in recent years, some NCCI and some member insurers have focused significant resources on doing a better job with assigned risk policies. But part of the problem is that they focus those resources in ways that don't necessarily make life easier for policyholders.

The unique aspect of alternative employers like temporary agencies and PEOs is that their policies can have lots of classifications on them. Where a typical manufacturer might have only three or four classes, a temp agency or PEO can have dozens or even hundreds. And the workplace exposures of employees can change in an instant, if the policyholder signs up a new client that is in a different kind of work.

The standard workers' compensation insurance policy just wasn't designed with such alternative employers in mind. The policy was really designed to work for more traditional kinds of employers. But instead of developing policy forms that would address these problems, the insurance industry has just tried to shoehorn alternative employers into the existing policy format, with predictable difficulties ensuing.

The real trap for such alternative employers is that underwriting of assigned risk policies can often be a bit cursory, as nowadays NCCI and insurers concentrate much more effort on the audit. So, they are less concerned that a policy isn't written with all the appropriate classes and rates, because they figure they can just catch any problems at the audit. But doing a stringent audit for such employers, when the underwriting process tends to be the opposite and the classification rules are complex and arcane, is a recipe for disaster for policyholders.

So it is vital for alternative employers to expend some considerable effort in learning the complexities of the classification system. This is not an easy task. The Workers' Compensation classification system, as we have mentioned earlier, does not correspond with any other classification system, such as SIC codes. Even insurance professionals make mistakes in assigning classifications, because of the complexity. Yet if an alternative employer does not make this effort, its insurance company may be demanding huge additional premiums after doing an audit, because it has changed classification codes. During the course of the policy, the alternative employer has priced its charges to clients based on the classes and rates on the policy, not realizing that the insurance company might come in after policy expiration and double the rate being charged for some kinds of work. Needless to say, this is not a situation in which any sane business owner wants to find him or herself.

If you are an alternative employer and you find yourself in such a situation, review the audit billing done by the insurer very, very carefully. Because of the complexity of the classification system and the insurer's limited understanding of the work done for your clients, many of the classification changes sought may not really be valid. Depending on what your state insurance regulations say, you may also have some protection there from changes made on the audit.

The insurance industry does not make the classification system user-friendly, so be prepared to have to do some heavy lifting to get good information. As mentioned earlier, many agents and brokers are not as knowledgeable as you might hope in this regard. And since it is your company that will ultimately have to deal with the audit premium, no one else has as much incentive to get things right as you do.

How to Check Your Company's Workers' Compensation Classifications

1. List the classification codes used on your workers' compensation policy.

2. Compare these with the classifications used on the audits of recent past policies. Any changes? If so, look more carefully into the reasons for this change.

3. Examine the definitions for your classifications with the appropriate rating bureau for the states involved (NCCI for most states or the independent rating bureau for non-NCCI states). Your agent or broker should be able to give you copies of the definitions of the classifications involved. Make sure your company's operations seem to fit these definitions.

4. Make sure to check if there are any "state special" classifications that may apply to your operations in some states.

5. Call the rating bureau and see if there has been an inspection of your operations in recent years. If yes, request a copy of the inspection report so you can review it and make sure the description of your operations is accurate.

6. If there is any question about the accuracy of the classification assigned to your operations, discuss this with an experienced and knowledgeable classification expert at the appropriate rating bureau. See if this person agrees with the results of your inspection.

7. Contact competitors in your same line of work, if feasible, to see how they are classified. If they are classified in a less expensive class than your company, they may be willing to share this information. Business groups and associations for your field of work may also have information on this subject.

8. Discuss the classification with the experienced agent, broker, or consultant to determine if your classification may be wrong. Do not request an NCCI inspection without first determining the cost of such a request. NCCI

inspections are often fairly expensive, with costs possibly running close to $1,000. You may not wish to incur this expense. You may be able to correct a classification error in other ways without paying for an NCCI inspection. Non-NCCI rating bureau inspections tend to be less costly.

9. If you can't get the rating bureau to change your classification and you feel you belong in another class, you can request an appearance before the appeals board in your state. Contact your state's insurance regulators to find out the details about how to request an appearance. There is no cost involved with appearing before the appeals board.

A Complicated Case of Classification Correction

Correcting classifications isn't always easy, but if you're convinced that the change is correct then perseverance can pay off handsomely, as this case illustrates.

The agent had appealed the classification used for this employer before we got involved. This attempt was unsuccessful, but the employer wasn't ready to throw in the towel. They contacted my office for further assistance and we got to work.

Our review of the inspection report showed that it accurately described the employer's operations. However, we couldn't justify the higher-rated classification that had been assigned, based on our reading of the pertinent manuals. This particular employer was based in Indiana, and Indiana has a unique relationship with NCCI. Technically, Indiana operates an independent rating bureau, but that rating bureau follows NCCI manual rules pretty closely and relies on NCCI for a lot of services. At that time, the NCCI office that had handled the inspection and classification assignment was based in Illinois. (Since then, NCCI has consolidated its operations down in Florida). Based on our different interpretation of the classification description, we sent a copy of the inspector's report, along with appropriate sections from the NCCI Scopes® Manual, to a senior classifier at NCCI. He reviewed this and agreed that the classification decision had been in error. He then assigned the lower classification we felt was more appropriate. But things got complicated.

Remember, this employer was headquartered in Indiana, a state that is technically independent of NCCI. And even though NCCI had agreed with us that a less expensive classification code was warranted, the independent Indiana rating bureau didn't want to go along with this decision. In their files, they had found a copy of an old decision made by Indiana's governing committee, their precursor to modern appeals boards. In the late 1960s, this particular employer had appealed before this governing committee, and it had assigned the expensive classification. Indiana said that NCCI did not have the authority to overrule that earlier decision by the committee-even though that decision was nearly twenty-five years old at that time.

But we went back to the governing committee and presented the same evidence that had persuaded NCCI to agree with us. The committee agreed that the new, lower classification was warranted and approved its use for this employer. The lower classification was ultimately approved for use in all states in which this employer operated, with a reduction in annual premium of about 25 percent.

The moral of this story? When you're sure you're right, keep on working the system, even when things get complicated. The odds are that you can prevail, if you just keep at it.

QUICK REVIEW
- Mistakes in classification are one of the most common causes of overcharges in workers' compensation premiums for employers.
- Rating bureaus like NCCI have authority to determine proper classification for employers and can overrule the classification decisions of the insurance company.
- Even rating bureaus can make mistakes in assigning classifications, so employers need to be involved in

reviewing and researching if classifications used are really correct.

- If a classification mistake is suspected, employers often need to work with the rating bureau, not the insurance company, to get the problem corrected.
- The classification system is complex, particularly for employers such as temporary agencies or employee leasing companies. Particular effort may be needed to avoid overcharges due to misclassification by insurance companies.

CHAPTER 6

EXPERIENCE MODIFICATION FACTORS

When I do presentation on the subject of experience modification factors, I often use a graphic of Egyptian hieroglyphics up on the screen. It usually gets a chuckle of recognition from some in the audience who get my little joke: to a lot of folks who buy insurance (as well as a lot of folks who sell insurance), the calculation of experience modification factors is about as understandable as that ancient Egyptian writing. Perhaps that's why problems with experience modifiers constitute the second most common source of premium overcharges that I see in my consulting practice.

Most employers who pay more than a few thousand dollars per year for workers' compensation insurance are familiar with the experience modification factor, sometimes called an EMR for experience modification rating, or just mod. It can be found down toward the bottom of the premium calculation, right after manual premium and before premium discount. The experience modifier is designed to adjust the current premium based on prior losses. This is done by comparing loss information for a particular employer from three prior years (typically) with expected losses (calculated based on average losses of similar companies) for those same prior years.

Expected losses are calculated by taking the audited payrolls for those same past years and multiplying them by an *expected loss ratio* (ELR). The ELR for each classification is figured by averaging the losses of all businesses in that classification in a state per hundred dollars of payroll. So the ELR for classification 8810 (clerical) in Illinois is calculated each year as the average loss per hundred dollars for payroll for all employers in Illinois reporting payroll in code 8810.

DECIPHERING YOUR EXPERIENCE MOD

If your company is large enough to be experience rated (most companies paying more than $5,000 per year in Workers' Compensation premium get experience rated), then you should be receiving a worksheet each year from the rating bureau that calculates your modifier. Yes, the same rating bureaus that write the rules about classification also are in charge of calculating experience modifiers. And those same rating bureaus write the rules about classification also are in charge of calculating experience modifiers. And those same rating bureaus write the manual of rules that governs how modifiers are to be calculated. For most states, the rating bureau is NCCI, but again, some states that allow private insurance **don't use the NCCI rules:**

California, Delaware, Indiana, Massachusetts, Michigan, Minnesota, New Jersey, New York, North Carolina, Pennsylvania, Texas, Wisconsin

These states sill calculate experience modifiers for employers; however, the formulas that these non-NCCI states use to calculate modifiers differ a little from the formula used by NCCI. Employers don't really need to understand all of the fine details of these formulas in order to check their mods, but in this chapter, we'll give you the tools you need to be able to check your company's modifiers and spot common mistakes that increase mods improperly. And remember that the monopoly fund states also don't use NCCI. These states (North Dakota, Ohio, Washington, and Wyoming) use their own formulas to make adjustments to Workers Comp charges for employers.

Common Misconceptions About Modifiers

Over the years, I've heard a lot of things said about experience modifiers that just aren't true. Perhaps most common is that "the state" calculates them. As you may have gathered, this just isn't so (at least, not in most jurisdictions). Rating bureaus are not part of state government. The biggest rating bureau, NCCI, is a not-for-profit corporation that serves member insurance companies. It's a private corporation. Even the non-NCCI rating bureaus are not really part of state government, although some of them are established by state statute and are more quasi-governmental than NCCI.

Another inaccuracy I've heard about experience modifiers is that they compare our past losses with your past premiums. Again, not really true. As mentioned above, the mod formula compares your past reported losses (subject to some important limitations) with *expected losses.* Those expected losses are calculated by multiplying your audited payroll for those same past years times statewide expected loss factors for each classification code.

Past Years' Payroll Audits Should Match Modifier

Since past audited payrolls are used to calculate experience mods, this is the easiest part of experience modification factors for employers to check on their own. The information used here should match up exactly with the audited payroll information on your past years' audit billing statements for your past workers' compensation insurance coverage.

Remember, workers' compensation insurance begins by the insurer estimating which payroll amounts fall into which particular classifications. After the policy ends, the insurer does an audit—either by sending out its own auditor to review your payroll records or by asking you to report actual payrolls to it (usually the case for smaller employers). You then receive an audit billing statement should match up exactly with the payroll numbers used to calculate your experience mod. If they don't match, it may well indicate that incorrect information was used to calculate your modifier.

Intrastate or Interstate Modifier

If your business has always operated in just a single state, you'll get an *intrastate* modifier, calculated using expected loss data for just that one state. But if you've operated in more than one state, you may well get an *interstate* mod.

Most states coordinate with NCCI so that companies that operate in multiple states get a single integrated experience modifier. An interstate modifier combines payroll and loss data for multiple states and the resulting experience mod applies to your current policy for all states that participate. Even some states that maintain separate non-NCCI rating bureaus take part in the interstate rating mechanism.

For example, in Wisconsin the Wisconsin Rating Bureau calculates modifiers, but if Wisconsin employers have operations in other states, they may qualify for interstate rating. Then NCCI will calculate the mod for them, utilizing payroll and loss data for both Wisconsin and other states. This is a fairly recent change, though. Ten years ago, Wisconsin didn't coordinate with NCCI for interstate rating, and some other states still operate that way.

Stand-Alone Modifiers
California, for instance, does not (as of this writing, 2009) coordinate with interstate experience rating. So a company's California payroll and loss data will not be integrated into its interstate mod, and its separate California mod will be calculated based solely on past payroll and losses from California operations. The resulting modifier will apply only to California premium calculations, even if it's as part of a policy that covers other states as well. Delaware, Michigan, New Jersey, and Pennsylvania also operate the same policy of not coordinating with interstate rating. For these states, separate "stand-alone" modifiers will apply to premiums for those states, assuming that the employer meets the premium size requirements in each state to be eligible for experience rating.

REVIEWING YOUR EMR WORKSHEET
Take a look at the sample experience modification rating worksheet that follows (Figure 6-1). This is a mod worksheet for a fictitious company using the formula and worksheet layout used by

NCCI. Modifiers calculated by non-NCCI rating bureaus will use formulas and layouts that differ in some details, but the general principle will be similar.

In this sample worksheet, the expected loss ratio (ELR) for Class 9052 is 1.23 (although on the worksheet it looks like 123). This means that the average claims of everyone in Class 9052 were computed to be $1.23 for every hundred dollars on payroll. So, by multiplying the audited payroll reported in Class 9052, we get the expected losses for a company of its size in its state. In the second year year (06/28/03) shown on this sample worksheet, payroll of $1,223,843 in Class 9052 generated $15,053 of expected losses. This amount was arrived at by dividing the payroll

The D-Ratio
As you can see from the sample worksheet, there is another column immediately to the right of the expected loss ratio, the *discount ratio* (D-ratio). This is a further calculation done to expected losses to determine how much of those expected losses are *primary* and how much are *excess* (these terms are explained below). This is done to reflect similar differentiation of actual losses into primary and excess. The D-ratio determines what percentage of expected losses is considered primary. I know this gets a little technical, but it's an important part of the NCCI experience rating formula, so let's review it so that worksheets become more understandable.

WORKERS COMPENSATION EXPERIENCE RATING

NAME
OF
RISK

EFFECTIVE DATE 06/28/06

RISK IDENT. NO

STATE   SOUTH CAROLINA

1 CODE	2 ELR	3 D-RATI	4 PAYROLL	5 EXPECTED LOSSES	6 EXP PRIM LOSSES	7 CLAIM DATA	8 IJ	O F	9 ACT INC LOSSES	10 ACT PRIM LOSSES
CARRIER			POLICY NO			EFF-DATE	06/28/02		EXP-DATE	06/28/03
9052	123	23	1149762	14142	3253		5	F	24890	5000
9807	ADDITIONAL	PREMIUM	(0)(	0)			5	0	48986	5000
							6	F	178	178
POLICY-TOTAL			1149762	(SUBJECT) PREMIUM =		36832	)		74054	
CARRIER 13781			POLICY NO			EFF-DATE	06/28/03		EXP-DATE	06/28/04
8810	014	22	23655	33	7		5	F	6000	5000
9052	123	23	1223843	15053	3462		6	F	279	279
9807	ADDITIONAL	PREMIUM	(0)(	0)			6	F	347	347
POLICY-TOTAL			1247498	(SUBJECT) PREMIUM =		36682	)		6626	
CARRIER 13781			POLICY NO	WC7687202		EFF-DATE	06/28/04		EXP-DATE	06/28/05
8810	014	22	24260	34	7	09067832	6	F	165	165
9052	123	23	1258923	15485	3562					
9807	ADDITIONAL	PREMIUM	(0)(	0)						
POLICY-TOTAL			1283183	(SUBJECT) PREMIUM =		37733	)		185	

RATING REFLECTS A DECREASE OF 70% MEDICAL ONLY PRIMARY AND EXCESS LOSS
DOLLARS WHERE ERA IS APPLIED

•••••••••••••••••••••••••••
•••• REVISED RATING ••••
•••••••••••••••••••••••••••

RATING REVISED TO REFLECT APPROVED RATING VALUES

(ARAP) IF APPL : 1 19

(A)	(B)	(C) EXPECTED EXCESS (D-E)	(D)	(E)	(F) ACTUAL EXCESS (H-I)	(G)	(H)	(I)
011		34456	44747	10291	64876	18450	80167	15291

• Total by Policy Year of all cases $2,000 or less.
Limited loss.
C Catastrophic loss.
D Disease Loss.
E Employers Liability Loss.

		11 PRIMARY LOSSES	12 STABILIZING VALUE	13 RATABLE EXCESS	14 TOTALS	
PAGE NUMBER 1	ACTUAL	(D) 15291	(C) X (1-W) + (G) 49116	(A) X (F) 7136	(J) 71543	(15) EXP.MOD. (J) / (K)
DATE 10/05/06	EXPECTED	(E) 10291	(A) X (C) 49116	(K) 3790	63197	1 13

In its experience rating formula, the NCCI recognizes that not all claims dollars should be counted equally. One employer might have a single, unlikely event that costs $100,000, while another employer has a pattern—five separate claims, each $20,000. The two employers have each had the same dollar total of claims, but the experience rating formula is designed to discount that single $100,000 claim. So the employer with the five $20,000 claims will have a higher modifier than the employer with the single $100,000 claim, all other things being equal.

The single large claim could well be atypical, a fluke that's unlikely to recur, while the five $20,000 claims indicate a pattern that is more likely to be repeated in the future.

The NCCI experience rating formula discounts reported claims over a certain amount, so to be consistent the expected losses need to have that same discount applied. The D-ratio reflects how much of expected claims (on average) exceed that primary cutoff. Currently, the NCCI experience rating formula discounts each individual claim over $5,000. That's why at the far right of the worksheet there are two columns that contain actual reported losses for this company. The first column shows "Actual Incurred Losses." Take the second claim listed, for $20,000. In the column labeled "Actual Primary Losses," that claim is shown for only $5,000, because on the first $5,000 of the claim is counted as primary.

Actual Incurred Losses
This is one of those great insurance terms that are often poorly understood by people buying insurance, yet it is an important concept that makes a lot of difference in the cost of workers' compensation insurance. Incurred losses include not just what the insurance company has actually paid out for the claim, but also the *reserves* that the insurance company has established for the claim. Reserves represent what the insurance company thinks the ultimate cost of the claim will be. It is an educated guess at best, but in the experience rating formula, those best guesses get counted exactly the same as hard dollars actually paid out.

Medical-Only Claims Discounted

The current NCCI experience mod formula also heavily discounts *medical-only* claims. That is, claims for which the only cost is medical care, without any lost-time benefits being paid. In calculating an NCCI experience modifier, the dollar amount paid for these claims is discounted by 70 percent. This means that only 30 percent of the cost of medical-only claims is actually counted in computing a modifier under the NCCI formula. (Remember, non-NCCI states don't include this feature, as they follow different ratings formulas.) This discount was instituted by NCCI to encourage employers to turn in all claims to their insurer, even minor ones. In the past, some employers would pay such small claims themselves without reporting them to the insurer, with the idea of holding down their future experience modifier. The problem with such a practice is that sometimes minor claims can balloon into major claims; then, if the insurance company wasn't notified in a timely manner, it can deny responsibility for the claim. So unofficially "self-insuring" small claims isn't a good idea, especially if your experience modifier is not calculated by NCCI. Additionally, many states have approved so-called *small-deductible* programs, in which an employer can officially self-insure small medical-only claims. If you want to self-insure small medical-only claims, it's best to do so officially. You get a premium credit (if your state has approved a small-deductible plan) and you avoid the possibility of having an insurer deny responsibility for a small claim that later turns out to be not so small.

Combination of Entities

Under the rules of experience rating, business entities that have more than 50 percent common ownership are supposed to be combined. That is, the last payroll and data for all such entities are supposed to be combined into a single experience modification factor. But problems and errors can also occur in this area, so business owners and managers are well advised to review this area carefully to make sure that mistakes aren't making the modifier higher than it really should be.

Remember, it's not just the employer who can request that the rating bureau determine if separately rated entities can be combined. The insurance company can also initiate the process, but sometimes the system doesn't follow the rules carefully.

Of course, sometimes the problem occurs in just the opposite direction: sometimes companies are combined for experience rating when they really shouldn't be and the resulting experience mod is higher than it should be.

Changes in Ownership
Folks who have been working with Workers' Compensation insurance may remember a time when, if a company's ownership changed, the experience mod reset back to 1.00. But that changed a long time ago. Under current NCCI experience rating rules, a change in ownership doesn't mean that experience resets, unless the company's operations also change enough to change the classification assigned. Of course, if the change in ownership involves a merger or acquisition of another entity that already has a published experience mod, then the new combined entity should get a modifier that is the result of the combined loss and payroll histories. But if new ownership takes over a company and that new owner doesn't have a published experience mod, then the business continues to have the modifier it's earned from its past experience.

More recently, I worked with two private schools in the New England area that had been combined for experience rating, even though they only had 50 percent common ownership. What was particularly interesting in this case was that separating the two entities produced a lower mod for both schools even though one had a better loss record than the other. Normally, one would expect that separating two such entities would lower the mod for the one with the better loss record and produce a higher mod for the other, but not in this instance. Due to some quirks in the formula, both schools benefited from having their experience mods calculated separately—a large benefit for one and a lesser benefit for the other.

Fathers and Sons and Experience Mods: A Legacy

A few years back, I was called in to review the Workers' Compensation premium charges for a small masonry contractor. The company had been started a few years earlier by two young men. As a new business, it had started out with a 1.00 experience modifier, as new businesses should under the experience ratings rules. However, in my review I found out these two young men had formed their new company by combing two companies that had been owned by their fathers. So this "new" company wasn't really new after all, but instead a combination of two old companies. Under the rules, the "new" company should have had experience mod calculated based on the combined experience of the fathers' companies. This experience had been favorable, so the proper mod for the "new" company was significantly lower than 1.00.

The insurance agent and the insurance company had not done a very good job of explaining how these rules of experience rating worked, so the two partners were unaware that they should have inherited the favorable experience of their fathers' companies. They had been given the appropriate form to fill out (the NCCI ERM-14), but no one had explained why they should fill it out or how, so it had gotten lost among various other papers relating to their insurance. So I had them fill out the ERM-14 and send it to NCCI. Then I followed up and made sure the resulting lower modifiers were calculated for all appropriate years and then that the insurance company revised those premium charges and refunded all the overcharges that had resulted from the use of the higher, incorrect modifiers.

COMMON MOD MISTAKES

Here are common mistakes we find in experience modifiers and their application:
- Missing or inaccurate data
- Increase in experience modifier applied late in states that prohibit such increases

- Mistakes in combination of entities—either combined when they shouldn't have been or not combined when they should have been
- Modifier not revised to reflect change in classification
- Insurer does not report reimbursements it has received for certain claims such as Second Injury Fund payments or subrogations
- Insurance company does not apply a revision from NCCI that lowers the experience mod

Let's take a closer look at each of these kinds of mistakes and how to correct them.

Missing or Inaccurate Data

Just recently, I worked with a small residential masonry contractor. In reviewing their recent experience modification factor worksheets, I saw that a year of data was missing. I checked with the contractor and found that in the missing year, losses had been low; in fact, they had no claims that year. However, the payroll had been significant. So I set about getting that missing data incorporated into their mod calculation. That was easier than usual, because a phone call to NCCI revealed that it had the missing data, but just had somehow not incorporated it into the mod calculation. The addition of this data reduced the contractor's mod from a 1.00 to a .91.

Now, it isn't usually that easy to correct missing data, because normally it's missing because an insurance company has failed to file what's called a *unit statistical report*—a unit stat report, as it's often called—and typically the rating bureau, like NCCI, won't take action to get the carrier to file that missing report. So the employer has to contact the insurance company and then persuade or cajole those folks into filing the missing report with the rating bureau. Of course, before doing so, it would be in the employer's interest to determine that the result would produce a lower experience mod. Performing this calculation is pretty technical, so an employer would probably be well advised to ask its agent (or a consultant like me, if the agent can't do this) to perform the calculation to make sure the corrected mod would be lower.

In recent years, data is sometimes missing because a past insurance company is no longer in business. If that's the case, you can probably provide the missing data to NCCI or another rating bureau in a form other than a unit stat report. If you can document the audited payrolls and classes used in the missing year, along with the claims for that year, the rating bureau should be able to incorporate the missing data. Similarly, if data is missing because your company was covered by some kind of self-insurance program, you can report those past payrolls and losses to the rating bureau and get them incorporated into your mod.

Increases in Modifier After Policy Inception

In some states, the rules allow an insurance company to increase the experience modification factor for a policy after it starts, but not all states allow this. The easiest way to determine whether your state prohibits such practices is to contact your state's department of insurance (see the directory in Chapter 1). If you think that your insurance company must already know which states allow this and which states don't, you would be mistaken.

A few years ago, I reduced the Workers' Compensation premiums for a client by almost $600,000 by catching such a mistake. The experience modifier had been calculated correctly, but it had been calculated late and endorsed on to the policy months after it had begun. In Tennessee, where this client operated, this is prohibited by a section of the state insurance regulations. Once we pointed out the mistake to the insurer, it corrected the mistake, but if we had not done so, the insurer would have pocketed almost $600,000 in premium charges to which they were not entitled.

Mistakes in the Combination of Entities

Earlier in this chapter, I shared two case histories about these kinds of mistakes, one about a company whose mod should have been combined from two prior companies and the other about two companies that had been combined improperly. Generally, two entities are required to be combined if they have more than 50 percent common ownership. (Pennsylvania does not make this a requirement, but rather an option that the employer can choose.)

So if your company was formed in recent years by combing entities, you may well want to take a close look at the modifier used on your policies since that combination.

Conversely, if your experience modifier has been calculated on the basis of combining two or more separate entities, you may well want to verify that this was really done properly and check if separating the entities would be beneficial to one or both.

I mentioned that Pennsylvania does not require commonly owned businesses to be combined. This was an issue in a recent case. There, several related entities were combined for the experience rating, because the insurer wasn't aware that the rules were different in Pennsylvania. Being accustomed to the way things are done in NCCI states, the insurer initiated the process of combining the companies without getting the consent of the policy holder. As it turned out, the policy holder found it preferable to have the two companies experience-rated separately, so we had to work with the carrier and the Pennsylvania rating bureau to untangle the improper combination.

Again, keep in mind that calculating the effect of making changes in combination of entities is a technical process; you will probably need the assistance of someone with experience in this to make sure the end result will benefit your company

Modifier Not Revised to Reflect a Change in Classification
This is also a relatively common mistake. When an insurer makes a change in classification code on a policy, the experience modifier used on that policy is supposed to be recalculated in a reciprocal fashion. So if an insurance company changes your classification

to something more expensive, a good part of that increased rate (not all of it, but a good part) is supposed to be offset by a lower experience modification factor. In essence, the experience modifier should be recalculated as if your company had always been in this more expensive class. But again, I often find that the insurers do not initiate this. They tend to worry about getting the classification change done and don't make sure the rating bureau makes the reciprocal change in the modifier.

So if you company is subject to a classification change to a more expensive class and you can't successfully fight that change, then you at least want to make sure the experience modifier has been revised to reflect the updated classification.

Insurance Company Does Not Apply a Revision From NCCI That Lowers the Experience Mod

When an experience modification factor is recalculated by NCCI, it often times happens either during the term of the policy or even after the audit has been completed. If the recalculation results in a lower experience modification factor than what was used on the policy or audit. However, we've seen insurance companies, who are sent every revision by NCCI and other rating bureaus, simply not apply lower experience modification factors. This is an easy thing for employers to check over. NCCI and other rating bureaus will usually send out copies of any experience modification worksheets that they have revised. Whenever an employer receives a revision to a past experience modification factor, they should compare it to the modification factor on their policy or audit. If the revision is lower, the employer should ask the insurance carrier to apply the revised mod.

OTHER STATES MODIFICATION WORKSHEETS

The earlier sample modifier worksheet used the NCCI experience modification factor formula, but remember that some states don't use the NCCI experience rating formula and their mod worksheets can look a little different. Figure 6-2 shows a sample California experience modification factor worksheet.

This second experience mod worksheet shows the same kind of information as the first, only laid out in a little different format. Instead of showing payroll and loss information for each year in one block, this worksheet breaks payroll information and loss information into different areas.

One other important difference you may note on this California experience modifier worksheet is that the medical-only claims are not discounted as they were in the NCCI calculation. Also, the California formula discounts actual losses above $2001. So some of the details of the formula are different from the NCCI calculation, but the calculation is still done in a very similar fashion, by comparing actual historic losses for a particular employer with the expected losses that are calculated using historic payroll information.

WORKERS' COMPENSATION INSURANCE RATING BUREAU
OF CALIFORNIA
EXPERIENCE RATING FORM

PAGE 1 OF 1

ISSUED

11/18/02 1 1 03

STATE CMPNSTN INS FUND

SAN FRANCISCO

1619104 2

4034 CONCRETE PRODUCTS MFG
#5606 CONTRACTORS - EXECUTIVE SUPERVISORS
8232 BUILDING MATERIAL DEALERS-COMMERCIAL
#-IF/ANY

CLASS CODE	YR 01 PAYROLL	YR 00 PAYROLL	YR 99 PAYROLL	YR 98 PAYROLL	EXPECTED LOSS RATE	EXPECTED LOSSES	'D' RATIO	PRIMARY EXPECTED LOSSES
5213	537988	546113	485632	61361	4.16	67854	.17	11535
5208	00	00	176		2.93	5	.17	1
4034	214664	256586	203357		7.11	47965	.19	9113
8742	64354	152997	164576		.49	1871	.22	412
8810	154961	147497	131802		.43	1867	.23	429

EXPECTED LOSSES (f) = (d) - (e): 98072
EXPECTED LOSSES (d): 119562
PRIMARY EXPECTED LOSSES (e): 21490

CLAIM NUMBER	TYPE	S	POLICY YEAR	ACTUAL INCURRED LOSSES	PRIMARY ACTUAL LOSSES	CLAIM NUMBER	TYPE	S	POLICY YEAR	ACTUAL INCURRED LOSSES	PRIMARY ACTUAL LOSSES
99290793	T	F	99	3289	2877						
12369	M	F	00	129270	8538	UNDER $2001			99	2045	2045
21120	M	O	00	175000	8654	12963	T	F	00	2256	2194
						UNDER $2001			00	408	408
NA161412	N	F	01	4869	3692	UNDER $2001			01	1250	1250

ACTUAL EXCESS (c) = (a) - (b): 288729
ACTUAL INCURRED LOSSES (a): 318387
PRIMARY ACTUAL LOSSES (b): 29658

RATING PROCEDURE

TOTAL PRIMARY ACTUAL (b)	'B' VALUE	'W' VALUE	RATABLE EXCESS LOSSES - W x (c)	(1-W) x (f)	TOTAL (g)	
29658	10000	.19	54859	79438	173955	021112LSL

TOTAL EXPECTED LOSSES (d)	'T' VALUE	INDEMNITY AND MEDICAL COMBINED	TOTAL (h)	
119562	10000	ENTER TABLE III WITH EXPECTED LOSSES (d)	129562	134 %

A Husband and a Wife and Two Companies

A husband and a wife each owned separate temporary employment agencies. ABC Temps (not the real name, of course) was
owned 100 percent by the husband. XYZ Temporary Services (also

not the real name) was owned 100 percent by the wife. Both companies had been insured through the assigned risk mechanism in their state, on separate policies.

But XYZ had much worse experience than ABC. The insurance carrier requested that NCCI review the matter. The result was that NCCI ruled that the two companies were combinable for experience rating purposes. This greatly increased premiums for ABC, based on the poor past loss-experience of XYZ.

However, by appealing this ruling to their state department of insurance, we were able to get the NCCI decision reversed. After all, the NCCI experience rating manual said that to be combined two entities had to have more than 50 percent common ownership. These two separate corporations had 0 percent common ownership.

However, NCCI had relied upon another section of the manual that stated that a transfer of assets between two entities was also a basis for combination. XYZ had placed some workers who had formerly been placed by ABC, so NCCI decided that this constituted the transfer of an asset.

But the NCCI manual did not define what constituted an "asset." We argued (successfully, it turned out) that the temporary workers placed by these two separate agencies could not constitute an asset as these workers were not owned by the temporary agencies that, thus, did not constitute an asset of either company.

Unreported Reimbursements
In the past few years, we've stumbled onto what may well be one of the most costly causes of experience modification factor errors: insurance companies failing to report to NCCI (or other rating bureaus) reimbursements they receive for certain claims.

It began with some work we did in South Carolina, where our firm was commissioned to study the impact of that state's Second Injury

Fund on Workers Compensation premiums of smaller employers. That study found that in a majority of cases, smaller employers were not receiving any benefit from reimbursements paid by the Second Injury Fund there to insurance companies. In part, this was because many small employers were too small to be eligible for an experience modification factor, which is the only direct mechanism for such reimbursements to be passed along to an insured employer.But the other thing we discovered was that, even when an employer was large enough to be experience rated, insurance companies often did not issue corrected unit statistical reports to NCCI. This meant that the employer's experience modification factor was not adjusted to reflect the reimbursement that the insurance company had received.

Here's how it works, in simplified fashion: a worker at ABC Electricians hurts his back. The insurance company ultimately pays out $100,000 for that claim. The cost of that claim gets reported to NCCI and is included in the data used to calculate experience modification factors for future policies of ABC Electricians.

But the insurance company for ABC files for reimbursement from the Second Injury Fund, because this particular back injury was actually just a re-injury of an earlier back injury for this worker. Ultimately, the insurance company receives $75,000 reimbursement, which means the net cost of this claim was only $25,000, not the $100,000 earlier reported. The insurance company is supposed to file a corrected report with NCCI, showing that the claim only cost $25,000. But very often, we have found that insurance companies are not making such corrected reports, leaving employers with experience modifiers higher than they really should be.

So anytime an employer becomes aware of their insurer receiving a reimbursement on a claim, whether from a Second Injury Fund or some other source (such as a subrogation) the employer should insist that corrected reports be filed with the appropriate rating bureau. An error of this type can inflate experience mods for

3 subsequent policy years for an employer, increasing premiums significantly.

As I said at the beginning of this chapter, experience modification factor worksheets can seem like hieroglyphics to many employers, but reviewing these calculations can be well worth the effort, as there can be significant mistakes buried in these rows of numbers.

QUICK REVIEW
- The Experience modification factor is the way insurance companies adjust current premiums based on prior years' losses and payrolls.
- Experience modification factors are calculated by rating bureaus based on loss and payroll information reported by an employer's past insurers.
- Errors by insurance companies regarding past losses and payrolls can cause experience modification factors to be wrong. Employers need to review the worksheets carefully to spot such errors.
- Changes in ownership can also affect experience modification factors. Employers should review the modifiers being used on their policies to make sure they take into account current ownership.
- Some states limit the ability of insurance companies to increase experience modification factors after a policy begins. **Employers should check what protection is provided by their particular state.** A change to a more expensive classification means the experience modification factor should be recalculated downwards. There is a reciprocal relationship between classification and modifier, but often when class change is made, the change to modifier is overlooked.
- Employers should make sure to watch for reimbursements their insurer gets for Workers Compensation claims, to make sure proper reporting is done to rating bureaus.

CHAPTER 7

THE PREMIUM AUDIT

Earlier in this *Field Guide*, we covered how the premium for a workers' compensation insurance policy is only an estimated premium when the policy starts. The actual premium for the coverage is determined through an audit. The audit is usually done after the policy has expired, although sometimes an insurance company will want audits done earlier, during the term of the policy, to make sure the estimated premium isn't too far off the mark. The premium audit that's performed after policy expiration is mainly about payroll—because for almost all kinds of employments, payroll is the basic unit that is applied to the rate to determine the premium.

For smaller employers, an insurance company may just ask that the employer fill out a form about the final payroll and send it in to the insurer, but for larger employers, they will want to send out a *premium auditor* to determine the actual premium for the policy period. In such cases, the premium auditor will contact the employer to schedule an appointment to come out and review payroll records and operations for the audit.

There has been some evolution in recent decades in the profession of premium auditor. When I first began working with the workers' compensation insurance, back in the mid 1970s, most premium auditors worked directly for an insurance company, but since then the trend has been for much of this work to be outsourced to third-party firms. A lot of the people working for these third-party firms are the same people who used to work directly for the insurance companies, but now they're under a lot more pressure to do the audits in less time. So more than ever, an employer that prepares wisely for a premium audit can benefit by avoiding overcharges.

PREPARE FOR YOUR AUDIT

It can be vital to spend a little time and effort preparing for your premium audit, because if the auditor can't readily determine from your records certain important details, he or she will just assume the worst-case scenario and bill you on that basis. As the auditor is under pressure to do the audit as quickly and efficiently as possible, he or she will resolve any unclear areas by assuming the worst. So, for example, if your payroll records don't let the auditor quickly and easily determine how much of your payroll is overtime, you won't get the adjustment that eliminates the premium portion of overtime pay. (Most states, but not all, allow for overtime pay to be reduced down to straight time when computing Workers' Compensation premiums.)

So before the auditor arrives, review your payroll records and make sure they allow the auditor to determine easily how much payroll for the year was overtime, so that the adjustment can be made that eliminates the premium portion of the overtime pay. If your company has situations where you pay more than time-and-a-half, make sure the payroll records allow the auditor to determine that readily. Double-time would be adjusted by half, as long as the payroll records allow the auditor to readily determine the actual amount of the overtime/premium pay.

I've sometimes consulted with employers whose records didn't spell out this vital information for the auditor, at least not in usable forms. Even though these employers used a well-known payroll service, the records didn't allow the auditor to determine overtime pay for the year easily. The overtime was broken out, yes, but only pay period by pay period—and only for each individual employee. The auditor would have had to spend a lot of time going through the records and compiling the overall overtime amount, and the auditor just didn't have the time to do that. So the insurance company did not exclude the premium portion of the overtime pay and, as a result, the employer paid significantly higher premiums.

So take the time to review your payroll records a couple of weeks before the auditor is due to stop by. See if you can determine, by looking at your actual records, the following kinds of information:

- Overtime pay summarized by department and calculated on annual basis
- For construction-type work, records kept of how many hours worked at different kinds of employment that are eligible for different classifications
- Separation of payroll for different departments that are eligible for different classifications
- Certificates of insurance for all subcontracted work
- Executive officers

Take the time to review the audit billing statements and audit work papers from recent past audits. This can give you an idea of what areas might be issues for your company in the upcoming audit. Make sure you've got a designated person available to answer any questions the auditor might have about company operations. Take some time to review the manual descriptions of the classifications on your policy, to anticipate any questions the auditor might have that could potentially lead to changes in classification.

Other Pay Differential Programs
Occasionally, I have worked with employers that had other kinds of pay differential systems in place for employers. So instead of paying time-and-a-half for overtime, they would do things like pay employees for an additional day (even though the employee hadn't worked that day). The problem with all such alternative schemes for pay differential is that the workers' compensation rules only allow for traditional adjustments to overtime pay (either time-and-a-half or double-time) and no other. So if you've agreed to pay an employee for time that the employee isn't actually working, that pay will be picked up when it comes time to compute your workers'

compensation premiums, even though the employee wasn't physically exposed to the workplace. It's the same for sick time and vacation pay—under the rules, all these things are picked up, even though the employee isn't physically present. In fact, all kinds of compensation to employees can be counted when computing the workers' compensation premium. Here again is the official list of what's counted as *remuneration* and what's not, per NCCI rules, as presented in Chapter 3:

Remuneration *includes*:
- regular pay, including salary or hourly;
- commissions;
- bonuses;
- overtime pay, less the premium portion;
- holiday, vacation, and sick pay;
- payments by the employer of contributions required by law to statutory insurance or pension plans such as Social Security that would otherwise be paid by the employee;
- piecework, incentive plans, profit-sharing plans;
- payments to employees for hand or power tools supplied by employees;
- rental value of housing provided to employees;
- value of lodging provided by the employer;
- value of meals provided by the employer; and
- value of store certificates, merchandise, or credits given to employees by the employer.

Remuneration *excludes*:
- tips and gratuities received by employees;
- payments by the employer to group insurance plans;
- value of special awards paid for invention or discovery;
- dismissal or severance pay, except for time worked or accrued vacation;
- value of employer-provided aircraft;
- value of employer-provided automobiles;
- value of employer-provided free or discounted aircraft flight;

- value of employer-provided incentive vacation (contest winner);
- employer-provided discounts on property or services;
- employer-provided tickets to entertainment events; and
- employer payments to military reservists called to active duty, payments that make up the difference between military pay and employee's pay prior to conscription;

CONTROL THE AUDIT PROCESS

One red flag I watch for when reviewing audits is if the audit was performed away from the company premises, at the accountant's offices. That's because the accountant, while he or she knows the payroll numbers well and has lots of records, may not always know the details of the work being done by the employer. And since part of the auditor's job is not just to determine payroll, but also to review the classifications used, if questions arise about the kind of work being done by the company or by certain departments, the accountant may not be able to give accurate information.

If your company uses subcontractors or independent contractors, make sure you have certificates of insurance on file documenting that these 1099 people have their own workers' compensation insurance. Make sure to get certificates before the audit, otherwise your company may well be charge for this exposure. Similarly, if you've used temporary employees or workers from a professional employer organization, make sure you have evidence that they were covered somewhere.

Remember that most construction-type companies can use more than one classification code for their operations; they can even divide the payroll of an individual employee between or among classifications. But the payroll records must document the actual hours spent by such employees in each of the workplace exposures. An estimate will not suffice. If the payroll records do not document the hours spent in each kind of work, all of an employee's payroll will go into the most expensive classification applicable.

CHECK YOUR WORK PAPERS

I mentioned earlier that it can be a good idea to review the audit work papers from prior years in preparation for a current audit. But not all employers get copies of the audit work papers—and that can be an expensive mistake.

Audit work papers are computerized records of how the auditor conducted the audit, listing the documents consulted, the auditor's description of his or her understanding of your operations, notes on any changes in classifications made, a detailed description of the payroll numbers and all adjustments (like overtime and executive officer limitations), and what's done by various departments and what classifications have been assigned to those workers. In other words, the audit work papers are a road map that details how the auditor arrived at the payroll numbers that will be used to determine the final audited premium for the policy.

Audit work papers are not automatically provided to policy holders. They have to be requested. If the policy holder requests a copy, the insurer will provide it, but if the policy holder doesn't ask, it typically isn't provided. So by all means, request a copy of the audit work papers from the auditor. Then review them carefully to make sure there are no mistakes or misunderstandings that have improperly inflated your premiums. The next case study illustrates how comparing one year's audit with the next can reveal questionable changes.

This client was a medium-sized manufacturer, with plants in several Midwestern states. The company was large enough to have its own corporate airplane, with a pilot and co-pilot on staff. The audited payroll for the pilot and co-pilot alerted me to a problem with the audit.

While reviewing the audits for several past years, I noticed that the payroll for the pilot and co-pilot's classification had jumped from $50,000 one year to $200,000 the next. When I questioned this, I was told there had been no big increase in the aircraft personnel payroll. So I began investigating the audit. This client, head-quartered in a small Iowa city, had used the one large accounting firm in the area for its payroll work. The premium auditor had gone to the accountant's offices to perform the workers' comp audit, so I went to those same offices to find out where those payroll numbers for the flight personnel had come from.

As I worked through the payroll records, less of what I saw made sense. The correct payroll for the pilot and co-pilot was still $50,000. However, a copy of an early trial balance I found in the accountant's files had mistakenly assigned $200,000 in payroll to the flight personnel. All of the other payroll numbers on the audit matched this trial balance, also. Yet the actual payroll records for the policy period did not match.

The trial balance had mistakenly been used as the basis for the audit. I am still not sure how much fault lay with the insurance company premium auditor and how much with the accountant. Obviously, no one had checked the final product very carefully. There were several significant errors in the audit besides the aviation payroll: the overtime payroll was off and several departments had been placed into the manufacturing class instead of the clerical class where they belonged.

The mistake in classifications occurred because no one at the accountant's office understood the actual duties of the various departments involved. These mistakes could have been avoided if a representative from the manufacturer's company had been involved with the audit. Then net result of all the mistakes had been a $7,500 premium overcharge, which could have been prevented by reviewing the audit and audit work papers more carefully.

COMMON AUDIT MISTAKES
In my work consulting with employers, the mistakes I find on premium audits fall into a couple of categories:
- Mistakes in adjusting overtime
- Mistakes in assigning payroll to different classifications

- Charging for subcontractors or independent contractors who have their own insurance

When reviewing audit work papers, here's a checklist of important things to review carefully:

- Make sure you understand the overall scheme of the audit. For example, did the auditor start with the total payroll numbers and then separate certain departments' payroll into other classes?
- Check the accuracy of the total payroll numbers.
- Check that overtime was adjusted back to straight time properly.
- Are limitations on executive officer payroll allowed?
- Is payroll for sole proprietor or partners excluded if they have not chosen to be covered for workers' comp?
- Are there any charges for independent contractors that had their own insurance in force?
- Were any non-payroll remuneration charges picked up that shouldn't have been?
- Does assignment of particular departments within the company to particular classifications seem reasonable and appropriate for the work done by those departments? Did the auditor properly understand the work performed by those departments?

Confusion with Independent Contractors

A few years ago, I was called in by an insurance agent to review the audit charges for one of his clients. The agent suspected that on prior policies, written by a different agent, the insurance company had overcharged the client, a fencing contractor, but the prior insurance company was insisting it was too late to make any changes in those audits.

As I dug into the case, I quickly discovered that the payroll audits had been performed at the offices of the client's outside accountant—again, a red flag. In this case, the accountant worked out of his home. When I went there and reviewed the payroll records, I discovered the accountant had a computer printout of IRS 1099 payments to independent contractors. One entry on the list caught my eye; it showed payments to someone I knew was actually a partner in the business.

The accountant had never properly understood the partner's status in the company. However, the partner was listed as one of the named insureds on the contractor's workers' compensation policy. The policy read, "John Smith and Joe Jones, dba Active Fence Co." Yet payroll for "Joe Jones" was being picked up as if he were an independent contractor.

In the state where Active Fence was located, partners are not covered for Workers' Compensation unless they choose to be. In this case, the partner had emphatically chosen not to be covered.

What went wrong here? The accountant did not properly understand his client. Also, the insurance company auditor did not look carefully at who was named as insured under the policy. This misunderstanding and this mistake caused Active Fence to pay significant premium overcharges for a number of years.

I also learned that a number of other independent contractors on that 1099 list were family members and friends who worked on a contract basis. However, they did not work as fencing contractors. Instead, they served as messengers and telephone solicitors for Active Fence. Their payroll belonged in the clerical class, not the fencing class. Because the accountant's records had simply listed them as independent contractors, the premium auditor had assumed they had been doing fencing work.

I also discovered that some of the other independent contractors, who actually did fencing work, carried their own workers' compensation insurance. The accountant had not known that either.

When it had all been straightened out, I had recovered about $5,000 in overcharges—a considerable amount for a small contractor that paid only about $10,000 a year for Workers' Compensation.

The fictitious audit work papers shown in Figure 7-1 were adapted from real ones done for one of my clients. The names have been changed, but the format is the real one used by a real insurance company.

The first page includes a brief description of the company's operations, information about the company's ownership, and a list of factors that the auditor has reviewed in preparing the audit. For example, this audit work paper indicates that the auditor has found that overtime is not a factor for this company's payroll (Key Question #9). It also indicates that the two corporate officers have chosen to exclude themselves from coverage, so their payroll should not be included in the premium computation. It also indicates that this company does not use subcontractors, temporary employees, or leased employees.

The second page shows the detail of the payroll found in the audit. Since this audit was of a relatively small company, it lists individual names rather than listing payroll by department. A larger company's audit work papers wouldn't show payroll for each individual but would instead list it by departments.

This is a relatively simple audit, but the work paper can be used to determine exactly how the payroll was developed and enables one to identify key areas where errors might have occurred. For example, if overtime pay was actually a significant part of pay for this company, one could identify from this audit work paper that overtime had not adjusted. If some of the individuals listed had not done masonry work, but instead were employed as clerical or salespeople, this could also be identified from the listing of the duties of individual employees.

The audit work papers used by different insurance companies reflect their own format, but all can be used to double-check how the auditor has arrived at the particular payroll and classification decisions that determine the audited premium. A little effort in reviewing these documents can produce significant savings.

Watch Payroll Allocation on Audits Carefully
One of the tricky things that an employer needs to watch carefully on a premium audit is how payroll is allocated by the auditor. Whether your company is large or small, keeping an eye on this detail can catch costly and avoidable overcharges. Consider this recent case from our files.

A Connecticut employer was in the business of landscaping and lawn maintenance. Under NCCI rules, these two types of work go into two different classifications, with the landscaping being charged at $10.45 per hundred dollars of payroll and the lawn maintenance taking a rate of only $5.29. A careful review of their audit work papers found that some employees who belonged in the less expensive class had been assigned in the audit to the more expensive class. This point was buried in the details of the work papers, but a careful review found it.

Once we were able to convince the insurance company that a mistake had been made, the premium charges were reversed, with a premium reduction to the employer of about 20 percent of the annual premium.

Taking the time to carefully review audit work papers can require some patience and determination, but can be well worth the effort. Remember, the auditor will usually not provide a copy of the work papers, unless you request them. If you request them, they will normally be provided without any fuss, but the employer has to remember to request them at the time the audit is done, as the insurance company may not keep them on file too long into the future.

CORRECTING AUDIT MISTAKES

OK, let's say you've reviewed your audit and audit work papers and you feel there's an error that you need to correct. The field auditor that performed the audit should have left his or her card behind, with phone numbers and maybe an email address. So as a first step, communicate to the field auditor the nature of the mistake you've found and ask that it be corrected. The auditor may be reluctant to make another trip out to your premises, so be prepared to fax or mail copies of any documentation that backs up your contention. For example, if you have certificates of insurance for subcontractors that weren't considered during the audit, send copies to the auditor.

If you don't get a satisfactory result from the field auditor, contact the audit manager for the insurance company. When dealing with insurance companies, I've often found that persistence makes the difference between getting your complaint resolved and getting ignored. Given the increased workloads a lot of insurance company people are dealing with nowadays, it can take a bit of persistence to get their attention focused on solving your problem. But if you genuinely believe you're right, stick to your guns; and if you're disputing an audit that hasn't been paid yet, you're in a relatively strong position. You probably want to pay the undisputed portion of the audit, but then you can insist the insurance company address your concerns before you will consider paying the undisputed portion.

If you can't get your problem resolved by dealing with the audit manager, you can always take your complaint to your state's department of insurance. Just make sure you can document whatever corrections you're trying to get made. With persistence and determination, you can get even overworked and unresponsive insurance company personnel to correct mistakes.

Surviving an Extreme Audit

Sometimes an employer can be subjected to a particularly intense and strenuous payroll audit process. This is usually done when the insurance company suspects that an employer has been getting away with paying lower premiums than are really owed. Temporary agencies and employee leasing companies are favorite targets of this type of "extreme" audit, but almost any employer could be targeted for such an investigation.

The terms of the workers' compensation insurance policy give the insurance company broad latitude to examine the books and records of an employer and set no specific limits on what kind of records and documents an insurance company may insist on seeing. Sometimes employers get upset by broad demands by insurance companies for records that the employer feels are none of the insurer's business. However, by terms of the policy, the insurance company has the right to inspect any business record that may have an impact on the premium.

If your company gets subjected to an extreme audit, resist your initial impulse to negotiate or play hardball. This will usually just make a bad situation worse. A better strategy is to cooperate as fully as possible.

Remember that if the insurance company can't get all the information and documentation they want, the manual rules allow them to estimate the premium on a "worst-case scenario" basis, and then bill you for that amount. Such worst-case-scenario premium calculations can take an employer's breath when they are first received, as the insurance company will typically be demanding a premium far in excess of what the employer expected.

To whatever extent possible, try to maintain a cooperative working relationship with the insurance company and the auditor. Don't take it personally. Reacting emotionally to a difficult premium audit can only create deeper suspicion on part of the insurance company and ultimately make it more difficult to resolve any audit dispute. Remain professional in all communication with the insurance company, whether in person, over the phone, or in writing.

Work closely with the auditor, and try to understand what questions he or she may be trying to resolve with the information requests. The main issues the auditor will be focusing on will be the nature of the work done, making sure that all appropriate payroll is picked up on the audit, and ownership of the company. Some auditors may make it difficult to remain professional because of their attitude or their demands for documents; but in the long run, employers are better served by keeping their cool and working to maintain a decent working relationship with the auditor and the insurance company.

I don't mean to make it sound like audit personnel are always unresponsive or difficult; in fact, a lot of the time they're very cooperative in fixing mistakes, but occasionally, I've encountered auditors who just didn't like to admit that a mistake had been made or who didn't want to take the time and effort to send someone back out to redo an audit. And if you should run into one of these problem situations, you'll need to be persistent to get your concerns properly addressed; but if you're in the right, stick to your guns and ultimately you should prevail.

TIMETABLE FOR CONTROLLING WORKER' COMPENSATION COSTS

Here's a timetable for taking action over the course of a year to control Workers' Compensation costs.

Nine Months Before Policy Inception- Review the incurred losses that will be reported to the rating bureau for use in the next experience modification factor. Negotiate lower claims reserves where possible.

Two Months Before Policy Inception- Check what the appropriate rating bureaus have on file for your company regarding proper classifications and experience modification factors. Review all existing inspection reports and experience mod worksheets for errors.

Policy Inception or Renewal- Make sure all competing proposals use the same payrolls, classes, and experience mods. Keep on file a copy of the winning proposal for comparison later with the policy when it is produced.

One Month After Renewal- Start preparing for the audit of expired policy review payroll records to make sure the auditor will be able to break out overtime and assign proper classifications to your various departments and workers.

During the Audit (Typically Three Months After Renewal) - Make sure someone knowledgeable about company operations is available to help the auditor. Make certain all certificates of insurance for independent contractors or subcontractors are on file and available. Request a copy of the auditor's work papers for review.

After the Audit- Review the audit work papers carefully. Check classifications, payroll computation, overtime adjustment, and description of your operations.

QUICK REVIEW
- Review payroll records in advance of the premium audit to make sure the records allow the auditor to give you all the credits for which you are eligible.
- Make sure the payroll records allow overtime pay to be broken out.
- Make sure certificates of insurance are on file for all independent contractors and subcontractors.
- Always request copy of the auditor's work papers after the audit is completed and check for problems before paying any additional premium.
- If the audit is done by a third-party, such as an accountant, make sure someone knowledgeable about your operations is available to make sure the auditor does not misunderstand what is done by the company overall and by various departments.

CHAPTER 8

CHOOSING AGENTS AND INSURERS AND CONSULTANTS

A few years ago, there was a serious scandal in the insurance world that was uncovered by (then) New York attorney General Eliot Spitzer. Mr. Spitzer has had his own ups and downs in the world since then, and I fear the scandal itself may have faded a bit from many memories. At the heart of the matter were allegations that the largest insurance broker in the world, Marsh & McLennan, engaged in bid-rigging practices that improperly inflated insurance premiums for commercial policy holders.

Some executives were convicted and everyone promised never to do such a thing again. The outrage over this scandal has largely subsided, but the initial response of the insurance industry, generally, was to decry the particular abuses ascribed to Marsh & McLennan and to deny simultaneously that this was more than just an isolated instance of broker misconduct. It's now pretty much just old news.

Wise employers should always remember what was uncovered here. Most Workers' Compensation coverage in the U.S. is sold by insurance agents or brokers; however, I've found that many purchasers of insurance don't understand the role of the insurance agent or broker as well as they might, and this sometimes contributes to problems with the cost of their workers' compensation insurance. So this chapter will endeavor to explain some of the lesser-known realities about insurance agents, brokers, and the insurance companies with and for whom they work.

AGENT, BROKER, OR PRODUCER—WHAT'S THE DIFFERENCE?

The terms *insurance agent* and *broker* tend to get blurred together, and the distinction can be made more difficult because the same individual or the same insurance agency may sometimes be acting as an agent of an insurance company and other times as a broker representing solely the interests of the policy holders. A newer term is used by some regulators, *insurance producer,* to reflect the fact that the distinction between insurance agent and broker can get fuzzy.

Technically speaking, an insurance agent is a licensed insurance producer who has a contract with a specific insurance company to sell its products. Some agents are tied to just one insurance company. This company is known in the insurance industry as a *direct writer.* An agent for a direct writer can only sell that particular insurer's policies. State Farm is an example of a personal-lines direct writing company. Liberty Mutual is an example of a direct writer that writes workers' compensation and other commercial lines of insurance.

An *independent agent* has contracts with multiple insurance companies and can choose which of those insurers to use for a particular client. So while an agent for Liberty Mutual could only present proposals from Liberty Mutual, an independent agent might be able to present proposals from Travelers, Fireman's Fund, and CNA. An insurance broker is technically not an agent of the insurance company, but instead represents the insurance purchaser, seeking out insurance coverage on their behalf. This difference between insurance *agent* and insurance *broker* can get further complicated because some states impose stricter regulations on the status of such insurance intermediaries. In New York, for example, all insurance producers are considered to be acting as brokers on behalf of clients. In Michigan, by contrast, anyone selling insurance has to be a licensed agent of a carrier.

In the particular instances cited by Attorney General Spitzer, Marsh & McLennan was acting as an insurance broker, seeking out insurance proposals for large corporate clients on a non-commission compensation basis. That is, Marsh was earning a fee from corporate clients for seeking out insurance proposals from various insurers. These proposals were supposed to be net of commissions, because Marsh was being paid a negotiated fee by its clients, but, unbeknownst to those clients, Marsh was also receiving so-called *contingent commission* payments from insurers for placing business with them. Marsh did not disclose these contingent commissions to its clients. Worse, Marsh allegedly steered business toward those insurers on the basis of which one paid the best contingent commissions, manipulating proposals from other insurers so that the clients did not actually receive the best quotes possible. The clients could not make an informed decision about the insurance options brought to them, because the broker had decided in advance which insurer would win the account based on contingent commission income to the broker. The prices of the other insurers were deliberately inflated in the process, to inevitably steer the insured to the insurance company that was desired by the broker.

Now that this has all been uncovered, a number of large insurance brokers have given up the practice of accepting contingent commissions. This was after several of them paid large settlements to regulators over the issue of improper contingent commissions. But agencies that are not as huge may well still engage in the practice.

Direct writers of Workers' Compensation often stress the level of loss control and other services they can offer. Since workers' compensation is their favored line of insurance, they pride themselves on providing better reports on claims and more comprehensive assistance in safety engineering. They will also often be willing to write the workers' compensation insurance without also writing the other commercial lines for an insured. Another advantage of working with direct writers of workers' compensation is that their personnel may be more familiar with Workers' Compensation insurance coverage and rating plans that the average independent agent.

The great drawback to using a direct writer, of course, is that the agent who sells its policies is an employee of the company. This may make the agent less able to represent your interests against the insurance company than an independent agent.

My Experience as a Direct Writer
Years ago, I began my career in Workers' Compensation as an agent for a direct writing insurer. A day came when a dispute arose between one of my accounts and the insurance company regarding how an audit had been performed and the resulting premium charges.

I believed that my client was right and I argued the client's case with my manager and with the district manager above him. At some point, the word came back to me, in essence, "You work for us. Shut up. We've made up our minds and that is the end of it."

I couldn't help that client, because I had no real leverage with the insurance company that employed me. That particular case stuck in my mind long after and eventually helped lead me to changing the focus of my insurance career so that I could help companies that have similar disputes with their insurance companies.

The direct writers of the world might well assure you that the experience cited above was an isolated case, but I don't think so. An agent for a direct writing company simply has much less leverage, on average, than an independent agent. Of course, even an independent agent has limits on what he or she can do to change the mind of insurance company underwriters and auditors. But the independent agent can always at least threaten to move the account to a different insurer, something no direct writing agent can do.

Independent insurance agents represent multiple insurance companies, so they're not tied down to just one single insurer, but independent agents don't have access to every insurance company; they typically have contracts with a limited number of insurance companies. Theoretically, an independent agent can also act as a broker—obtaining coverage for you from an insurance company with which he or she doesn't have a contract. Generally, independent agents will use their contracted companies first and use other markets only when and if they absolutely must.

Sometimes an independent agent will overplay how many insurance companies he or she can access. Keep in mind that when an independent insurance agency has a contract with an insurance company, he or she has made a commitment to that insurer to place a certain volume of business with them. Meeting sales quotas and maintaining specified loss ratios can enable an agent to earn additionally commissions, called *contingent commissions.* These are the commission payments that were involved in the Marsh & McLennan scandal, because these commissions allegedly were the reason Marsh steered clients to certain insurers, even though those insurers were not the lowest bidders for those clients.

A *broker* is an insurance producer who works solely as the representative of the policy holder and is not contracted with any insurance company as its agent. A broker may be compensated on a non-commission negotiated-fee basis or by commissions from the insurance company. Although the practice of receiving contingent commissions is under considerably scrutiny in the wake of Spitzer's revelations, as of this writing, many (if not most) commercial insurance agents and brokers still receive contingent commissions. Some large brokers like Marsh have foresworn contingent commissions in penance for their alleged wrongdoing and insurance regulators are considering taking some new actions in these areas, but at the moment, contingent commissions are still perfectly legal, yet controversial.

The simple truth that no attorney general or insurance commissioner can change is that human beings will always be tempted to place their own interests first. Insurance agents and brokers are susceptible to the same lapses in judgment and ethics as anyone else. So, while trust is an essential part of the insurance transaction, a wise insurance purchase would perhaps be well advised to keep in mind an old Russian adage that President Reagan once popularized, "Trust, but verify."

In recent years, most states have deregulated Workers' Compensation insurance considerably, on the theory that allowing insurance companies to compete on price would foster competition and ultimately reduce costs for employers. Sometimes it's worked, sometimes it hasn't—in part because the insurance transaction is always inherently unequal. The people selling the insurance have certain advantages that deregulation hasn't addressed—witness the problems uncovered by Attorney General Spitzer.

But insurance purchasers have certain strengths as well that can be maximized. The existence of both direct-writing and independent-agency insurance companies means that you can use them to compete against each other for your business. Just make sure that you don't let one intermediary (broker) control your access to all of the proposals from the different insurers. The kind of bid rigging alleged by Spitzer can occur only if an employer relies on one intermediary, who can then act as a gatekeeper and potentially manipulate the proposals from insurers.

Trust, but verify. So even though your broker or agent assures you that he or she can access any insurance company you want or need, make sure you protect yourself by dealing with more than one source for your insurance proposals. Not necessarily every year, but every few years you probably want to keep everybody honest by getting genuinely competitive quotes.

Picking an Agent or Broker

So how do you pick an agent or broker? It depends on your business, to some degree. A larger company may have need of greater resources from an agent. On the other hand, a smaller or medium-sized employer might not be served as well by a large agency, where your account may well end up being viewed as too small to warrant their best efforts. So try to work with insurance agencies that roughly match up with your own company's size.

Another important factor to take into account is whether a particular agent has experience with your kind of business. The insurance needs of a manufacturer can differ greatly from those of a construction company. Make sure you're dealing with an agency that has experience with your kind of business. Ask for references.

Professional designations can also be a useful method of choosing between agents. For example, to attain the designation of *Chartered Property Casualty Underwriter* (CPCU), a person must pass a series of ten examinations administered nationally, meet certain minimum requirements for experience in the insurance industry, and must adhere to a code of ethics. Some agents may have the designation of CIC (*Certified Insurance Counselor*). Although it takes fewer examinations to attain this designation, it is also a useful benchmark in evaluating the knowledge and professionalism of agents.

Professional designations are far from the only criteria one should use, but all other things being equal, these designations should be given due consideration. They are among the few objective benchmarks in the insurance industry beyond those for salesmanship.

Don't just consider the individual agent. Find out about the agency as well—how large it is, how many accounts similar to yours it handles, how large a staff it has, and how experienced the particular people are who will be assigned to your account. You might want to arrange a visit to their offices so you can get a feel for the agency.

One final point: make sure the agent and agency understand that they will have to make full disclosure of all commissions they would earn on any proposed program—including disclosure of all contingent commissions.

CHOOSING AN INSURER

Once upon a time it was a lot easier to evaluate the financial stability of an insurance company. You checked its rating from A.M. Best, a world-wide insurance-rating and information agency founded in 1899. As long as an insurance company had some kind of A rating, it was probably going to be OK. But over the course of the past ten years, we've seen some major insurance companies that had fine Best's ratings just before beginning a precipitous decline into liquidation. So, ratings services like A.M. Best can give a good picture of an insurer's recent past stability, but keep in mind that those ratings can have a short shelf life.

Here's a listing of the major insurance company rating services:
A.M. Best Company
Ambest Road
Oldwick, NJ 08858-9988
Phone: (908) 439-2200 Website: http://www.ambest.com

Standard & Poor's
55 Water Street
New York, NY 10041
Phone: (212) 438-7200 Website: http://www.standardandpoors.com

---

Demotech
2941 Donnylane Boulevard
Columbus, OH 43235-3228
Phone: (800) 354-7202 Website: http://www.demotech.com

Weiss Ratings
15430 Endeavor Drive
Jupiter, FL 33478 Phone: (800) 289-9222 Website: http://www.weissratings.com
Moody's Investors Service
99 Church Street
New York, NY 1007
Phone: (212) 553-1658 Website: http://www.moodys.com

Generally speaking, these rating services rate insurance companies on such things as their liquidity, leverage, investments, profitability, loss ratio, and return on assets. Since the Best rating system is perhaps the most widely used, let's take a look at what the Best rating tells you.

The traditional letter ratings that Best gives insurers are called "Best's Ratings." Insurance companies that receive a letter rating have met certain criteria set by Best for quality and quantity of data. If an insurance company does not submit a sufficient quality of data, it receives instead a numerical "Financial Performance Rating." Most insurance companies rated by Best also get a rating outlook that indicates the *potential* future direction of that company's rating. Best also shows the financial size rating for all insurance companies it reviews, based on capital, surplus, and reserve funds.

If an insurance company fails to qualify for a rating opinion, Best assigns it an "NR" or "Not Rated" classification. The highest Best ratings would be A++ and A+ (Superior). The next ratings are A and A- (Excellent), followed by B++ and B+ (Very Good). The ratings decline from there to C and C- (Weak). D (Poor), E (Under Regulatory Supervision), and F (In Liquidation).

Just keep in mind that the recent shift from soft market conditions to hard market conditions exposed some of the weaknesses of the insurance rating system. Some well-known insurance companies saw their Best ratings fall precipitously. For example, one would have had to watch the insurance trade press fairly closely to track exactly how far and how fast the ratings of Fremont Compensation declined in its last year or two before it was placed into liquidation.

So if the financial ratings systems have to be taken with a grain of salt, what else can you do? For one thing, it depends on what stage of the insurance cycle things are. If you've been buying commercial insurance for a while, you know about the cycle of commercial insurance pricing. In the soft market, insurers are competing aggressively for business, mainly by discounting their prices. This typically goes on a bit too long for the good of insurance companies. Then some outside event triggers the inevitable abrupt return to hard market conditions. The last time this occurred was right around the latter part of 2001. External events such as the collapse of the dotcom stock bubble, the terrorist attack of 9/11, and record low interest rates served to shift the insurance market from soft to hard in fairly short order. And along the way, some well-known insurance companies disappeared forever. Remember Reliance Insurance? Fremont Compensation? How about Superior National?

So if the insurance market has been soft long enough that even you, as the insurance purchaser, are thinking that things are getting a little extreme, it may be the time to avoid insurance companies that are the most aggressively cutting prices. It isn't that hard to monitor the state of the insurance market nowadays. You do not have to rely on information provided by your agent or broker, although that is one source. An employer can easily access information on the commercial insurance market on the internet, where there are many free sources of insurance news. (See our list of insurance resources in Chapter 12).

Insurance, especially workers' compensation insurance, may seem like a commodity purchase, but it isn't completely. And if your workers' compensation carrier goes under while you're relying on it, it can be a real painful experience. Even if it goes under a year or so after you leave it, you may find its liquidator aggressively seeking to re-audit your past policies to recoup premiums that they think were missed by the now-insolvent carrier.

As of this writing, however, we're not in a soft market. We're still living with a hard insurance market, although it seems ready to soften somewhat, barring further outside shocks, such as another serious terrorist attack or some unexpected financial crisis. The market has been hard long enough for just about all of the fallout from the last soft market to have passed. The insurance companies that survived the last soft market have had several years now of record high premiums and record profits, so most insurers at the moment are feeling fairly restored and reinvigorated. There are some exceptions, however, so employers should not relax their vigilance about insurer solvency and stability.

But during a hard market, employers have to be prepared to endure large jumps in insurance costs, restricted coverage, and reduced competition for their business. As the hard market matures, new places typically enter the market, attracted by the high rates the hard market allows. This has started happening already with this latest hard market.

Using Competition to Lower Costs

Whatever the state of the insurance market, employers can use competition for their business to hold down costs and obtain the best coverage. So long before your insurance program expires, begin the process of interviewing and selecting agents or brokers to work on your account. Begin at least six months before your current policy expires and then winnow the field down to two or at most three qualified agents or brokers, along with a direct-writing carrier. If your business is in the construction field or some other field that's somewhat more difficult to insure, it may be difficult to work with more than two independent agents or brokers and a direct writer.

Allocate Markets

It is vital that you, as the insurance purchaser, retain control over which insurance companies may be used by which independent agent or broker. You must make sure anyone involved in the process agrees in advance to abide by your decisions regarding allocation of the insurance markets. If you do not, your incumbent agent could well "block the markets" for any other independent agent. The agent does this by making submissions to every conceivable insurance market for your account, even if that agent isn't going to work seriously with that insurer on your behalf. Once an insurance company gets a submission from one agency for your account, it cannot work with another agency to produce a quote for you.

Some years ago, I was working as an expert witness in insurance-related litigation. In the course of that work, I had access to the files of the insurance agent/broker that had written workers' compensation and other commercial insurance for a particular insured for years. While reviewing the file, I came across a document prepared by that agency. It was a form for keeping track of how effectively this agency had "blocked markets" on the account. It was titled "Market Blocking Checklist" and listed every conceivable insurance market, with spaces to indicate whether or not it had been blocked. This form wasn't for keeping track of all the markets the agency was working with in order to get the best possible deal for the client. It was designed to make sure that no viable markets were left available for any competitor agency to use.

The way market blocking works is that an agent sends in a submission with enough information to lock up that particular insurance company, but then the agent doesn't send in enough information to satisfy the underwriter or doesn't respond quickly to request for additional information or documentation. The agent does enough to keep the insurance company tied up, but not enough to get a quote or at least not a truly competitive quote. And in the process, he or she blocks any other independent agency from using that insurance company.

I'm happy to report that the particular insurance agency involved in that market-blocking activity is no longer in business. The principal of that agency was convicted in federal court this year for misappropriating clients' premiums that were supposed to be in trust. But beware, this agency was far from being the only one to indulge in market blocking. To avoid being victimized by this tactic, allocate specific insurance markets to each independent agent working on your account. If anyone violates your allocation by approaching a market reserved for another agent, use a broker of record letter to assign the insurance company to a broker whom you designate and authorize to work with that company on your behalf.

If you can afford it, you may want to consider hiring an independent consultant to help you manage the process of selecting agents and agencies and allocating insurance markets among them. An independent consultant can act impartially in your best interests to harness the competition among agents and insurers to produce optimal result for you. Particularly if competing agents squabble over which one gets access to particular insurance markets, having an informed but independent arbitrator involved can make the process work more smoothly.

You can use the form exemplified in Figure 8-1 to help choose among competing agents or brokers on a basis other than price.

Figure 8-1

Individual Agent/Broker name:
Agency/Brokerage name
Independent agent or captive agent?
Number of employees at agency/brokerage (if independent)
Volume of commercial insurance written by agency/brokerage annually
How long has individual agent/broker been with this agency?
How long has individual agent/broker been in business?
Individual agent/broker's position within company
Professional designations of individual agent/broker
Professional organizations individual agent/broker belongs to
Other clients of this agent/broker in same of similar field to yours
Who else in the agency/brokerage will be involved in servicing your account?
Can agent/broker offer referral to other clients for whom he or she has successfully resolved a dispute with an insurance carrier?

Figure 8-1 (continued)

Has agent/broker ever been personally involved in changing Workers Compensation classification for a client? If yes, obtain details.

Has agent/broker been involved in correcting an experience modification factor for a client? If yes, obtain details:

Does agency/brokerage accept contingent commissions?

Is agency/brokerage willing to disclose fully all compensation it will receive from insurers for writing your account?

Questions for References Provided:

How happy are they with quality of service from agent/broker and from the agency/brokerage? What is reference's opinion of agent/broker's ability to represent insured's interests with an insurance company?

Why did reference decide to deal with this particular agent/broker and this particular agency/brokerage?

In a similar vein, you can use the profile form shown in Figure 8-2 to help in choosing between competing insurance companies on a basis other than mere price.

Figure 8-2

Insurer Name:

Is insurer part of a large group of insurance companies?

Is insurer direct writer or working through independent agent?

Current Rating from A.M. Best

Current Rating from Standard & Poor's

Insurer able to write insurance in all states in which your company operates or is likely to operate in near future?

Any states where insurer cannot write coverage

How long has the insurer been writing insurance in your state?

References of other policyholders in your line of work

Will insurer write Workers Compensation insurance without also writing other lines of insurance?

Figure 8-2 (continued)

Questions to Ask Insurance Company References
How does this insurer appear to set reserves on open claims—"worst case scenario" consistently or more reasonable and open to reconsideration?
Any particular problems with this insurer regarding premium audits?
Have loss control recommendations from this insurer been useful and practical or unreasonable and excessive and impractical?
How long has this insurer written coverage for the reference?
Has this insurer been willing to stick with the reference even through occasional years of bad losses?

Insurance Consultants
Finally, let's discuss the selection and use of people like me (and my son, partner, and co-author, Scott), insurance consultants in general and premium review consultants in particular. Insurance consultants are pretty common creatures—if for no other reason than because many agents and brokers like to call themselves "consultants." And some of them may even actually occasionally act as consultants. But one has to be careful of any consultant that also sells insurance, as it can be difficult to advise a client about what's best for the client if there is also a second agenda—selling insurance to that client.

My own clear preference is that a consultant should not be in a position to sell you insurance or to be able to share in commissions behind the scenes. So in selecting someone to act as an insurance consultant, you really want to make sure there are no hidden agendas. Insist that the consultant commit in writing to you that the only compensation the consultant will accept for his or her work on your behalf is the fee you have agreed to pay the consultant.

A particular kind of insurance consultant has been emerging in recent years—the kind like the author of this book. I specialize in reviewing clients' workers' compensation insurance charges, looking to identify any overcharges due to technical mistakes in classification, experience modifier, or premium audit. When I started this work, back in 1983, there weren't very many people doing this kind of work. Nowadays, every time I check the internet there appears to be several new companies offering to do what I do. And while I don't mind the competition (it keeps everyone on their toes), there have been some developments in my chosen field that concern me.

For one thing, this kind of work is unlicensed and unregulated at the moment. I've suggested to insurance regulators in my home state that this kind of work should be licensed and regulated like the sale of insurance, but they haven't been interested in taking on any new work. So even though existing regulations of insurance companies and insurance agents haven't prevented occasional rogues and worse from plying their trade, it gives consumers some protections. The premium review business lacks even rudimentary oversight and regulation. That may have some positives, because insurance regulators sometimes are a little too close to the insurance industry. If the insurance industry had its way, maybe there wouldn't be any independent premium review consultants like my competitors and me.

Problems with Consultants
I've learned the one or two horror stories over the years. There has been at least one outright unethical and scurrilous premium audit review firm that I know used to do major national marketing of its services. Fortunately, it appears to have gone out of business. Unfortunately, I understand that one of the principals in that firm has set up shop under a new corporate name.

That company offered, just like my company, to review current and past workers' compensation premium charges for policy holders, recover any overcharges, and thereby earn a fee based on how much it recovers. The problem was that this company would try to obtain refunds for clients by misrepresenting the nature of the work done by those clients or by some of the clients' workers. It was essentially counseling its clients to participate in premium fraud.

As if that weren't bad enough, I learned of another way in which this competitor differed from my company: it would present its findings of (theoretical) savings, tell the client what needed to be done to recover those savings, and then insist on payment of a fee before those savings were actually realized.

I learned of one Chicago-area company that dealt with these people. They paid them a substantial fee based on a report that said the client had been misclassified and should request an NCCI inspection to trigger the change. However the consultant was wrong and NCCI inspection didn't result in a lower class—it produced a more expensive class. And it couldn't be corrected, because the higher class was really correct for this client under NCCI. The client was never able to recover the $20,000 it had paid this consultant for the savings that turned out to be negative.

I also learned, from contacts within the insurance industry, that this consultant often had clients write to the insurers with false information about the work to be done by those clients, attempting to obtain premium refunds that weren't legitimate.

Now, many other premium review companies that I know of currently appear to operate ethically and legitimately. But there are some companies out there that I know who engage in practices that I find questionable. One company locks clients into a contract that cannot be cancelled by the client for a number of years. Others outsource the professional work because they don't have the actual expertise in-house. I have seen another company where the fine print of their contract stipulates that any reduction in experience modifier or premium reduction or refund that the client receives is *assumed to be the result of the consultant's work*. Beware such fine print, as the consultant may seek a fee for a refund or reduction that you had coming to you independent of any work by the consultant.

So here are some suggestions for employers. First, never misrepresent the nature of your work or the work done by some of your employees. If any consultant suggests that you provide false or misleading information to your insurer or a rating bureau, you need to stop working with that consultant immediately and report the matter to insurance regulators in your states. Deliberate misrepresentation of information to lower workers' compensation premiums improperly is a felony in most states, and insurance companies are on the watch for it.

When considering using a premium review consulting firm, there are some important questions that need to be answered first, to make sure you're dealing with a reputable and ethical company. Here are some of those important questions (Figure 8-3).

Finally, beware of extravagant claims by premium review consultants. I've been doing this kind of work for over twenty-five years now, and I estimate that I find significant overcharges for clients in something like one third to one half of the programs I examine. The exact percentage fluctuates over time, but consistently ranges within these parameters. I have heard of some consultants in this field who claim to recover money for 90 percent of their clients. If it's true, they're to be congratulated. But all of my experience tells me that such claims are probably greatly exaggerated. If 90 percent of all workers' compensation policies have significant overcharges, then we have an even more serious problem than I thought. It's bad enough to find overcharges one third of the time—that argues that the insurance system isn't even really trying to find and correct such mistakes on their own, but I find claims of 90 percent recovery rates to be suspect, so perhaps so should you.

Figure 8-3

How long has the company been in business?
Who are the principals of the company?
What are the professional credentials and experience of the principals?

Figure 8-2 (continued)

Obtain at least three references and check them.

To what professional insurance societies or associations do the consultant or company principals belong?

What is the fee basis for the consultant's work?

Can client choose between contingent fee or hourly rate?

Make clear (spell out in writing) that a contingent fee will only be due if and when you actually receive the reductions or refunds.

Is the consultant willing to put his or her findings in writing and to communicate those findings directly to insurance company auditors, underwriters, and/or insurance regulators?

By all means, *get references and check them!* You might also want to **check with your state in insurance regulators**, to see if they have any record of complaints being filed against a company that you're considering. Remember, an ethical premium review company can do you a lot of good by finding and recovering substantial premium overcharges that your company isn't even aware have occurred. But an unethical premium review company can cost you money and time pursuing bogus refunds or, even worse, get you involved in premium fraud.

QUICK REVIEW

- Make sure you understand what kind of insurance producer you are dealing with—independent agent, broker, or captive agent.
- Choose your insurer carefully, as well as your insurance producer. Turmoil in the industry has caused some well-known insurers to fail in recent years.
- Manage competition among insurance producers and insurance companies with a firm hand to produce best results from competitive bidding.
- Be objective in selecting the best insurance producer and agency for your company.
- Be careful in selecting insurance consultants; this area of the industry is lightly regulated, at best.

CHAPTER 9

SHOPPING FOR THE BEST COVERAGE AT THE BEST PRICE

HOW TO EVALUATE INSURANCE PROPOSALS

A common problem in comparing differing insurance proposals is finding a common yardstick to measure them. Of course, you want to obtain the best coverage at the lowest price. But anyone who's been through the process will know that it can be very difficult to figure out which proposal provides the best coverage, because often there will be significant variation in the fine details. How does one tell which differences are important and useful and which ones are not? And when it comes to cost, be careful, because sometimes the proposal with the lowest apparent cost turns out to be more expensive than some of the other quotes would have been.

Some business owners try to standardize the coverage part by telling agents and brokers to quote the insurance "apples to apples" with the expiring policies. But the problem with this approach is that the expiring policies might have serious deficiencies. It's really not in your best interest to discourage a sharp insurance agent from pointing out significant problems in your expiring coverage. But how do you tell which differences are important and which are nitpicking?

One approach is to develop a set of insurance specifications to be used by those bidding on the insurance. Set out a standardized schedule of overages and make sure all proposals are consistent with it. These specifications should also spell out clearly and explicitly the basis for computing the premium, such as payrolls, sales, and experience modification factor. You can make clear that you welcome suggestions for improving coverage, but these should be shown as options. Any additional costs associated with those optional recommendations should be required to be clearly identified. This way, you can obtain competing proposals that are standardized in terms of coverage and that avoid any lowballing by agents.

In Insurance parlance, a lowball quote may seem cheap when you look at the premium dollars, but may not be so cheap if it's based on lower payrolls or sales estimates.

In the case of workers' compensation insurance, to avoid lowballing you want to make sure that all proposals spell out in detail exactly how the estimated premiums have been calculated. This means that the proposal must show all payroll estimates in each classification, with each rate for each classification, along with the experience modification factor and any other credit or debits used to calculate the premium.

An Example of a Lowball Proposal

How does lowballing work? It simply involves making some adjustment in the estimated payrolls or rates or modifications that affect he proposed premium and then obscuring the fact. For example, consider two proposals for workers' compensation insurance:

	Proposal A	Proposal B
Clerical payroll	$560,000	$560,000
Shop payroll	$1,200,000	$1,200,000
Experience Mod	1.02	1.02
Premium	$65,789	$96,492

Now, the bottom-line premium on Proposal A looks clearly better. And they both use the same payroll estimates and the same experience modifier. So Proposal A will obviously save money, right? Not necessarily.

Notice that these proposals don't really specify what class codes and rates are being used. It turns out that Proposal A is using a different class code (with a lower manual rate) than what is being used by Proposal B.

Proposal A

Code	Payroll	Manual Rate	Premium	
8810	$560,000	.50	$2,800.00	
3629	$1,200,000	4.65	$55,800	
			$58,600.00	Manual Premium
			1.02	Experience Mod
			$59,772.00	Modified Premium
			10%	Schedule Debit
			$65,749.00	Standard Premium

Proposal B

Code	Payroll	Manual Rate	Premium	
8810	$560,000	.50	$2,800.00	
3632	$1,200,000	7.65	$91,800.00	
			$94,600.00	Manual Premium
			1.02	Experience Mod
			$96,482.00	Modified Premium
			$96,492.00	Standard Premium

Maybe the agent producing Proposal A thinks that a lower class really is appropriate for this policy holder and he's gotten an underwriter to issue a proposal using this lower class. For example, if Proposal B is using code 3632 for the shop operations, but Proposal A is using code 3629, there's a hidden assumption built into this proposal. Maybe this agent is particularly smart about classifications and he's figured out that this insured really does belong in a lower class. But take a look at the full details of how each proposed premium was really calculated.

If the agent were wrong in Proposal A about the insured being eligible for code 3629, Proposal B would actually save money, because Proposal A has a ten percent schedule debit built into it, while Proposal B does not. Proposal A also does not take into account the fact that if this insured really is eligible for code 3629, the 1.02 experience modifier should be higher than 1.02, because the 1.02 mod was calculated on the basis of code 3632, not 3629. The increase in experience modifier would not offset all of the rate savings from the lower classification code, but it might well offset something like 25 percent of the rate difference.

Agent might try to lowball a Workers' Compensation proposals in various ways. Simply using lower estimated payrolls (and keeping the class codes the same) would give one proposal an unfair advantage that won't hold up. Remember, the actual payroll is going to be determined with an audit, so the illusory savings produced by depressing the payroll estimate will vanish then.

To make sure you aren't being lowballed, make sure all proposals for workers' compensation insurance spell out all the following elements of the premium calculation:
- Classification description
- Code number
- Estimated payroll by classification
- Manual rates
- Experience modifier
- Scheduled credit or debit applied
- All other premium credits used
- Premium discount factor

TYPES OF WORKERS' COMPENSATION POLICIES

And of course, all of the above elements cover only the variables of a *guaranteed-cost* proposal. If the competing plans are *loss-sensitive*, then you will also need a detailed projection of cost at various loss levels. So let's review how to compare competing loss-sensitive proposals.

Back in Chapter 2 we briefly reviewed different kinds of workers' compensation insurance policies, including the above-mentioned loss-sensitive policies. But let's get into more detail now, so we can review how to compare such plans specifically.

RETROSPECTIVE RATING
As we had mentioned in Chapter 2, one of the most common types of loss-sensitive plans is Retrospective Rating (or Retro, as the plans are often called). Retro plans can have great variation, but let's start with the basics that they all have in common.

All retro plans make subsequent adjustments to standard premium, based on losses that occur during the policy. Standard premium is your regular workers' compensation insurance premium, calculated the same as a guaranteed-cost policy, but before application of a premium discount factor. So standard premium gets computed via payroll placed in specific classifications, with rates per hundred dollars of payroll, adjusted by the experience modification factor and any other credits or debits that apply.

A retro plan then adjusts that standard premium according to a predetermined formula that factors in the losses that occur during the policy period. Depending on the cost of those claims, the retro premium might be less than standard premium (in which case the insurance returns money back to you), more than standard premium (in which case the insurance company bills you for the additional premium), or it could work out to be just the same as the standard premium.

Traditionally, most retro plans use incurred losses to figure retro premiums. Incurred losses include not just the amounts the insurance company has actually paid out to date on claims, but also the reserves they estimate for what they think will be the ultimate cost of those claims. Those loss reserves figure into the calculation just as much as the actual paid losses.

Another kind of retro, called a *paid-loss retro*, counts only the claims costs actually paid by the insurance company. Ultimately both kinds of plans should end up at the same place, everything else being equal, but a paid-loss retro offers cash flow advantages to the policy holder. Paid-loss retro plans tend to be more available from insurers in soft insurance markets, but I've also seen companies continue to offer them to select accounts during hard markets.

Retro plans make their premium adjustments well after the policy has ended. That's why they're called Retrospective rating—as they "look back" at a prior policy period. The first retro adjustment is made using loss numbers valued six months after the policy has expired. So for a policy that ended December 31, 2008, the first retro adjustment would use loss numbers valued as of June 30, 2009. Of course, that doesn't mean that the adjustment will be calculated on June 30. It typically takes a few additional months for the calculation to be made and sent out.

So for this hypothetical plan, the first retro adjustment might be sent to the policy holder in September 2009. After that, there will be annual subsequent recalculations—each done using revised loss numbers as of June 30 or each year. So sometime in September 2010, our hypothetical policy holder would receive a revised retro adjustment calculated using losses values as of June 30, 2010. And the same would happen in 2011 and 2012, either until all claims are closed out and finalized or until policy holder and insurer agree on a negotiated final retro adjustment. Typically, if there are still open claims, the insurer will come up with its best projected loss numbers and propose a final retro calculation using these numbers. If the policy holder agrees, the insurer would then close out the retro so there would be no further adjustments. But if the policy holder and insurer can't agree to terms, the retro could undergo further adjustments, possibly producing significant additional premiums in future years for that policy that ended in 2008.

There's generally an accepted framework for calculating these retro premium adjustments. One element is the *basic charge*. This is a heavily discounted insurance charge. Traditionally, this has been expressed as a percentage of standard premium. Thus, a basic of .15 means that the basic premium would be 15 percent of standard premium.

The next part of the retro calculation is the losses. Remember, this could either be *incurred* losses, or just *paid* losses. Either way, the insurance company doesn't just charge the loss number. It charges a *loss conversion factor* (LCF) to the loss numbers. The LCF is a percentage add-on to the loss numbers. So an LCF of 1.15 would mean that the loss numbers would be multiplied by 1.15—in other words, a 15 percent additional charge.

So far, we've identified two elements of a retro adjustment—the basic premium and converted losses (losses times the LCF). These get multiplied by a *tax factor*. This is a premium tax charged by the state; it varies from state to state from year to year.

Now's let's run some numbers for a hypothetical retro. For simplicity's sake, let's continue using a simplified retro formula. Under this kind of retro formula, you would add the basic charge to the converted losses and then multiply that sum by the tax factor. Let's assume, in our hypothetical retro, that there was only one state involved and the tax factor for that state was 1.07. So you would add the basic factor to the converted losses and then multiply that sum by 1.07, to get the retro premium for this simplified ratio.

Let's say the standard premium for the account was $100,000. With a basic charge of .15, the basic premium would be $15,000. Now let's assume that incurred losses are $50,000.

Multiplying that by the LCF of 1.15 produces converted losses of $57,500. Adding the basic we get:
$15,000 + $57,500 = $72,500

Multiplying this by the tax factor we get
$72,500 × 1.07 = $77,575

This would be the retro premium for this plan.

So far, we've been examining a simplified retro formula. Years ago, insurance companies actually wrote retro plans that were this simple. But over the course of the past ten or fifteen years, such simple retros have been complicated by many insurers. Still, if you understand the basic retro formula as detailed above, it will help you understand some of the complications that insurers have introduced in recent years.

The older, simpler kind of retro formula served insurers and insured pretty well for decades. But needless to say, insurers eventually decided that such simple retros needed to be made more complicated (and of course, more expensive). So they came up with ways to inflate the loss cost further by coming up with *allocated loss adjustment expenses* and *unallocated loss adjustment expenses.* These are additional charges for certain expenses associated with handling claims.

It culd be argued that the loss conversion factor already charged for such expenses, but insurers want to be able to make additional charges for their expenses. Allocated loss adjustment expenses are loss adjustments and handling costs that can be allocated to a specific claim. So in retro plans that include this charge, the loss figure includes not just what's paid out and what's reserved, but specific handling charges for those claims as well. Unallocated loss adjustment expenses are charges for costs that aren't associated with specific claims.

Another part of retro plans that can be added optionally is a *loss limitation*. This places a cap on the amount of any single claim that gets counted in the retro calculation, so that a single very expensive claim doesn't do too much economic damage when figuring the retro premium. There is, of course, an additional charge for this limitation.

Two other important factors in any retro calculation exist: the *minimum* and the *maximum* charges. The minimum charge is, as its name implies, a floor to the retro premium. It is the minimum premium that will be due under the plan, even with zero losses. Conversely, the maximum charge is the ceiling on the retro premium. It is the maximum amount that can be charged for the plan, no matter how high the losses are.

Of course, since retro plans are designed by insurance companies, the minimum and maximum premiums aren't fixed dollar amounts. Historically, they have been defined as percentages of standard premium. Remember, standard premium is the Workers' Compensation premium developed for a company using the regular guaranteed-cost rules—rates times payroll, adjusted by experience modification factor and other credits and debits, but without the premium discount factor. So a minimum premium of .30 would mean that the minimum premium would be 30 percent of standard premium and a maximum premium of 1.40 would mean that the maximum premium would be 140 percent of standard premium. And since standard premium for a policy is known only after the audit, the dollar amounts of the minimum and maximum premium charges can't really be known until the audited standard premium is known.

Remember also that as your standard premium varies significantly from what was estimated when the policy began, the basic charge may vary also. Although maximum, minimum, LCF, and other retro factors are set with the policy begins, the basic factor is actually calculated through a complicated formula that takes into account the size of the premium. If your actual standard premium is significantly lower than originally estimated, the basic factor used on the retro adjustment may be higher than originally stated. If your audited standard premium is significantly higher than originally estimated, the basic factor under the plan may be lower than originally stated.

LRARO Rating

In 1991, NCCI began filing with state regulators a new concept in its retrospective rating manual—Large Risk Alternative Rating Option (LRARO). Most states (but not all), have approved this change to the retrospective rating manual. The new sections of the manual made up only a few paragraphs, in contrast with the hundreds of pages in the rest of the manual that deal with other, more traditional retro options. But those few paragraphs added language to the effect that for large policyholders, the factors of a retro plan could be negotiated between the insurance carrier and the policyholder.

Think about it. For decades, a manual consisting of hundreds of pages had been used to detail how retro plans worked and how factors had to be calculated and applied to compute premiums. But suddenly two or three paragraphs inserted into that voluminous manual allowed insurance companies to disregard all those detailed manual rules and just negotiate the terms of retro plans with policyholders. And if you've ever purchased a large complicated Workers Compensation insurance policy, you know that such negotiations tend to be pretty one-sided.

Worse yet, over the years since 1991, the definition of what constitutes a "large" policyholder has been ratcheted downwards. The original rationale for these LRARO plans was that they would offer large sophisticated insurance buyers greater flexibility in insurance pricing. But since the introduction of LRARO, the threshold for qualification has been lowered in many states, so that now these plans are being offered to policyholders with only a few hundred thousand dollars in premium, rather than the original threshold of $1,000,000.

Some insurers have taken the advent of LRARO to mean that "anything goes" when it comes to Workers Compensation retro plans, but this is not really true. Some states have deregulated things to the point where an insurer can literally file any kind of loss-sensitive plan and then use it shortly thereafter. But not all states have taken this approach. The state-by-state mosaic of Workers' Compensation insurance means regulation is a patchwork of different approaches. If your company does business in a number of states you need to be aware that some insurers take shortcuts with the regulatory approval process. In their desire to offer multi-state employers a single policy covering all (or most) states, I have seen some insurers attempt to get around state insurance regulations and offer rating programs that were not really allowed in some of the states that were covered by the policy.

Side Agreements

One technique used by insurers to attempt to skirt state regulations on retro plans is the use of a separate side agreement that purports to define how premiums can be calculated under the policy. But these side agreements are not part of the policy and thus really cannot alter the terms of the policy. The standard Workers Compensation insurance policy makes this clear in its fine print. It states, "The only agreements relating to this insurance are stated in this policy. The terms of this policy may not be changed or waived except by endorsement issued by us to be part of the policy." Yet I have seen side agreements drafted by insurers that do indeed attempt to change the terms of the policy—because these side agreements would contain a formula for computing premium charges that differ radically from those in the policy. The insurance company would insist that the policyholder sign the side agreements and then use them as the basis for computing premiums, even though the policy itself contained a different formula that would have produced lower premiums.

Insurance regulators, in my experience, tend not to question the legitimacy of such side agreements, even when they clearly contradict the terms of the policies. However, my experience as an expert witness in litigation cases that involved this issue has been different.

In those cases, often involving insurers suing policyholders for large additional premiums, I have pointed out that the side agreements violate the terms of the policies. In those cases, the insurance companies have tended to settle (on terms favorable to the policyholders) before the case can go to trial. So it would appear that insurance companies themselves recognize the shaky legal ground they're on when they use side agreements to re-write the terms of the policies.

Not all side agreements attempt this insurance sleight-of-hand. With some policies, such as paid loss retro plans and Large Deductible plans, a side agreement may be legitimately used to contractually spell out funding agreements contractually between the policyholder and the insurer, so that the insurance company has a guarantee that it won't be left holding the bag for claims that should rightfully be the responsibility of the policyholder. But a side agreement that materially changes the terms of the policy may well not stand up to a legal challenge.

Why would an insurance company go to the trouble of drafting a side agreement that differs from the terms of the policy? Why wouldn't the insurer just endorse the policy itself to use the premium formula contained in the side agreement? The answer is that if the insurance company wants to use a retro formula that isn't approved in some states, it can't endorse such a plan onto the policy. So some insurers have chosen to attempt an end-run around regulators. They still have to file the policy forms they use, but they don't have to file the side agreements. The only problem, as noted earlier, is the policy language makes clear that only endorsements to the policy can change the terms of the policy. Any attempt to make a change in the policy via non-policy agreements is prohibited under the terms of the policy itself.

If your insurance company asks you to sign a side agreement for Workers Compensation insurance, take a close look at it. Compare the premium formula contained in the side agreement with what's actually on the policy. If there is a difference between the two, you may want to consider carefully the ramifications of the (quite possibly more expensive) side agreement.

Comparing Retro Proposals

When you're comparing competing proposals of retro plans, you want to identify the key components and make sure all are using the same Standard Premium as a starting point. Then run each plan through hypothetical loss levels and compare the resulting retro premium charges.

One thing to watch for: some retro plans that utilize side agreements define the Minimum and Maximum factors differently than has historically been the case with approved retro plans. Historically, Minimum and Maximum premiums were expressed as a percentage of Standard Premium. However, some side agreements instead define Minimum and Maximum as a rate times payroll. They also may define Basic premium as a rate times payroll, rather than as a percentage of Standard Premium. This change means that a policyholder loses certain protections imbedded in NCCI manual rules and state statutes that limit increases in classification codes or experience modifiers. When Maximum and Basic are expressed as a percentage of Standard Premium, that means that Standard Premium must be calculated in accordance with those NCCI and statutory limits. But removing the connection between Standard Premium and Maximum and Basic means that the insurer can disregard those protections, as Standard Premium is no longer the basis for computing Maximum or the Basic premium.

When Maximum and Basic premium charges are divorced from Standard Premium, it means that correcting errors in classifications and experience modifiers is pointless. Correcting such mistakes would still adjust Standard Premium, but this adjustment would no longer affect the charges owed to the insurance company.

No wonder some insurers have circumvented insurance regulators with these side agreements—it enables them to tilt the odds further in their favor when it comes to premium charges.

Large Deductible Plans

Another type of loss-sensitive policy that is often offered to large employers is the Large Deductible plan. This type of policy calls for the policyholder to essentially self-insure claims up to an agreed upon limit. For example, a Large Deductible policy with a $100,000 limit means that the employer is responsible for reimbursing the insurer for each claim, up to the first $100,000 per claim. Anything above $100,000 would be the responsibility of the insurer, but most claims would typically fall below this threshold.

We discussed these plans in Chapter 3, but now let's go into a little more detail about them and consider how to compare competing Large Deductible policies.

Remember, in a Large Deductible policy, the insurance company is still responsible for paying all claims. This is different from the way deductibles work in other lines of insurance. Insurance regulators want to make sure that payments to injured workers remained the ultimate responsibility of the insurance company, regardless of whether or not the policyholder lives up to the agreement to reimburse. So Workers Compensation deductibles are set up so that the insurance company is responsible for the claim even if the policyholder fails to pay.

So Large Deductible programs usually have side agreements that obligate the employer to pay for the claims that fall under the deductible limit. And those agreements normally specify a dollar amount for each claim, as well as an overall aggregate limit. The aggregate limit sets a maximum amount for all claims in the aggregate for which the employer is responsible. Not all Large Deductible plans feature an aggregate limit, but many do.

One tricky area is that many of these agreements state that the aggregate deductible amount is either a stated dollar amount or a rate per hundred dollars of payroll, whichever is higher. So if audited payrolls are higher than the estimated payrolls, the aggregate deductible limit will also increase.

In addition to paying for claims under the deductible limit, the employer will also have to pay an insurance premium. This is a highly discounted premium, commensurate with the fact that the employer is actually responsible for a large share of the losses under the policy. The discounted insurance premium represents, at least in theory, a charge for the insurance company's risk of claims above the deductible limits.

In actual practice, it can be difficult to discern just how rational and objective insurers are in determining the discount factors for Large Deductible policies. There is no oversight or regulation of these discounts, no objective standards that insurers must hold to. So it is not uncommon for the discount factor applied from one year's policy to the next to vary significantly, even when there is no change in deductible limit, employer, or insurance company. So for the 2008-09 policy, Amalgamated Insurance Group might use a .70 discount factor for Superior Staffing, Inc. with a $1,000,000 deductible limit (meaning that Superior pays only 30 percent of the Standard Premium.). But for 2009-10, Amalgamated might insist on applying .65 factor for Superior, even though the deductible limit is still $1,000,000 (so now Superior must pay 35 percent of the Standard Premium).

I have sometimes even found insurers changing the discount factor that's used on the audit to something more expensive than what was on the original policy.

These factors are essentially "negotiable," although, as with much that passes for negotiation over commercial insurance, it is often a very one-sided negotiation.

When comparing Large Deductible plans, compare the Standard Premium computations and the discount factors of each, as well as the specific deductible limits being proposed. Note whether the plans call for flat dollar amounts in the aggregate deductible limit or have limits that are adjustable based on payroll. If adjustable, make sure the payroll estimates used in both plans are the same and are reasonable estimates for your coming year. Lowball payroll estimates can make a big difference not only in the insurance premium charges, but also in the amount of the aggregate deductible limit.

For example, one client was a large road construction contractor that had purchased a Large Deductible policies for several years running from a large and well known direct writer. I got called in when a dispute arose after they had left the carrier for a different insurance company. The old insurer was now claiming the contractor owed about $1,000,000 in additional charges, mainly for claims that had fallen under the deductible limits. In fact, the insurer had filed suit against the contractor seeking that million dollars.

When I reviewed the policies and deductible billings, something curious emerged. The insurer had changed the aggregate deductible limits after the policies had begun. In one year, it had changed the aggregate deductible limit well after the policy had *expired*.

The terms of the original policies were clear in that they set aggregate deductible limits as flat dollar amounts. But later endorsements changed this so that the deductible amount was either the flat dollar amount or a rate times payroll, whichever was greater. And since payrolls had increased over the original policy estimates, the aggregate deductible limits also increased.

However, state insurance regulations in this instance prohibited making changes in deductibles that would increase premiums after policy inception. So, I was able to report to my client that they didn't owe a million dollars to the insurance company—and that the insurance company actually owed them about four million dollars back in overcharges.

Ultimately, the insurance company settled for something pretty close to that four million dollar refund.

QUICK REVIEW
- Utilize insurance specifications to minimize problems with competitive bidding on insurance.
- Watch out for "low ball" insurance proposals.
- Understand all factors of a retro style policy before agreeing to it. A poorly designed retro can be a very expensive mistake.
- Be sure to understand how the terms of a side agreement may be attempting to change the terms of the policy improperly regarding premium computation.
- Compare all loss-sensitive plans carefully and objectively. There can be many confusing details in these plans and an employer may need outside professional advice to avoid purchasing a plan that is not suitable.

CHAPTER 10

MANAGING WORKERS' COMPENSATION COSTS
BETWEEN RENEWALS

So far we've covered what employers need to do when they're shopping for Workers Compensation insurance and what they need to do when the policy ends and the audit is being done. But in between those two events there are many important steps that employers also need to take to control their Workers Compensation costs and make sure their coverage is right.

First and foremost, employers need to be active in managing claims. Although many larger employers have learned the hard way about how important this can be, it's surprising how many companies don't take as much responsibility in this area as they could. Taking your eye off this ball can be a very costly mistake.

First off, make sure you have procedures in place to report all workplace injuries promptly to your insurer. We covered this earlier in our section on experience modification factors, but it bears repeating: if you don't report an incident to your insurer on a timely basis, the insurer can later deny responsibility for the claim. That's why it's important to report all workplace injuries, even minor ones, because sometimes minor injuries develop into major losses. Remember that under the current NCCI experience rating formula, medical-only claims are discounted by 70 percent, so minor medical-only claims are not going to have a serious effect on your experience mod.

Many states now have small-deductible plans in place, so if you want to self-insure small claims, do it the right way by endorsing the small deductible onto your policy. That way, you can still pay for small claims yourself but be protected in case something some of them turn into something major.

Some states have enacted managed care provisions into their Workers Compensation systems, but many have not. In states where employees are free to choose their own treating physicians, employers can still exercise some influence over where employees are treated initially. Your insurance company can possibly help recommend local clinics and doctors that will provide proper medical care and attention to employees at reasonable cost. Just be sure to listen to feedback from your workers about such medical providers. If honest and reliable workers are telling you they think a medical provider is cutting corners or discouraging genuine claims for genuine injuries, you may want to make a change. In the long run, creating the perception that legitimate injuries are not being well-handled by the providers you utilize can backfire, encouraging adversarial attitudes in your employees and ultimately driving up your costs.

Most of your employees aren't looking to make their workplace injury some kind of lottery win. If you can get them good and competent medical care promptly, with a physician or clinic that you trust is not going to unfairly slant diagnosis and treatment one way or the other, you can go a long way towards controlling medical costs.

After a claim is turned in, don't leave everything to the insurance company. Make sure you do your own follow up with your employee. If the employee is having difficulty with claims personnel at the insurance company, you want to know about it right away so you can intervene. A wise manager will do everything possible to make an injured worker feel that the company is on his or her side and that the employer is working with the employee to make sure the insurer is treating them fairly. Creating bureaucratic obstacles to your workers receiving fair and prompt treatment may sometimes serve the insurance companies' interests, but it often does not serve the employer's interests in the long run.

Do whatever you can to make sure that any difficulties or hard feelings towards the insurance company are not transferred to you, the employer. Make sure your employees understand that Workers Compensation is a cost of doing business, not just an entitlement of workers, and that unnecessary and inflated claims aren't paid by some faceless distant bureaucracy—they are paid by your company ultimately, and higher Workers Compensation costs reduce the revenues on which everyone at the company relies.

Your claims costs will ultimately greatly influence your insurance premiums, either on the current policy if it's loss-sensitive, or on future policies through the experience modification factor.

It's been pretty well documented that when employees retain an attorney, the ultimate cost of the claims tends to rise. So it can be in the employer's interests to remove the need for your employees to bring in an attorney to whatever extent you can. That may mean putting pressure on an insurance company that is handling claims slowly or in a manner that is antagonizing your workers. You probably know your people better than the insurance company does, so make sure you protect your people from any problems in the insurance claims adjustment process. The more your employees perceive you as being on their side, helping them to get fair and equitable treatment from the insurer, the better the odds that your claims will not be unnecessarily inflated.

When any of your employees cannot do their regular duties due to injury, do your best to find them some alternative light duty. An employee who is sitting at home watching daytime television will see plenty of ads from attorneys who would love to take their case. Finding light duty work wherever possible can be a very cost effective way to hold down the costs of Workers Compensation claims.

Keep track of your company's critical date for the insurer to report loss data to the rating bureau for use in your next experience modification factor. Remember, your insurer will essentially 'take a snapshot" of your loss information, including reserves, six months after policy expiration. So if your policy expires January 1, the insurer will be reporting your losses and loss reserves as of July 1.

So review open claims for excessive reserves well in advance of that critical reporting date, so you can negotiate with your carrier about appropriate reserves. Once those figures get reported to the rating bureau, any later lowering of reserves won't affect the next modifier, but only the one calculated after that. So don't let that critical window of opportunity close without checking your open claims carefully to see if there are any loss reserves that can be lowered.

Second Injury Funds and Experience Mods
Some states maintain Second Injury Funds. These funds reimburse insurance companies and self-insured employers when it is determined that a recent Workers Compensation claim was due, in whole or in part, to some pre-existing workplace injury. These funds then pay a reimbursement that can be a large percentage of the cost of the new claim. Although states have been debating whether or not to keep these SIF operations, and some have discontinued them, some states still operate them.

Back in 2006, our consulting firm was retained to do a study of the South Carolina Second Injury Fund. We discovered something surprising. Many smaller employers received no benefit from the reimbursements paid by the SIF in South Carolina. For some small employers, this was because they were too small for experience rating. And experience rating is the only real mechanism for an employer to get the benefit of a SIF reimbursement paid to an insurance company. But what we also found was that even for employers large enough to be experience rated, in many instances, the insurance companies were not making the revised reports to

NCCI about the reimbursements. That meant that the employers' experience modification factor was not revised to reflect those reimbursements, making the modifiers higher than they should have been.

This was a troubling finding, and one that received some serious notice in the South Carolina press and became part of a larger struggle against increasing Workers Compensation rates in the state. Subsequent to our report, the South Carolina legislature passed legislation that requires insurance companies to certify to SIF that revised reports have been filed with NCCI about these reimbursements. But it is still possible that some employers are not getting the revised modifiers they are entitled.

So if you operate in a state that maintains a Second Injury Fund, watch carefully if any of your claims are eligible for reimbursement. If they are reimbursed, make sure your insurer files a corrected unit statistical report with NCCI or other appropriate rating bureau.

Certificates of Insurance

Earlier in Chapter 7 we reviewed how important it is to have all your certificates of insurance on file from any subcontractors, temporary agencies, or employee-leasing firms you use. But the best time to be working on this isn't just before your audit, but rather all during the year to make sure that those subcontractors or others that owe your company a certificate provide them on a timely basis.

Remember, a certificate of insurance is a written assurance that someone else is providing Workers Compensation insurance for certain workers. If you don't have a copy of the certificate available when your insurance company's auditor shows up, you will be charged for those workers. So make sure you initiate proper procedures in your office to follow up with those who owe you certificates.

While you're at it, make sure you have someone on your staff who is trained to read and understand certificates properly. If some third party owes your company a certificate, there is probably some contractual basis for it. That contract should spell out the details about the insurance coverage that is required. Review the certificate carefully to make sure the insurance described matches up with the requirements of your contract. What kind of information should be checked? The effective dates, the financial strength of the insurer, and any additional requirements your company may have imposed should be verified on the certificate.

Keep in mind something else about certificates: they can't change the coverage actually provided by the insurance policy they are describing. If the certificate is inaccurate, and the actual policy is different in some important way, the existence of the certificate doesn't somehow obligate the insurance company to live up to what's described on the certificate. It's one of the great ironies and weaknesses of the insurance system—a lot of time and effort is expended providing certificates of insurance, but only the policy itself determines the actual coverage (if any) provided.

So if a policy gets cancelled early for non-payment, it won't make any difference that you have a certificate of insurance showing that coverage was in force. You may well have the basis for legal action against the party that was contractually obligated to keep the insurance in force, but that can be an expensive and time-consuming effort with no guarantee of success. If a company can't afford to pay its insurance, what are the odds you can successfully recover anything through litigation?

Similarly, if the certificate states that your company has been added as an additional insured under a subcontractor's policy, but the actual policy is not so endorsed, the certificate does not actually give you the coverage. Only the policy can do that.

So what can you do? One solution is to request a copy of the policy itself or at least pertinent parts of it, showing effective date and any additional insured requirements. This may still not completely protect you if the policy gets cancelled mid-term, but it gives you a more solid basis for verifying coverage than a certificate.

Many states now produce online listings that verify if Workers Compensation coverage is in place. This can be a way to verify that a certificate of insurance for Workers Compensation insurance is really worth the paper it's printed on.

Ghost Policies and Certificates

There's nothing supernatural about the problem of "ghost policies" in Workers Compensation. This can cause significant problems and disputes at audit time, and create increased premiums for unwary employers who are victimized by them.

A ghost policy" is a Workers Compensation insurance policy written for a sole proprietor that actually excludes coverage for that sole proprietor. Such a policy would cover any employees that the sole proprietor might hire, but otherwise charges minimum premium only (usually less than a thousand dollars) as the insurance company is told that there are no workers other than the sole proprietor.

Why would a sole proprietor purchase such a policy? To meet the contractual requirements of his clients. In many states, an insurance company is entitled to charge premiums for any worker who might legally file a Workers Compensation claim under the policy. That means that, in many states, independent contractors and subcontractors that don't have their own insurance can file claims under the policies of those that hire their services. But in many of those same states, sole proprietors and partners are not required to insure themselves for Workers Compensation, and in fact are automatically excluded unless they elect to insure themselves. So clients that hire such contractors often require the contractor to provide evidence that the contractor has his own Workers Comp insurance in place.

The ghost policy meets that contractual requirement—it enables the sole proprietor to produce a certificate of insurance that shows Workers Compensation insurance in place. What is often left off such a certificate, however, is the detail that the policy only covers other workers and not the sole proprietor. But insurance companies have been getting wise to this, and charging employers on their audits when certificates of insurance turn out to be "ghostly".

To guard against this, insist that any certificate of insurance for a sole proprietor or partnership spells out that the sole proprietor or partners are covered under the policy. That way, you won't end up paying for Workers Compensation coverage for that contractor when your audit is done.

Fluctuations in Payroll

Since the payrolls (and classifications) on the policy are estimated at the outset, sometimes those estimates, even when made with the best effort, turn out to be off the mark. You could find yourself with actual payroll running substantially lower than the policy estimates—or substantially higher. In such cases, it may well make sense to get the policy's estimates adjusted midterm, rather than waiting for the eventual audit.

Particularly if your actual payrolls are running significantly lower than the policy estimates, your company may find it imperative to get the policy estimates revised downwards. But be warned: this can be a touchy negotiation with your insurer. Insurance companies hate to be left holding the bag at audit time. From hard experience, they know that sometimes it can be difficult or impossible to collect a large bill for an additional premium that's been developed at the audit, so they're reluctant to lowball on the payroll estimates.

To get your policy's payroll estimates lowered during the course of the policy may take some time and effort on your part. With persistence and some documentation, you should be able to get your insurer to work with you on this, but be prepared to encounter some initial resistance. You will probably have to make a convincing case for changes in business conditions since the policy estimates were first arrived at. Still, by working with your agent, you should be able to get some accommodation.

If your payrolls are running substantially higher than estimated, you may be tempted just to let things ride and take advantage of the cash flow advantage. But there can be dangers in this approach. Allowing substantial additional premium to ride until the policy expires means that you have to be sure your company's cash flow will enable you to pay the entire additional premium all at once. Endorsing the higher payrolls onto the policy midterm will space out your payment of that additional premium and help you keep current with this expense.

Temps, PEOs, and Subs
Earlier, we covered temps, PEOs, and subcontractors in our discussion of certificates of insurance. Remember that just because a company has contractually agreed to provide Workers Compensation coverage for certain workers doesn't mean that it has actually done so. Recent years have seen some extreme fluctuations in the state of the commercial insurance marketplace, and these have hit staffing companies particularly hard. Staffing companies are companies such as temporary agencies or employee leasing companies (known as PEOs, or Professional Employer Organizations).

A few years ago, one of the largest PEOs in the United States went out of business unexpectedly, in large part because of problems with obtaining Workers Compensation insurance. It had contractually agreed to cover large numbers of workers at its clients' operations, but in fact it did not have coverage in place for months and months. Eventually, these problems led to the failure of the PEO.

If you contract with a PEO or other alternative employer, then this other employer typically will have responsibility for providing insurance on workers at your company. But if something goes wrong and that other company doesn't actually provide the

Workers Compensation insurance, your company will be liable for the exposure. This means that injured workers will be able to make a claim against your company, even though you have contracted with the PEO or temp agency. It also means your insurance company will be entitled to charge premiums for all those workers, even though the cost of that coverage had been included in the fees you paid the PEO or temp agency.

Many PEOs and temporary agencies find it difficult to obtain voluntary market Workers Compensation insurance—particularly in hard insurance markets. Assigned Risk plans insure many smaller temporary agencies, but PEOs (employee leasing companies) often don't find assigned risk coverage very conducive to their business plans. Many PEOs use lower Workers Compensation costs as a key selling point to prospective clients, but it's difficult to offer lower Workers Comp costs if your policy is written through an Assigned Risk plan.

That was the dilemma facing that large PEO referenced earlier in this chapter—the one that went out of business. Although Assigned Risk coverage was always an option, the PEO didn't pursue that coverage because it just would have been too expensive—the PEO couldn't offer any cost savings to its clients. So instead it pursued all kinds of complicated strategies to try to obtain voluntary market coverage. These strategies had worked in the soft insurance market, but when the insurance market tightened up, the PEO's old voluntary market carrier had gone into liquidation abruptly.

One solution many PEOs have turned to in recent years has been Large Deductible policies. Carriers have been often willing to offer Large Deductible policies to PEOs when other voluntary market coverage has been impossible to obtain. Where it can get tricky is that PEOs normally bill their clients on a Guaranteed Cost type arrangement. As long as claims are reasonable, this arrangement can work well. But if claims get out of control, the PEO can find itself squeezed between the fixed charges coming from clients and escalating claims costs owed to the carrier. This can be a recipe for disaster.

If push comes to disastrous shove, the PEO may find its Workers Compensation coverage cancelled for non-payment on relatively short notice. Clients of the PEO may not be aware of the problem until coverage is gone and they are left to scramble for new coverage on their own.

So when using a PEO arrangement, it's wise to ask for detailed information about exactly how the PEO has met its Workers Compensation obligations. Remember, a certificate of insurance won't detail the kind of policy that's in place. It may not say, for example, that the policy has ais Large Deductible. So you may not be able to spot a potential problem just by examining the certificate.

Fronting

Another practice in the insurance industry that could cause unforeseen problems is called *fronting*. It's an unregulated practice; insurance commissioners are aware of it, but don't know exactly how widespread it is. By its very nature it's deceptive, although legal—and practiced by many large and reputable companies. Here's how it works.

Relatively large employers can find it advantageous to use a *captive insurance company*—a company owned in whole or in part by the policyholder. So ABC Corp. can set up an insurance company based offshore (or in some U.S. jurisdictions) to write its insurance. The problem is, states regulate which insurance companies are allowed to write Workers Compensation insurance and captives often don't pass muster. Or if they are approved in one state, they may not be approved in all the other states in which ABC Corp. needs insurance. But creative insurance folks came up with a solution to that problem: fronting. If you can get a large and well-known insurance company to write your Workers Compensation insurance, but then reinsure all your claims with your captive, you get the best of both worlds. The claims are actually being paid by your captive, and most of the premiums are going to the captive (the fronting insurer keeps a small cut as a "fronting fee," typically five to ten percent of the premium). But to the outside world, your Workers Compensation isn't written by ABC Corp. Captive, but instead by Giant Well Known Insurance, Inc.

Now technically, should the captive be unable to pay the claims, the fronting insurance company would be on the hook for them. But fronting companies are usually careful to make sure the captive meets financial standards and provides sufficient guarantees sufficient to make it unlikely.

Still, the practice is inherently deceptive. Your company might well have certificates of insurance that state that a large and well known insurance company is writing the Workers Compensation insurance for a contractor performing work for you, but the actual responsibility for paying claims rests instead with some offshore captive insurance company located in the Cayman Islands. And you can't tell the difference.

At the moment, there isn't much you can do about the situation. Even if you were to get a full copy of the policy from the large well-known insurer, you wouldn't be able to tell it was a front. Will these elaborate arrangements ever create problems for the insurance system? Will they create problems for your company? No one really knows for sure. Insurance regulators have been debating this issue for years (decades, actually). To date, the limited regulations that have been adopted have been vague and narrowly focused on certain specific lines of insurance. Florida has adopted some regulations that specifically address and limit fronting, but this state is exceptional in this regard.

The only lesson one can draw from these practices is that even though you think that a particular insurer is responsible for the Workers Compensation for some other business, you can't assume that there isn't some other insurance company actually responsible for the claims. In general, fronting has worked without creating major problems—so far. Of course, at the time of this writing, we're in the midst of the worst financial crisis since the Great Depression. The major insurance company AIG has imploded and is limping along on government life support, and becoming a focus of public outrage over financial excess and risk. So just because fronting hasn't yet blown up in anyone's face may not mean that it won't sometime in the future.

Tracking Endorsements To Your Policy
Finally, here is one more fundamental thing the cost-conscious employer needs to do to control Workers Compensation costs: carefully track all endorsements that you receive during the course of the policy. Because Workers Compensation policies always start out with estimated premiums, the insurance company typically will make changes to those estimates by endorsing the policy.

For example, after the audit of the prior policy is completed (typically a few months after the succeeding policy has started) the insurance company may want to endorse that new policy to the same payroll and classifications as were found on that audit.

Let's say that the policy effective January 1, 2009 had the estimated premium shown in Figure 10-1. But in early March, 2009, the 2008 policy is audited, resulting in the audited payrolls and premiums shown in Figure 10-2. (By the way, all premium numbers are rounded, per insurance industry practice, to nearest dollar.)

Figure 10-1 Estimated Policy Premium for 2009 at Outset

Classification	Code	Payroll	Rate	Premium
Machine Shop NOC	3632	$565,000	$7.43	$41,979
Outside Sales	8742	$125,000	$0,86	$1,075
Clerical	8810	$450,000	$0.55	$2,475.
			Manual Premium	$45,529
			Experience Modifier	.92
			Modified Premium	$41,887

Figure 10-2 Audited Premium for 2008

Classification	Code	Payroll	Rate	Premium
Machine Shop NOC	3632	$627,456	$7.25	$45,491
Outside Sales	8742	$125,554	$0,80	$1,004
Clerical	8810	$466,789	$0.49	$2,287
			Manual Premium	$48,782
			Experience Modifier	.90
			Modified Premium	$43,904

Typical insurance company practice, if the 2009 policy has been written by the same insurer as the 2008 policy, would be to endorse the newer policy up to the same payrolls as had been found during the audit of the prior policy. So now the 2009 policy would be endorsed as shown in Figure 10-3.

Figure 10-3 2009 policy endorsed to reflect 2008 audited payrolls

Classification	Code	Payroll	Rate	Premium
Machine Shop NOC	3632	$627,456	$7.43	$46,620
Outside Sales	8742	$125,554	$0,86	$1,080
Clerical	8810	$466,789	$0.55	$2,567
			Manual Premium	$50,357
			Experience Modifier	.92
			Modified Premium	$46,328

Notice that the estimated payrolls for 2009 now matches what was found on the audit for the 2008 policy, but the premium is higher because thee 2009 policy is using different manual rates for each classification (and the experience modifier is higher in 2009 than it was in 2008).

This is a fairly routine endorsement that's done to a policy. But suppose that the increase in payrolls wasn't so incremental. Suppose that the 2008 audit had found $2,627,456 in Machine Shop payrolls—but the year was up and down; during the first half of 2008, business had boomed, and then dropped off during the second half. That hasn't been so uncommon in the Great Recession of 2008-09. So if 2009 were continuing that same unfortunate trend, the audited payrolls for 2008 might be an unreasonably high estimate for 2009 If this is the case, you need to start negotiating, explaining immediately to the insurance company about why 2009 payroll estimates shouldn't be based on the audited payrolls for 2008.

Or consider a different scenario: the 2009 policy starts out as shown in Figure 10-3 but five months into the policy the insurer endorses the policy to use a 1.45 experience modification factor in place of the .92. In Chapter 6, when we were covering experience modification factors, it was mentioned that some states place limitations on how late in the policy an experience mod can be increased. So depending upon which state the policyholder is in, this endorsement that increases experience modifier might be acceptable or it might be improper. But you can't rely on your insurance company to be aware of the different rules that apply in the various states. It might seem like they should be, but in my experience, insurers tend to be a little careless about this.

So to make sure your company isn't overcharged because your insurance company conveniently forgets what the proper rules are for your state, you'll have to take an active role in protecting yourself. Even your insurance agent may not be aware of what the particular rules are for your state. Your best option may be to contact your state's insurance regulators and review the pertinent rules with someone knowledgeable there.

If you find your insurance company has violated the rules that pertain in a particular jurisdiction, you will want to respond promptly to the endorsement, in writing, pointing out exactly how and why the endorsement fails to comply with regulations. If this doesn't get results, file a written complaint with your state's insurance regulators. This can be done online in many states.

There are two types of regulations that you may need to check to see if premium-increasing endorsements (such as increases in experience modifier) are proper. One kind of regulation is contained in a state's statutory insurance code. State regulators are most familiar with this kind of regulation. The second type of regulation that may be of some help is within the manual rules of the rating bureau for your particular state. State insurance regulators may not always be as familiar with these manual rules as they are with the statutory insurance code, so you may need to consult the rating bureau as well as state insurance regulators, to learn the rules for a particular state. In NCCI states, check the rules in the *Basic Manual* that limit how late in the policy experience modifiers can be increased. For non-NCCI states, check that the appropriate rating is used with that state, as indicated in Chapter 1.

Sometimes insurance underwriters will change classification codes mid-policy, via endorsement. If the change in classification serves to increase premiums by adding an expensive classification not originally on the policy, you may want to do the same kind of checking as discussed above for experience modifier changes. Many states limit the time frame in which classification code changes that increase premium can be made—many states, but not all. Some states will allow such an endorsement to be made early in a policy, but not later, while other states will not allow such an endorsement at all once the policy has begun.

Get Your Policy and Review It
While we're on the subject of reviewing policy endorsements, there is a related matter that every business owner and manager should keep in mind. It's something that drives both policyholders and insurance agents crazy sometimes—late policy production. If your policy is effective July 1, 2009, you shouldn't have to wait until April 2010 to get your copy of the policy. Yet such extreme delays in receiving a Workers Compensation policy are not unheard of.

Sometimes this is the fault of the insurance company. Sometimes it is the fault of the insurance agent. But no matter whose fault it is, it is important to you, the policyholder, to insist that your policy be produced to you within a reasonable time—say within three months of the effective date.

If you don't get a copy of the policy in a reasonable time, it is more difficult to catch your insurance company making an improper increase in experience mod or classification. Insist on getting your policy in a timely manner. Then review it carefully to make sure it conforms to the proposal you accepted. Check classifications, rates, experience modifiers, and all credits and debits to make sure they are as originally proposed. Check named insureds to make they are accurate and complete. Check all coverage extensions and endorsements to make sure everything you originally ordered has been incorporated into the policy. And if not, insist that the policy be corrected to conform to the proposal.

Here's an extreme example of what can happen when a policy doesn't match the proposal.

This case occurred in the early 1990s, when I was consulting with a Fortune 100 manufacturer of heavy equipment. This manufacturer in downstate Illinois had come up with an insurance program for its manufacturing suppliers—that is, smaller companies that made parts for the bigger manufacturer. My part of the program was to review Workers Compensation classifications, audits, and premiums for those suppliers, but the overall program actually also sought to sell insurance to those suppliers. As it turned out, one supplier had purchased insurance through the program, only to find out that the rates on the policy weren't going to be the rates shown on the proposal. It turned out that the people working on the insurance program were based in Wisconsin, but this supplier was in Illinois. The agent had somehow used Wisconsin rates in the proposal, but when it came time to produce the policy, the insurance carrier balked, saying that there was no way it could use manual rates anywhere near what had been quoted. It was shaping up as a major problem this fledgling insurance program, but I got to play hero for both the policyholder and the program. It turned out that the supplier had been misclassified for many years; once the classification mistake was corrected, the actual premium was even lower than the in the proposal. The policy used Illinois manual rates, but the manual rate for the proper classification more than made up the difference.

The above problem surfaced fairly soon after the policy had begun. But sometimes insurance agents aren't so quick to own up to a mistake. Although most insurance agents are very good about checking over policies when they come in, sometimes it can be difficult to tell when the agent is being less than forthright.

A few years ago, in my hometown of Chicago, an extremely well-known and well-connected insurance broker was convicted in federal court of misappropriating millions of dollars from clients. One of his schemes reportedly was to "shortstop" audits that produced return premiums for clients. The insurance company would issue the credits to the agency's account, but the agent wouldn't forward those refunds on to policyholders. And because this particular broker was extremely well-connected politically, I suspect that some of those policyholders found it politic not to ask too persistently about their refunds. Eventually, the federal prosecutor asked about them when the whistle was blown by disgruntled employees. But this isn't the only instance I've found over the years of such unethical and illegal behavior by insurance producers. I have seen some other instances—relatively rare, thank goodness—of agents or brokers somehow forgetting to forward return premiums that were due policyholders. And sometimes with complex accounts, an "oversight" would cause premium refunds to get lost in the complicated insurance billings.

One of the most successful insurance salesperson I've ever known also ended up serving federal time for misappropriating clients' premiums. When I started in the insurance business, I was told to tag along with this guy as he made his rounds, as our manger hoped I might learn a little of whatever magic this agent seemed to possess.

I left that insurance company a few years later without ever having learned too many of that guy's secrets—but I saw enough to know that he was very persuasive, very charming, but he also cut a lot of corners and played a lot of angles. He tended to be very good at telling people what they wanted to hear, rather than what was true and accurate.

I didn't learn how many corners he was cutting until years later when I talked with another insurance broker who had done business with him. I learned that another broker's agency had been in the middle of being acquired by my old "friend's" agency, until the other broker discovered that moneys were being misappropriated from his agency even before the deal was finished. And that's how the one-time Golden Boy ended up going to jail.

(He's still as charming and persuasive as ever, it would appear. The last time I Googled his name, I found he was out of jail and had set up shop on the internet as some kind of consultant to the trucking industry. He was very upfront about being a convicted felon who had learned his lesson, so perhaps there's hope for him. But I still wouldn't want to buy insurance from him.)

What's a little frightening is that I have been told that these two cases are somewhat unusual—in that the miscreants did jail time. Most insurance agent infractions, so I'm told, are handled more discreetly; the money is returned and everything is taken care of behind closed doors.

The scandal over the well-connected broker had almost followed that pattern. Initially, our state's department of insurance had merely told the broker to return the money and all would be forgiven. To be fair, that really wasn't what the department of insurance wanted to do—our then-governor ordered the DOI to do it. That particular former governor of Illinois, by the way, is currently also serving time in a federal penal institution, for other offenses.

The point of all this is that, although the vast majority of insurance people are extremely ethical, conscientious, and honest, the occasional rogue can sometimes get away with a lot of financial shenanigans before getting caught. And sometimes it is the best and most persuasive salesperson who is the least ethically rigorous. So, as was stated earlier in this book, "Trust, but verify."

QUICK REVIEW
- Stay in active communication with injured workers—don't let the insurance company monopolize all contact. You want to know if any employee is having problems

with the insurer that may increase the ultimate cost of the claim inadvertently.

- Remember that Certificates of Insurance provide only limited assurance that an independent contractor or subcontractor really has its own Workers Comp insurance.
- Review payroll estimates mid-policy to make sure they are still reasonable. Adjust them if necessary to avoid large premium surprises at audit.
- Exercise care when using employee leasing or temporary agencies to make sure they have valid Workers Compensation coverage for workers they provide to you.
- Keep a careful eye on all endorsements to your policy during the policy period to make sure you understand why they are being made and that you receive all endorsements that are supposed to be part of the policy. Also watch out for changes in classification or experience modifier that may be prohibited by your state rules.

CHAPTER 11

ALTERNATIVE APPROACHES TO TRADITIONAL INSURANCE

So far, we've been reviewing insurance coverage for Workers Compensation exposures. Insurance is the most common way for employers to handle their Workers Compensation obligations, but it's not the only way. A number of alternative approaches to handling this business exposure exist, which this chapter will discuss

SELF-INSURANCE
Most states gives employers the option of self insuring their Workers Compensation obligations. But self-insurance is not the same thing as having no Workers Compensation coverage. Self-insurance means that the state has approved an employer to handle its Workers Compensation claims itself, instead of buying an insurance policy. But since states retain their keen interest in making sure that injured workers are going to be taken care of, they impose restrictions on employers. Essentially, a company has to be approved by state insurance regulators to be self-insured. The requirements for approval vary state to state, but only North Dakota prohibits self-insurance of Workers Compensation although Wyoming offers it only on an extremely limited basis.

Harking back to our concept of Workers Compensation being a state-by-state mosaic, keep in mind that to qualify as a self-insurer you have to do it on a state by state basis. In many states, self-insurance is practical only for larger companies, so self-insurance might not be practical, even for a good-sized employer. A company might qualify for self-insurance in some states, but still require insurance in other states where it has smaller operations. As an example, take Alabama. That state's requirements for self-insurance are:

- Provide audited financial statements
- $5,000,00 minimum net worth
- Current assets-to-current-liabilities ratio 1.0 or greater
- Positive net income

States will typically require that a company post some kind of financial guarantee, usually a *surety bond,* to make sure that claims are paid, along with excess insurance to cover claims above the amount guaranteed.

Some companies specialize in helping employers put together a viable self-insurance program, so you would still have to deal with outside insurance people. After all, with a self-insured program, you're going to need experienced people to handle the claims and you're going to need excess insurance, to limit your exposure to the claims costs. If you investigate self-insurance, you may find that although it is possible to reduce your ultimate cost of Workers Compensation, it will be just as complicated as negotiating a large insurance program.

To qualify as a self-insurer, you'll need to meet the particular requirements of each state in which you wish to be self-insured. You'll have to provide a financial guarantee, such as a surety bond. You'll need to establish a funding mechanism to provide funds to pay claims as you go along. You'll need to purchase excess insurance. Fortunately, there are specialists in self-insurance that can assist you with all of these things, so you can take a one-stop-shopping approach.

A good source of information about self-insurance for Workers Compensation can be found on the Internet at www.SPECandAGG. com.

GROUP SELF-INSURANCE

A more recent approach in many states has been the approval of group self-insurance plans. These programs allow an employer to meet its Workers Compensation obligations within a state by joining a multiple-employer program. From an employer's point of view, such programs look and feel a lot like buying traditional Workers Compensation insurance. But there are very important differences that employers need to be aware of before entering such programs.

Initially, group self-insurance programs typically offer significant savings over what is available in the insurance marketplace. So the initial going in-cost can look very attractive, especially when compared with assigned rick rates.

But those same low rates can later cause problems for employers that have entered these programs. Because the true cost of Workers Compensation claims can take years to be known, these programs can be vulnerable to being devoured by escalating costs as time goes on.

A few years ago, a very large and well known group self-insurance program in Kentucky had fallen prey to such problems. And employers that had been members of the program started receiving very large assessments to make up the shortfalls.

That's the potential problem with such programs. All members of the group are liable not just for the cost of their own claims, but also for the claims of the entire group. So if things go badly, you may receive a very large bill from the group, even if you haven't been a member for a few years.

My home state of Illinois has had similar problems with group self-insurance programs. A decade or so ago, these programs were established with great fanfare as a cost-saving alternative to traditional insurance programs. Many business groups established such plans and marketed them aggressively to their members. But regulatory oversight was not as tight as it should have been, so many of these plans have gone belly up, leaving members and past members with very large and unexpected assessments to make up shortfalls.

Group self-insurance programs may offer short-term savings, but it can be very difficult to know if the particular program you're contemplating is going to encounter problems in future years. Being a member of a group self-insurance program that isn't charging sufficient rates is like having a ticking time bomb under your desk. Given the very mixed records of such programs, any employer that decides to become to become a member had better realize the potential risk he or she is accepting. Although rates right now may seem very attractive, the liability of members as a whole can be a very unpleasant surprise down the road.

"VIRTUAL" WORKERS' COMPENSATION INSURANCE
Another recent development in the field is what I call "virtual" Workers Compensation insurance. This approach uses separate insurance products to attempt to produce coverage for an employer that comes close to meeting Workers Compensation obligations without actually using a Workers Compensation policy, Instead, it uses a combination of other insurance products like health insurance, disability insurance, and life insurance to cobble together a product that provides benefits for employees that come close to those provided by a Workers Compensation policy.

These programs have been developed and marketed to companies that find traditional Workers Compensation insurance to be very expensive. The problem is that in many states these "virtual" Workers Compensation programs do not meet an employers' legal obligation for Workers Compensation under state law.

However, Alabama has recently allowed such programs to be offered to employers in the state with approval of insurance regulators. They call them "alternative Workers Compensation plans." However, even the Alabama Department of Insurance notes this is a new provision of the the Workers Compensation law that is untested in courts. The department also notes that it is unclear which *guaranty association* would guarantee such alternative coverage in the event that an insurance company becomes insolvent.

As time goes on, other states may give official approval to such alternative Workers Compensation program, but you would be well advised to check carefully with your insurance regulators to determine whether or not such programs have any legitimacy in your state. Some insurance agents have marketed these programs within states that have not approved them, so an employer should not assume, just because some insurance agent is offering such an alternative program, that it must be legal and legitimate within the state. Just the opposite may be true, and you could be exposing your company to fines and sanctions from insurance regulators if you have not met state requirements regarding your Workers Compensation obligations.

GOING BARE

Some small employers may be tempted to not purchase Workers Compensation insurance or utilize any other approved method of meeting state-imposed obligations. They "go bare," as the saying goes. Some states allow this legally, although most do not.

Technically speaking, in most states, a business that doesn't have any employees (a sole proprietorship or a partnership) doesn't have to buy insurance for the sole proprietor or partners. Of course, the business has the option of buying insurance for those business owners anyway. But once a business has employees who aren't owners of the business, most states require that they either buy insurance or meet their obligations through some other means.

But some states allow very small employers not to purchase insurance. Alabama, for instance, does not require insurance if the employer has four or fewer employees. Illinois does not require that commission only sales people are covered by Workers

Compensation insurance. Texas gives all employers the option of not purchasing insurance.

But keep in mind that just because the state doesn't require insurance, this doesn't mean that your business won't be held liable for claims. You will indeed be held liable for workplace injuries or illnesses of your workers—and these liabilities can be substantial. So going bare always involves an element of risk, because you are creating significant potential liabilities for your company.

Another issue that often comes up for such employers is when a client requires proof of Workers Compensation insurance. I've often heard small employers question why their customer can require Workers Compensation insurance from them when the state does not.

The answer is really pretty simple. Those customers understand that even though the state does not require a Workers Compensation policy, the liabilities to injured workers' remain. And those customers understand that they could well be liable for workplace injuries of employees of companies they contract with for services. So even though the state may not require your small business to have a Workers Compensation policy, your customers may well require it contractually before they will hire your company.

PROFESSIONAL EMPLOYER ORGANIZATIONS (PEO)
Another alternative to purchasing a Workers Compensation policy is to utilize the services of a professional employer organization (PEO). This is also known *as employee leasing.* If you enter into an arrangement with a PEO, those people who have been working with you directly for you for years will now receive their paychecks from the PEO, which will also provide such benefits as Workers Compensation coverage.

Historically, lower Workers Compensation cost has been one of the major selling points of PEOs. There is a certain logic to this, because a PEO should be able to achieve certain economies of scale and Workers Compensation can theoretically be purchased at a lower unit cost when the policy is larger. But there have been some significant problems with PEOs and Workers Compensation insurance over the years.

The insurance industry has generally not welcomed the development of PEOs and has not been enthusiastic about underwriting such companies. Because a PEO can be a conglomeration of hundreds of different workplace exposures, it's difficult to effectively classify an underwrite a policy for a PEO.

Another major problem with Workers Compensation insurance for PEOs- experience modification factors. Experience modification factors are designed to adjust the cost of current Workers Compensation insurance based on recent past losses of a particular employer. But an employer that shifts to a PEO arrangement for its Workers Compensation coverage can escape the effects of its own loss history.

Experience modification factors use the claims history of a company in calculating an adjustment factor for that company's premiums. But if an employer moves to a PEO, that employer is now insured under a policy whose experience mod has been calculated from the loss history of that PEO and its members, not that particular employer.

For example, take Wonder Widgets, a company that has a 1.25 experience mod factor that will be effective on its Workers Compensation policy effective July 1st, 2009. That experience mod is based on the losses that Wonder Widget had during its policies that ran from July 2005-2008. But if it goes with a PEO effective July 1st 2009, its insurance is now written through a policy purchased by the PEO, which has an experience mod of .98, based on the loss-experiences of its client companies.

The concern of some insurance regulators and insurance companies is that this enables Wonder Widget to escape the financial consequences of its poor loss record. This can have the effect of reducing or eliminating the incentive to manage workplace safety.

Many states have thus enacted requirements that PEOs use the individual experience modifiers developed for their client companies, which has increased the complexity of Workers Compensation insurance programs administered by PEOs.

The biggest risk involved with using PEOs is that, because they sometimes have difficulty finding and maintaining Workers Compensation insurance (particularly in hard insurance markets), behind-the-scenes difficulties can sometimes arise that employers won't find out about until it's too late. If you're relying on a PEO for workers' compensation coverage, but that PEO loses its insurance, you might end up lacking coverage while the PEO scrambles to recover its coverage. Remember, if the PEO loses its coverage, then you're back to being responsible for your employees. If you maintain your own workers' compensation policy to cover your non-leased workers (such as clerical), you might find that your audit ends up charging you for coverage you thought the PEO was providing.

Administrative Services Organization (ASO)

There's a newer wrinkle in the world of staffing companies (like PEOs and Temporary Agencies) called Administrative Services Organizations, or ASOs. These offer a variety of HR related services to clients, just like PEOs, but an ASO doesn't become a "co-employer" the way a PEO does. We cover ASOs in a little more depth in Chapter 13, but for Workers Compensation purposes the main difference between an ASO and a PEO is that an ASO doesn't always offer Workers Compensation to clients, but when it does, the coverage is via an individual policy for the client.

The bottom line always to remember when considering any lower-cost alternative to regular Workers Compensation insurance is that there is a reason Workers Compensation insurance tends to be expensive- —claims. Lower-cost alternatives may save some money in the short term, but sometimes they end up being much more expensive in the long run, when all claims costs are finally accounted. Just ask all those Kentucky employers that are now receiving huge assessment bills for their group self-insurance program.

A guaranteed-cost assigned risk policy may seem expensive (and it often is), but in the long run it might turn out to be the most cost-effective approach. A proper Workers Compensation insurance policy relieves you of all responsibility for whatever claims may arise from your Workers Compensation liabilities. In spite of all the problems with this insurance product, it is a tested means of transferring these risks to a third party. Sometimes clever solutions to fundamental problems get a little too clever.

Larger employers may well have more complex alternative programs presented to them. These may involve some form of "fronting," as discussed in Chapter 10, and may involve *captive insurance companies*, as explained in Chapter 10, or *rent-a-captive*, which is basically an arrangement to lease the services of a captive insurance company. These alternatives are probably less risky than some of the others already reviewed, but still rely on complex arrangements. When coupled with effective loss control, such programs may be able to offer some price stability over time, when compared with the fluctuations of the commercial insurance market. Typically, such programs cannot match the savings that may become available during the soft insurance market, but can avoid the extreme price increases that come when the market moves to hard conditions. Additionally, these programs can provide viable coverage alternatives for employers that have difficulty finding traditional insurance at competitive rates.

QUICK REVIEW
- An insurance policy isn't the only way most states allow an employer to meet its Workers Compensation obligations. Be aware of the alternatives such as self-insurance and group self-insurance.

- **Beware of "virtual" Workers Compensation insurance programs, as only a few states recognize them as actually meeting an employer's Workers Compensation obligations.**
- Be aware of the potential problems of using employee leasing to solve Workers Compensation obligations
- Make sure you understand your state's requirements before going without Workers Compensation coverage. Only a few states allow employers to "go bare" without insurance, although some states allow very small employers to go without insurance.
- Be aware that even if your state allows your company to operate without Workers Compensation insurance, you run the risk of expensive claims from injured workers for which you would then be liable. Being exempt from purchasing Workers Compensation insurance does not shield an employer from responsibility for injured workers.

CHAPTER 12

CLAIMS, SAFETY, AND OTHER RESOURCES

So far we haven't addressed Workers Compensation claims costs too directly. . We've reviewed how the costs of claims impact your experience modification factor and loss-sensitive policies, but we haven't really gotten into what an employer can do to control the costs of claims. But once you've mastered all the other techniques and recommendations in this book and used them to address Workers Compensation costs, there remains one last area where an employer can wring out unnecessary costs: claims.

Traditionally, the insurance industry has tended to focus on claims first and foremost as the way to reduce Workers Compensation costs. But I've held off on discussing this area, because the traditional approach tends to focus so exclusively on claims control and ignores all the other important areas that we've been covering earlier. Besides, I think the insurance industry likes to focus on loss control so much partly as a way to distract policyholders from all the other problems that can inflate premiums. And of course, controlling claims costs also makes insurance more profitable for the insurance companies.

But the traditional focus on claims costs does have a legitimate point: the cost of Workers Compensation claims is one of the biggest drivers of costs for Workers Compensation insurance and there are things that employers can do to address the issue.

If your company is one of those fortunate enterprises that incur few Workers Compensation claims, count your blessings. Either you're extremely lucky or you're doing some important things right—maybe a little of both. Both even well-managed and safety-conscious companies can have problems with Workers Compensation claims. But there are some things you can do about it.

First, Know Thy Claims

A recurring theme of this book has been "Trust, but verify." And this certainly applies to your claims at least as much as it does to all the other areas we've been covering. Unless your company somehow has so few claims that you know each of them intimately without any effort, your first course of action should be to have a full-blown review of all claims that have occurred in recent years. First, if you are a fairly large company with many employees and many claims, check to make sure every one of those claims really belongs to you. Occasionally, an employer can get tagged with a claim that really doesn't belong to his company. It's somewhat rare, but it can happen.

If you're a multi-state operation, you may want to check that claims have been reported for the proper state and location. This can be particularly important if some of your states of operation utilize NCCI experience modification factors and other states don't. If a claim properly belongs to a state that doesn't integrate with the NCCI experience modification factor, getting it assigned to the proper state will lower your NCCI experience modifier (which affects multiple states). For example, an expensive claim that properly belongs in Michigan will affect only the stand-alone Michigan experience modifier. But if that expensive claim gets reported as if it belongs to an NCCI state, that claim will drive up the interstate modifier that applies in all NCCI states.

Also check that your insurance company is pursuing subrogation possibilities for claims that may have that potential. It's not uncommon for insurers to be lax about this. If some third party may be liable for a Workers Compensation injury, the cost of the claim can be reduced by the amount the Workers Compensation insurer recovers from that third party. For example, if a salesperson is injured in an auto accident while performing his duties, there may be subrogation possibilities against the other party in the accident.

Similarly, there may be the potential to recover from a Second Injury Fund. Some states maintain such Second Injury Funds to reimburse self-insured employers and insurance companies for the costs of claims that represent aggravations of prior injuries. As mentioned earlier, our study of insurance companies' reporting of South Carolina SIF reimbursements found that many insurance companies were not properly giving credit for those reimbursements on the experience modification factors for employers. That is, the insurance companies were getting reimbursements from the Second Injury Fund but they were not always making the appropriate corrected reports to NCCI that would revise experience modification factors to reflect those reimbursements.

Reimbursements due to subrogation or Second Injury Funds allow prior experience modification factors to be revised. But for this to happen, the insurance company has to file a corrected unit statistical report with NCCI (or other rating bureau). Our consulting work often finds that insurance companies have failed to make such corrected reports, resulting in experience modifiers higher than they should have been.

Our work has also found that insurance companies often do not pursue all the subrogation possibilities open to them. So employers need to keep on top of their claims and discuss with their insurance companies which open claims may have subrogation potential. And when your insurer does make a subrogation recovery or receives a reimbursement from a Second Injury Fund, you need to follow up and make sure the corrected report is sent to NCCI.

Another important thing you can learn by reviewing claims is the pattern behind your claims. Identify the patterns of what kinds of injuries are causing frequent or expensive claims, then you can then start to take steps to reduce them.

Finally, closely review all claims with large open reserves. Don't accept as gospel the insurance company's reserve determinations, as there is far more art than science in the way insurers set reserves. Be as demanding and as skeptical as you can be in determining why the insurance company has set reserve levels as high as they are. If necessary, bring in outside claims experts, either from your insurance agency or as independent consultants, to review those expensive reserves. Remember, for the experience modification factor, reserves count exactly the same as the amounts actually paid out by the insurer. Similarly, many loss-sensitive plans base charges on incurred losses, which again treat reserves the same as paid out claims amounts.

You have a right to insist that your insurance company handle claims in a competent and professional manner—particularly if you are on a loss-sensitive type policy. If disputes over loss-sensitive premiums end up in litigation (as they sometimes do), you may be able to insist that your insurer be able to demonstrate competence in setting reserves, pursuing subrogation, and in adjusting and settling claims.

Second, Know Thy Workers
Another effective technique to control claims costs is to utilize pre-employment physicals where possible. It's perfectly reasonable to make sure that prospective new employees are physically able to perform the work in question. However, be careful not to run afoul of the Americans with Disability Act (ADA). The ADA impacts employers with twenty-five or more employees and requires that pre-employment physicals not be given to job applicants until after a conditional offer of employment has been extended. So only those potential hires that are otherwise qualified for employment may be subjected to a pre-employment physical exam.

To avoid problems, make the conditional offer of employment in writing. Set forth all conditions that a candidate will have to meet before you will actually offer employment, such as the pre-employment physical and pre-employment drug screening. Also make clear that the employment will be on an at-will basis.

Return-to-work programs, also known as *modified work* or *light duty policies,* can be an essential part of your company's claims control efforts. Some employers dislike these programs or feel that it's difficult to find appropriate light work for recovering employees. But these programs can reduce the costs of claims significantly. Consult with specialists at your insurance company and/or your insurance producer to get help implementing return-to-work programs. And if you can't get appropriate help form these sources, consider shopping for other sources of insurance that do provide this kind of support service. If this is not practical because of the size or type of your business, you may well want to consider bringing in some outside assistance on your own. If your company is experiencing significant Workers Compensation losses, you need to take action to get them under control.

Third, Promote Safety

Not only do you need to manage carefully the cost of injuries that occur, you also need to take steps to prevent injuries from happening. Effective loss control or safety management can play a vital role in reducing the incidence, and thus the costs, of claims.

Again, there may be significant resources available from your insurer or agent. If not, shop around to see if you may be able to gain such resources by switching carriers or agents. This is an area where doing business with the lowest-cost provider may not always be cost-effective in the long run.

Consultants & Claims Costs

I've mentioned that in the past, our company sometimes got involved when a client reviewed how claims had been adjusted, settled, and/or reserved. Yet claims costs are not my own area of expertise—we specialize in checking premium charges. In those cases, we normally were teamed up with an independent consultant who specialized in such reviews. And we have seen that such reviews often find significant instances where insurance companies have set reserves too high, missed subrogation potential on claims, and caused claims to settle for more than was necessary by making mistakes in adjusting the claim.

Typically, such a review is practical only for larger employers on loss-sensitive plans, as these consultants charge by the hour and these projects can take some time to do properly.

But recently, we were asked to review a situation where a claims consultant worked on a contingent-fee basis, and had billed a client a significant contingent fee. The client hadn't paid as they didn't feel the consultant had really produced the savings claimed. And our review supported the view of the employer.

What was alarming was that the fine print of this consultant's contract, essentially stipulated that any change in reserves over time would be assumed to be the result of the consultant's work, thus entitling the consultant to a contingent fee. This was troubling as nothing in the materials I had reviewed indicated that the changes in reserves had been due to any particular negotiation or finding by the consultant.

Reserve amounts routinely change over time, as revised information on a claim becomes known. So the simple fact that reserves on certain claims changed over time after the consultant was hired was not prima facie evidence that the consultant had caused these reserve changes.

So as a general rule, I'm a little leery about contingent-fees for such work. This is so, even though my own company does a fair bit of contingent-fee work.

But our contingent-fee agreement makes it clear that we are only entitled to a fee if we produce savings for a client that the client would not have obtained without our efforts. This other consultant's agreement contained no such detail. In fact, as mentioned above, this other agreement required that changes in claims reserves would be assumed to be due to the consultant and would entitle the consultant to a fee.

Also, we generally offer clients the choice between a contingent-fee and a hourly rate fee. I tend to be suspicious of firms that insist on only offering a contingent-fee approach. So I would advise clients to lean towards an hourly rate approach for such work, unless the contingent fee contract spells out that fees will be based only on savings that the client would not have received without the involvement of the consultant.

Other Resources

The internet can be a wealth of information and resources—but sometimes that wealth of information can be overwhelming. Performing a Google search for "Workers Compensation insurance" produces so many different links, many to those selling insurance, that it can be difficult to find really useful resources online. Here are some that we've found useful.

www.cutcomp.com

This is the website for our company, Advanced Insurance Management LLC. And while it (naturally) provides information about our consulting services, it also contains a lot of useful information on Workers Compensation insurance generally.

www.ncci.com

The website of the National Council on Compensation, Inc. Although access to their online manuals requires a subscription, there is also some free material about Workers Compensation insurance that can be useful and informative.

www.dmoz.org/Business/Human_Resources

This is the Open Directory Project Listing of Human Resources links.

www.HR-Guide.com
A large collection of links to useful HR materials on the internet

www.cdc.gov/NIOSH
Homepage for the National Institute for Occupational Safety and Health—much useful information here, although it tends to be technical and oriented for safety professionals

www.OSHA.gov
Homepage for Occupational Safety and Health Administration—more useful resources, these presented in a somewhat more user-friendly format

http://www.hss.energy.gov/healthsafety/wshp/chem_safety/
Chemical safety handbook from the U.S. Department of Energy

http://www.saftek.com/safety.html
Online compendium of safety related links

http://www.toolkit.com/tools/index.aspx#Worker_Safety
Model safety program and other information from business owner's toolkit

QUICK REVIEW
- Review large open claims regularly to make sure reserves are not excessive.
- Make sure your insurer follows up on subrogation potential and reimbursements from Second Injury Funds.
- Make sure your insurer properly reports subrogation recoveries and reimbursements from SIFs to rating bureaus like NCCI.
- Shop around with insurers and agents to obtain loss control and safety services.
- Be careful of contingent-fee arrangements with claims review consultants.
- Take advantage of free loss control and safety resources available on the internet.

CHAPTER 13

NEW DEVELOPMENTS IN WORKERS' COMPENSATION

When I started in the field of Workers Compensation insurance, new developments seemed to come around on timescales best measured in decades. In other words, things didn't change very much, very quickly. But things are a little different now. The pressures created by the costs of Workers Compensation coverage have made new developments come along much more rapidly.

Pay As You Go

Perhaps the latest wrinkle in the field is "Pay As You Go." This is somewhat related to the field of PEOs or employee leasing, but is different in some aspects. With Pay As You Go, companies can obtain Workers Compensation insurance without the usual large deposit premiums and the potential surprises of premium audits. Billings are done on a monthly basis based on actual payrolls, so there shouldn't be unhappy surprises after the policy ends.

These programs are typically offered by payroll companies in conjunction with other services, so they are much like the services offered by PEOs. But with Pay As You Go, even some insurance companies are getting into the act themselves, partnering up with companies such as Intuit.

This appears to be the latest new trend in the Workers Compensation field, and it would seem to offer potential benefits by making monthly Workers Compensation billings direct from monthly payroll records, avoiding the need for large down payments and audit surprises. The only potential drawbacks I can see are that it adds a layer between the employer and the insurance company, and it weakens or eliminates the insurance agent's ability to assist the policyholder. As with PEOs, these programs can only be as good as the company providing the service. If a problem develops between the insurance company and the company actually selling the service, it may take a while for the employer to become aware of the problem.

This is such a new development that it may take some time for all the possible benefits and problems to fully manifest. These programs certainly offer the possibility of smoothing out the payment of Workers Compensation insurance, but do not resolve the underlying problems that have been the subject of this book.

ASOs: Administrative Services Organizations

Another relatively new buzzword in the field of Workers Compensation insurance is "ASO" which stands for Administrative Services Organizations (or sometimes Administrative Services Outsourcing). These companies provide services somewhat similar to those of a PEO (Professional Employer Organization), but are different in some key aspects. Generally, an ASO will handle certain human resources tasks such as tax filing and payroll, but will not provide Workers Compensation insurance or health insurance by becoming a "co-employer" with the client company.

However, many ASO type companies are now offering the "Pay As You Go" option for Workers Compensation insurance, so this line is starting to blur. But a key distinction is that under Workers Compensation insurance offered by an ASO, there is no "co-employment," so the policy is solely in the name of the client company. With a PEO, the client company is often insured under a master policy in the name of the PEO (but regulations in many states mandate individual policies for each client even when insured through a PEO).

For Workers Compensation purposes, the key distinction between an ASO service and PEO is that the ASO may or may not offer Workers Compensation insurance to clients, and when the ASO does so it will be offering individual policies to each client company. In a PEO, Workers Compensation coverage is provided to client companies via a master policy negotiated by the PEO, although some states require the insurance company to issue a separate policy for client companies. Furthermore, if the PEO loses its Workers Compensation coverage, coverage is lost for all client companies. Under an ASO format, each client company has its own separate policy direct with the insurance company, and independent of the ASO. The ASO handles billing that is coordinated with other payroll services, but is not a co-policyholder with the client company. This means that the client company retains all the legal rights a policyholder has in relation to the insurance company. In a PEO relationship, the policyholder is technically the PEO, and the client company may well not have the same protections that are provided to policyholders.

States Clamping Down on Employers
Another emerging trend in Workers Compensation is for states to enforce requirements for Workers Compensation coverage much more aggressively. Employers large and small are finding that state agencies are levying record fines and sometimes seeking criminal prosecutions for employers that do not meet the statutory requirements for Workers Compensation. For most employers, this means a valid Workers Compensation insurance policy. (Only Texas allows employers legally to go without valid Workers Compensation coverage, and even there it is not generally recommended.)

States are also increasing prosecutions of employers for what is viewed as improper avoidance of Workers Compensation premiums. This is why it's vital to never knowingly misrepresent the nature of the work done by your company and your workers. Not only will your insurance company likely figure it out in the long run, when they do figure it out they will not only seek back premiums from you, it may also **result in a criminal prosecution**.

Certainly it is in everyone's best interests for the authorities to police employer compliance with workers' compensation statutes.

Those employers who cheat the system gain unfair cost advantage over employers who play by the book. But employers need to beware because, in my experience, sometimes those in the insurance industry are a little too disposed to see fraud in the actions of policyholders, while dismissing the mistakes of the insurance industry itself as mere innocent mistakes. Occasionally, prosecutors may be misled by insurance company personnel into believing innocent actions by some employers to be deliberate acts of fraud.

That's why we stress so much that employers need to be scrupulous and careful in their dealings with insurance companies over Workers Compensation insurance premiums. An employer needs to exercise vigilance, because **overcharges happen routinely.** But in resisting those overcharges, employers need to be careful that they do not inadvertently give ammunition to those who would accuse them of fraud.

Here are our recommendations to employers to avoid such problems:
- Never knowingly give inaccurate or incomplete information to insurance company auditors or underwriters.
- Never deal with insurance producers who suggest you should reduce premiums by misleading an insurance company about the nature of your work.
- Document all information provided by your company to insurance company underwriters and auditors, so that a written record is preserved of what information your company provided, and to whom and when.
- Refrain from working with consultants who advise providing inaccurate or incomplete information to insurance company underwriters or auditors—these consultants may end up involving you in activities that could lead to criminal prosecution,
- When estimating payrolls and classifications on an insurance application, always review recent past years'

audits to make sure your estimates are consistent with these.

- If your estimates on an application need to be different from recent past audits, be sure to fully explain why these changes are justified.

- Keep your insurance company informed about changes in ownership of your company—this can impact your experience modification factor, and thus your premiums.

- Keep your own file documentation about the basis of your estimates. If a question should be raised years later, you may need to provide credible answers about the process you went through.

In the past, some employers apparently have felt it was acceptable to be less than exact when describing the work done by some of their employees or how their payroll was distributed among various kinds of work. Once upon a time, this might have been viewed by some as just sharp business practice, doing unto the insurance companies what many employers have felt the insurance companies did unto them. Fudging some information given to insurance companies in order to hold down costs may have not been uncommon, but it is definitely inadvisable. Not only might it cost your business money, it might create a criminal liability for the business owners or managers.

Competitive Bidding & Fraud

This new world of stepped-up enforcement and prosecution means that employers need to be more careful than ever in the competitive bidding process. If an overzealous insurance agent or broker utilizes lowball payrolls or payroll allocations, an insurer could possibly claim that an employer colluded with the agent/broker to defraud the insurer by providing fraudulent information concerning operations, classifications, or payrolls. So in competitive bidding situations, an employer should carefully review the underlying basis for any proposed Workers Compensation insurance premiums to make sure all estimates are reasonable and consistent with what's on other proposals. You should carefully examine any radical deviations in these factors. You don't want to penalize a good insurance producer who has figured out a legitimate change that reduces your premiums, but you also don't want to be dealing with someone who is trying to game the system to get your business.

PEOs & Fraud

Criminal prosecutions of Professional Employer Organizations also continue to be a trend in Workers Compensation insurance. States now regulate such enterprises more closely than in the past, but oversight in many states is still loose. Some PEOs have suggested to their clients that they possessed Workers Compensation skills far beyond those of mortal men (to paraphrase that old Superman intro), but have sadly fallen to earth, leaving insurance companies and clients jointly upset. So when considering utilizing the services of a PEO (again, essentially employee leasing), an employer needs to learn as much as possible about the PEO and the insurance company providing the Workers Compensation coverage.

Many PEOs now obtain their Workers Compensation coverage via Large Deductible policies. This does give them the benefit of obtaining valid Workers Compensation coverage at affordable cost. And if claims costs remain under control, such programs can offer significant benefits to the clients of such PEOs. But if claims costs get out of control, it can induce a death spiral at the PEO that cannot be reversed, one that ultimately can deprive clients of needed Workers Compensation coverage on short notice.

QUICK REVIEW
- "Pay as You Go" Workers Compensation programs can avoid large down payments and audit surprises.
- ASOs—Administrative Services Organizations—offer outsourced HR services like PEOs do, but Workers Compensation through ASOs is individualized.

- Employers need to be careful to avoid placing themselves in jeopardy of criminal prosecution over Workers Compensation coverage and premiums.
- When using PEOs, employers need to exercise caution to avoid being victimized by unstable or unreliable service providers

CHAPTER 14

DIFFERENT EMPLOYERS, DIFFERENT STRATEGIES

The Workers Compensation market poses some unique problems for employers of different sizes and types. Although employers of all kinds can be affected by most of the areas covered earlier in this book, I wanted to focus here on some particular tips for employers at both ends of the size spectrum, and for employers in certain kinds of enterprises.

For Small Employers

Here are some particular areas that small employers probably should focus in on, to help reduce their Workers Compensation costs.

Determine if You're in an Assigned Risk Plan

This is probably the biggest cost-reduction technique many smaller employers can utilize. That's because, in many states, the cost of being insured in the Assigned Risk Plan is much, much higher than the same coverage would cost in the voluntary market. Yet amazingly, small employers often don't realize that they're being covered through an Assigned Risk policy.

Sometimes an insurance agent handling the workers' compensation insurance for a small employer doesn't make it clear that the policy procured is an assigned risk policy. I think sometimes an agent doesn't like to admit that he or she can't get coverage in the voluntary market, so they find it easy to not explain to a small employer that coverage has been obtained via an Assigned Risk plan.

An Assigned Risk policy doesn't look different from any other workers' comp policy, except for some subtle differences. So make it a point to insist on knowing if your policy has been written through an assigned risk plan.

If you learn that you are in an assigned risk plan, check with your state's insurance regulators to see if assigned risk policies in your state have higher rates and premiums. If this is the case, then do everything in your power to find coverage outside the assigned risk plan. Talk with other agents, talk with employee leasing companies, investigate group self-insurance programs available in your state- —but don't let it be your agent's sole responsibility to get you out of the assigned risk plan. Your agent just may not have an alternative, but that doesn't mean that such an alternative doesn't exist.

Check What Credits May be Available to You in Your State. If you're not in the assigned risk plan, make sure your policy gives you whatever credits you might be eligible for in your state. If your state offers credits for a drug- and alcohol-free workplace, find out if you are eligible. If your state offers merit rating, see if you are eligible from an insurer. If your premium is of appropriate size, make sure you are getting the proper experience modification factor. If your state offers a small-deductible credit, look into obtaining this.

Insist on Getting Audit Workpapers After Any Audit. If the insurance company sends out an auditor to determine your final premium, make sure to request a copy of the audit workpapers so you can review them carefully and make sure payroll computation adjusts overtime properly and allocates payroll of different employees correctly. If your insurer has you self-report payrolls (rather than their sending out an auditor) make sure you adjust payroll to remove the premium portion of overtime pay (most states allow this). Also make sure you are allocating payroll properly among the various classes.

Check into Alternative Sources of Workers' Compensation. Many business and trade associations sponsor insurance programs that include workers' compensation insurance. Check into all organizations to which you belong or that you might be eligible to join that may offer sponsored insurance programs that could reduce your rates or premium.

Consider a PEO or ASO

A small employer may obtain to obtain savings on Workers Compensation coverage by signing up with a PEO or an ASO (see Chapters 11 and 13 for more details on these service providers). The key to using these third-party providers is to select a financially stable and reliable one (not always easy). Check references, check with your state insurance regulators, and find out all you can about the providers Workers Compensation program before signing up.

Tips for Large Employers

Large employers have their own particular areas to focus on, but don't completely ignore the tips for smaller employers, as some of these may also impact some larger companies. For example, in hard markets, larger employers can also be stuck in the Assigned Risk plan. And obtaining audit workpapers is important for any size company.

Competitive Bidding

An independent agent or broker may make the argument that he or she can access a large number of insurance companies, so there is no need to bring competing agents. But the fallacy of that approach was exposed years ago when then New York Attorney General Eliot Spitzer caught large brokers manipulating the system to deceive clients into thinking there was competitive bidding going on when it really wasn't competitive. An effective way to guard against such deception is to divide available insurance markets among several independent agents or brokers.

Review Common Ownership With Other Entities

Make sure the experience modification factor used on your policies has been calculated using data from all commonly owned entities (and only those entities that currently share 50 percent or more common ownership). Otherwise, your mod may be higher than proper because of incorrect payroll and loss data.

Read Side Agreements Carefully

As explained earlier, some insurers now offer loss-sensitive plans to large employers where premium formula is contained in separate side agreement that is not actually part of the policy. As a general rule, I advise clients to avoid such situations, as they often indicate that the insurer is using a premium formula that is unfairly advantageous to itself, one that has not been approved by state regulators.

Understand the Details of Any Loss-Sensitive Plans

Some of these plans can get extremely complicated and difficult to understand—even for the people selling them. When such plans are being proposed, make sure the agent or broker thoroughly explains how the plan will operate—and get those explanations in writing. Make sure your agent or broker understands that you intend to hold him or her responsible for any miscommunications or omissions in their explanation. You are relying upon your agent/broker to help you make an informed decision, you have a right to insist they fully and thoroughly explain the operation of the plan before you choose.

Keep a Watchful Eye on Loss Reserves

Many large employers end up on loss-sensitive policies, and many of these charge for loss reserves just the same as for actual paid claims. Any plan that is based on incurred losses is using paid claims and loss reserves together to adjust premium. Once you're on such a loss-sensitive plan, the insurance company may get a little lax, since they're playing with your dollars on such a plan, not theirs. Keep a close eye on loss reserves, subrogations, reimbursements from Second Injury Funds, and the way that claims are handled and settled.

Construction-Related Employers

For employers in construction-related work, Workers' Compensation is typically an even higher priority than for other employers. Rates tend to be high and the number of insurance companies interested in writing Workers' Comp for these employers tends to be lower. Additionally, many customers use experience modification factors as a rough benchmark of workplace safety. Finally, there are some kinds of workers' compensation insurance policies that typically are an issue only for construction-related risks.

OCIPs

Contractors may encounter projects where workers' compensation coverage is handled by separate policies that cover all the workers on that particular project. Such programs are known as *Owner Controlled Insurance Program* (OCIP), *consolidated insurance programs* (CIPs), or *wrap-up insurance programs* (wrap-ups). Such insurance programs cover the project owner and all contractors and subcontractors working on the project, rather than having each party provide coverage through separate policies.

These programs have been created to resolve some of the difficulties involved with all of these parties having their own policies. Making sure that all the contractors and subcontractors have met the contractual requirements for insurance can be a major undertaking. Consolidated insurance programs eliminate this chore, as coverage for all workers on a project is provided by a single policy.

In theory, OCIPs and their ilk offer some real advantages for large projects. An OCIP coordinates not only coverage, but also safety and loss control functions. In reality, though, these programs can have limitations. For instance, a contractor with effective safety and loss control programs may find that those used by the OCIP are less effective.

Another issue that can arise is that, while ideally an OCIP should cover everyone involved with the project, in the real world, it usually does not. An OCIP will typically exclude suppliers, vendors of materials, hauling firms, and blasting and demolition contractors. It can be important for construction companies participating in an OCIP to have a clear listing of who is covered under the plan and who is not.

Most importantly, from a cost control standpoint, contractors participating in an OCIP need to make sure their regular workers' compensation coverage coordinates properly so that they aren't charged twice for the same payroll.

When dealing with subcontractors, an OCIP can also cause some complications. A contractor will normally have certain procedures in place for handling and verifying certificates of insurance from subcontractors. But in an OCIP, the subcontractors may be required to file certificates with the OCIP broker or administrator. To avoid problems, a contractor should arrange that copies of all certificates be forwarded to the contractor as well.

Construction-related firms also need to make sure that data from OCIPs is filed with appropriate rating bureaus so that it is included in calculating the experience modification factors for those firms. Sometimes there can be delays in getting data reported from OCIP work, which can distort your experience modification factor. Remember, your company's data from OCIP work should be reported to rating bureaus for inclusion in your experience modification factor. This is different from a joint venture, which forms a business entity for which an experience modification factor will be calculated that will remain separate from your company's mod.

If you are the project owner utilizing as OCIP, you need to take steps to realize the cost-saving potential of the OCIP. For one, understand that because you as project owner are paying for the workers' compensation insurance, you have a greater need to make sure accurate payroll information is received from contractors and subcontractors. In an OCIP, the contractors and subcontractors may have less incentive to make sure records provided are accurate. So the project owner needs to pay attention to details such as the following questions:

- Has overtime pay been adjusted down to remove the premium portion?
- Have contractors and subcontractors kept adequate records so that payroll can be divided among appropriate classifications?
- Have payrolls been submitted for those exposures and operations that are excluded from the OCIP?

Project owners also need to check that proper rates have been applied in computing the premium. When the inception date of the OCIP is different from the inception date of the contractor's own workers' compensation policy, you should add an *anniversary rating date* (ARD) *endorsement* to the OCIP. This endorsement splits classifications, payrolls, experience mods, and other elements of the premium into pre-ARD and post-ARD, so that proper rates are applied to each. This makes sure that increased rates that may have applied after the contractor's ARD are used only for the post-ARD component and not the pre-ARD component.

Payroll Allocation

Whether your workers' compensation is through an OCIP or through your own policy, it is important to remember for construction-related risks that, unlike other kinds of employers, the payroll for individual employees is commonly divided among classifications—*where the payroll records allow.*

So it is vital to make sure that payroll records keep track of the exact time each employee spends at various job functions that you may be eligible for lower rates. If you do not keep track of the exact time spent in each job function, all of the payroll for that employee will be assigned to the classification that has the highest rate.

Contractor Credit Adjustment Plan

Another vital area of concern for construction-related risks is to make sure you receive all *contractors' premium adjustment credits* for which you may be eligible. Many states have separate programs that can produce additional premium credits for construction-related companies that pay relatively high hourly wages. But the *employer* needs to apply for these credits by submitting information about average hourly wages paid. This is different from experience modification factor calculations, which are done automatically by the insurance system. Contractors' premium adjustment credits will not be computed for you if you do not submit the proper form to the rating bureau. It is not uncommon for contractors to miss out on these credits because their agent or insurer has not properly explained the process to them.

Manufacturers

For manufacturing companies, perhaps the most important thing to keep in mind is that the single enterprise rule can hit you hard. That's the rule, discussed earlier in Chapter 5, that says that when determining classifications, NCCI and other rating bureaus classify your overall business enterprise, not the particular kinds of work done there. So janitors in a manufacturing plant get assigned to whatever the appropriate manufacturing class is for a particular company. For example, a janitor in a tire manufacturing plant gets assigned to the tire manufacturing classification, while a janitor in a machine shop gets assigned to the machine shop. Same thing for shipping and receiving people—they go into the governing classification.

For manufacturers, the only kinds of additional classifications usually allowed are for Standard Exceptions—clerical, outside sales, and (often but not always) drivers. And even then, those workers have to meet certain criteria. Clerical people have to be working in separate and distinct areas, for example.

There can be exceptions to this single enterprise rule, if a company is doing two things that are so different that they can't really fit into a single classification. But even then the operations have to be physically separated. So determining which governing classification is really right for a manufacturer can be critical. Manufactures may want to pay particular close attention to all the information on proper classification that's in Chapter 5.

QUICK REVIEW

- Small employers need to focus on getting out of the Assigned Risk plan if possible, as this can be the greatest cost savings available to them.
- Larger employers need to watch the details of loss-sensitive programs that may be proposed to them.
- Construction companies need to keep accurate payroll records to avoid problems with overtime and payroll allocation.
- Construction companies also need to coordinate regular coverage with OCIP coverage when applicable.
- Manufacturers need to examine governing classification closely.

APPENDIX A

GLOSSARY OF WORKERS' COMPENSATION TERMINOLOGY

ASO - Administrative Services Organization

ASO is a third party firm that provides certain outsourced human resources services such as payroll and taxes. They are similar to PEOs (Professional Employer Organization), but with some differences, particularly with how Workers Compensation coverage may be provided to clients. These differences are covered in more detail in Chapter 13.

Advisory Organization

"Advisory organization is a newer designation for organizations often known as rating bureaus (such as the NCCI). This new term, recently coined by the National Association of Insurance Commissioners, is meant to reflect more accurately the role of NCCI and other such organizations (like Insurance Services Office), which compile rating data and file policy forms for use by member insurance companies.

ALE - Allocated Loss Expenses

Insurance company costs for adjusting and settling claims, which can be identified with a specific claim, are allocated loss expenses. The ALE are often included in the claims costs used to adjust premiums in some loss-sensitive premium adjustment types of workers' compensation policies, such as sliding scale dividend plans or some retro- or retention plans.

ARAP - Assigned Risk Adjustment Program

ARAP is an additional debit charge placed on Assigned Risk policies (In NCCI jurisdictions) with experience modification factors higher than 1.00. The notable exception is Massachusetts, where ARAP stands for All Risk Adjustment Factor. This is a surcharge that increases premiums over and above the experience modifier, and in MA, the ARAP can be levied against all employers, not just those in the assigned risk plan.

Assigned Risk Plan

Sometimes called "the Pool," assigned risk plan is a mechanism established by individual states to make sure that employers can obtain workers' compensation insurance even if insurance companies are not willing to write such insurance on a voluntary basis. Assigned risk plans in many states carry higher rates than the voluntary market.

Audited Premium

The final premium for the policy term, produced by auditing actual payroll exposures is the audited premium.

Audit workpapers

The worksheets prepared by the premium auditor, which can be either hand-written or computerized, showing how the auditor arrived at the payroll numbers that are used to determine the audited premium are the audit workpapers.

Basic Manual

The *Basic Manual* produced by NCCI details rules governing premium computation of Workers Compensation insurance by NCCI member insurance companies. This manual of rules is filed with and approved by state insurance regulators, and is binding upon member insurance companies operating within states that use the NCCI system.

Carve-Out

A carve-out is an option allowed in California and some other states, where an employer and the union for the employer's workers agree to collectively bargain a separate schedule of workers' compensation benefits that differs from the statutory program imposed by the state.

Classification Code

Also called Class Code, this designation is the workers' compensation premium rate commensurate with the risk associated with that workplace exposure. For example, the classification code for an office clerk should carry a significantly lower rate than the code for a roofer. Misclassification is one of the most common causes of overcharges.

D-Ratio

In the experience modification factor calculation, this is a factor applied to the expected losses to determine what percentage of those expected losses are primary.

Direct Writer

A direct writer is an insurance company that does not work through independent insurance agents. The largest direct writer of workers' compensation insurance is Liberty Mutual. Agents for direct writers are employees of the insurance company, not independent agents.

Dividend

A dividend is the return of premium, calculated after policy expiration, based on the over-all performance of the insurance company or of a group of insureds. Dividends cannot be guaranteed in advance, although they are often shown on proposals for insurance.

Employers' Liability

Section B of the standard Workers' Compensation insurance policy shows the employer's liability, which is the part of the policy that has a dollar limit shown for the coverage. This section insures employers for liability towards employees that is not covered by the statutory Workers' Compensation provisions of the state (which are insured in Section A and have no set dollar limit on the policy).

Excess Losses

In the Experience Modification Factor, the amount a single claim is above the cut-off point for inclusion as a primary loss is an excess loss. In the NCCI experience rating formula, this threshold is $5,000. In other formulas used in non-NCCI experience rating, the threshold varies.

Expected Loss Ratio (ELR)

In the experience modification factor, ELR is a percentage factor applied to an employer's past audited payroll to calculate what the expected losses should be for a company of the same type and size as the employer.

Experience Modification Factor

Experience modification factor is an adjustment to Manual Premium, calculated by an advisory organization (also known as rating bureaus) such as NCCI, based on historic loss and payroll data of a particular insured. Also called Experience Modifier, X-Mod, Mod, or Experience Mod.

Experience Period

The window of time from which loss and payroll data is used to calculate an experience modification factor for an employer is the experience period. Normally this window is a three year period, starting four years prior to the effective date of the experience modifier. However, rating bureaus do not wait until three full years of data are in the experience period before producing an experience rating for an employer. If an employer reaches a certain, relatively low threshold of workers' compensation insurance premiums in any one of the three years in the experience period "window," this will make that employer eligible for experience rating.

Fronting

Fronting is an arrangement between two insurance companies to produce an insurance policy (usually workers' compensation) for a third party wherein one insurance company produces the official policy (for a fee), but cedes all losses from that policy to the other insurer. This kind of arrangement is used in situations where the insurer writing the risk is not an admitted company in a particular state, and the coverage needs to be written by an admitted carrier. In order to meet the statutory requirements, the first insurer pays a second (admitted) insurer to "front" the policy, even though the first insurer remains responsible for paying all losses arising under the policy. This kind of arrangement is often used by captive insurers when they are not admitted carriers in a particular state.

Governing Classification

The class code on an employer's workers' compensation insurance policy that generates the most payroll aside from standard exception classifications such as clerical or outside sales (unless there is no other workplace classification applicable other than a standard exception) is the governing classification.

Guaranteed-Cost

A Workers' Compensation insurance policy that is not subject to adjustment due to losses that occur during the policy term is the guaranteed-cost. In a guaranteed-cost policy, the only variable affecting premium that should change between policy inception and audit is payroll. This is in contrast to the various kinds of loss-sensitive plans, such as retrospective rating, retention plans, or sliding scale dividend plans, where there is a premium adjustment made based on losses incurred during the policy term.

Incurred Losses

Incurred losses are paid losses plus loss reserves for estimated future claims costs. Many loss-sensitive insurance policies adjust premium based on incurred losses rather than just on paid losses.

Indemnity Claim

A claim that includes not just medical payments but also payments for lost time by the injured worker is an indemnity claim. These tend to be more expensive than medical-only claims.

Interstate Rating

Interstate rating is an experience modification factor that applies across more than one state. Interstate ratings are calculated by NCCI for employers whose past Workers Compensation insurance policies show payroll in more than one state. Most, but not all states, participate in the interstate rating system. A few states, such as Michigan, Pennsylvania, and Delaware do not participate in interstate rating, but instead continue to calculate separate experience ratings for employers who operate in their jurisdictions, even if those employers also qualify for interstate rating. Those employers thus have one experience modifier applying to their operations in most states but a separate modifier calculated by the stand-alone state rating bureau. The separate stand-alone mod would apply only to Workers Compensationworkers' compensation insurance premiums developed for the employer's operations in that stand-alone state.

Involuntary Market

Involuntary market is another term for Assigned Risk policies. See also Residual Market.

Lost Time Claim

Lost time claim is the same as an indemnity claim.

Manual Premium

Workers' compensation premium calculated by multiplying payrolls by appropriate rates, before application of experience modifier, schedule credit, or premium discount is the manual premium.

Medical-Only Claims

Medical-only claims are those which the only cost is medical care, without any lost-time benefits being paid.

Merit Rating

A premium adjustment used in some NCCI states for employers too small to qualify for an experience modification factor is merit rating. It provides either a premium credit or a debit for such employers based on prior claims (or lack of them).

Modified Premium

Modified premium is the workers' compensation premium calculated after application of experience modification factor. It is similar to standard premium, but does not reflect any schedule credits or debits.

NCCI: The National Council on Compensation Insurance, Inc.

NCCI is the organization responsible in many states for determining proper Workers' Compensation classifications, experience modification factors, and collecting data used for ratemaking. NCCI also writes the manuals used in many states to calculate Workers' Compensation premiums, and administers the Assigned Risk Plan in many jurisdictions. NCCI is a private organization, not connected with government, although it is often mistakenly thought to be a governmental agency. In fact, it is a non-profit privately held corporation owned by major insurance companies, whose executives constitute a majority of the directors on NCCI's board.

Premium Auditor

The premium auditor determines actual exposure (remuneration) for a policy period, in order to determine the final audited premium. The auditor typically works either directly for the insurance company or for a third-party company retained by the insurance company.

Premium Discount

A premium credit, based on size of the premium paid is the premium discount. It is normally given automatically on voluntary market policies, although retrospective rating or sliding scale dividend policies usually do not have a premium discount.

Primary Losses

In the NCCI experience rating formula, the first $5,000 of any single loss is considered primary losses. The experience rating formula used by non-NCCI experience modification factors can vary—some states use a $2,000 threshold rather than $5,000.

Rating Bureau or Rating Organization

See Advisory Organization, or NCCI. Some states maintain their own separate rating bureau, although these often follow NCCI rules and use NCCI manuals. Currently, the states of California, Delaware, Indiana, Massachusetts, Michigan, Minnesota, New Jersey, New York, North Carolina, Pennsylvania, Texas, and Wyoming operate their own non-NCCI rating bureaus. Many of these largely follow NCCI rules for computing premiums and classifications, but California, Delaware, Texas, and Pennsylvania are notably different from NCCI in some aspects of classification and premium computation.

Remuneration

The basis for calculating Workers' Compensation premium is renumeration. Remuneration is primarily payroll, but may also include other forms of employee compensation. Workers' Compensation premium is computed by applying varying rates (for different classifications per hundred dollars of remuneration).

Residual Market

Residual market is another term for an Assigned Risk Plan or Involuntary Market. It refers to Workers Compensation insurance written through an assigned risk plan.

Retrospective Rating

A Workers' compensation insurance policy that makes a subsequent adjustment to premium, after policy expiration, based on losses generated during the policy period is retrospective rating. The adjustment can go up or down, within set parameters, based on the losses generated during the policy period.

Retention Plan

Similar to Retrospective Rating, this is a Workers' Compensation policy format that adjusts the premium, up or down, based on losses (and associated costs) that occur during the policy period.

Schedule Credit/Debit

A schedule credit/debit is a discretionary premium adjustment based on underwriters evaluation of special characteristics of a risk not reflected in the experience modifier. A schedule credit reduces premium, while a schedule debit increases premium.

Scopes® Manual

This manual is produced by NCCI and details what kinds of workplace exposures belong in particular Workers' Compensation classification codes, at least in NCCI jurisdictions.

Sliding Scale Dividend

A return of premium, after policy expiration, based on the actual loss-experience of the insured business is a sliding scale dividend. The size of the dividend varies with the actual loss ratio of the insured business.

Short Rate Penalty

A short rate penalty is applied by insurers when a Workers' Compensation insurance policy is cancelled by the insured before the expiration date of the policy. This penalty is steep in the early days of the policy, and gradually tapers off the closer the policy gets to the expiration date.

Standard Exception

Classifications that are normally not included in the governing classification are considered standard exceptions. These are clerical, outside sales, and often (but not always) drivers.

Standard Premium

remium after application of Experience Modifier and Schedule Credit/Debit, but before Premium Discount.

Voluntary Compensation

Voluntary compensation is an endorsement to the standard Workers' Compensation insurance policy that extends coverage to employees not required to be covered under the state's statutory Workers' Compensation provisions.

Voluntary Market

Workers' Compensation insurance written outside of the Assigned Risk Plan is in the voluntary market.

Workers' Compensation

Statutory systems enacted by states and other jurisdictions of the United States (such as the District of Columbia and Puerto Rico) obligating employers to paying specified benefits to workers who are injured or made ill in the course of their employment is workers' compensation. In the United States, many jurisdictions allow employers to purchase insurance policies to meet their statutory obligations. In many other countries, Workers Compensation is handled by government administered agencies.

APPENDIX B

RESIDUAL MARKET MECHANISMS IN VARIOUS JURISDICTIONS

A Residual Market System is the particular mechanism that a state uses to make sure that all employers can get workers' compensation coverage. Most states use an assigned risk pool mechanism, but some states use their state fund as the insurer of last resort for workers' compensation. Here's a state-by-state rundown.

The following states use an *assigned risk pooling system:*
Alabama
Alaska
Arizona
Arkansas
Connecticut
Delaware
District of Columbia
Georgia
Hawaii
Idaho
Illinois
Indiana
Iowa
Kansas
Massachusetts
Michigan
Minnesota
Mississippi
Missouri
Nevada
New Hampshire
New Jersey

New Mexico
North Carolina
Oregon
South Carolina
South Dakota
Tennessee
Vermont
Virginia
Wisconsin

Nebraska uses an Assigned Risk Program managed by a single insurance company.

The following states use a state fund as the workers' compensation insurer of last resort:
California
Colorado
Kentucky
Louisiana
Maine
Maryland
Montana
New York
North Dakota
Ohio
Oklahoma
Pennsylvania
Texas
Utah
Washington
West Virginia
Wyoming

Florida uses a *joint underwriting association*.

APPENDIX C

THRESHOLD REQUIREMENTS FOR WORKERS' COMPENSATION COVERAGE

The various states and territories of the U.S. set varying thresholds for requiring an employer to obtain valid Workers Compensation coverage (typically, a valid insurance policy) Those thresholds are:

Alabama employers with more than four full or part time employees
Alaska employers with more than one employee
Arizona employers with one or more employees
Arkansas most employers with three or more employees
California employers with one or more employees
Colorado employers with one or more employees
Connecticut employers with one or more employees
Delaware employers with one or more employees
D.C. Employers with one or more employees
Florida construction employers with one or more employees; non-construction employers with four or more employees
Georgia employers with three or more employees
Hawaii employers with one or more employees
Idaho employers with one or more employees
Illinois employers with one or more employees
Indiana employers with one or more employees
Iowa employers with one or more employees
Kansas employers with one or more employees unless payroll less than $20,000
Kentucky employers with one or more employees
Louisiana employers with one or more employees

Maine employers with one or more employees

Maryland employers with one or more employees

Massachusetts employers with one or more employees

Michigan employers with three or more employees or one who works thirty-five hours or more/week

Minnesota employers with one or more employees

Mississippi employers with five or more employees

Missouri employers with five or more employees, but construction employers with one or more

Montana employers with one or more employees

Nebraska employers with one or more employees

Nevada employers with one or more employees

New Hampshire employers with one or more employees

New Jersey employers with one or more employees

New Mexico employers with three or more employees

New York employers with one or more employees

North Carolina employers with three or more employees

North Dakota employers with one or more employees

Ohio employers with one or more employees

Oklahoma employers with one or more employees

Oregon employers with one or more employees

Pennsylvania employers with one or more employees

Puerto Rico employers with one or more employees

Rhode Island employers with one or more employees

South Carolina employers with four or more employees

South Dakota employers with one or more employees

Tennessee employers with five or more employees, coal mining one or more employees

Texas workers' compensation not required (but advised)

U.S. Virgin Islands employers with one or more employees

Utah employers with one or more employees

Vermont employers with one or more employees

Virginia employers with three or more employees

Washington employers with one or more employees

West Virginia employers with one or more employees; agriculture more than five employees

Wisconsin employers with three or more employees

APPENDIX D

THE ANNOTATED WORKERS' COMPENSATION INSURANCE POLICY

On the following pages you will find a copy of the standard workers' compensation insurance policy currently in use in U.S. jurisdictions. This is the 1992 policy version, drafted by the National Council on Compensation, Inc. (NCCI), but used in all states that allow private insurance, even the non-NCCI states. This is the oft-cited "fine print" that sets out the terms and conditions under which an insurance company insures an employer's workers' compensation obligations.

Of course, every employer that purchases workers' compensation insurance has a copy of this document. Few of them have probably actually read it. For the layperson, it can be a daunting task to try to read through such dense and legal language, even though this latest version of the policy has been made easier to read than earlier incarnations.

So here is a brief guide to some of the most important provisions of the policy, with explanations of what exactly is being promised by this contract.

We've talked a fair bit about *proper classification* earlier in this book. To see what the policy says about this, take a look under Part Five-Premiums, Section B, "Classifications." This policy section states:

> Item 4 of the Information Page shows the rate and premium basis for certain business or work classifications. These

> classifications were assigned based on an estimate of the exposures you would have during the policy period. If your actual exposures are not properly described by those classifications, we will assign proper classifications, rates, and premium basis by endorsement to this policy.

The "we" in this section refers to the insurance company. Notice that that the policy does not state that "we" (the insurance company) will "attempt to use the correct classification" or that "we will use the classification we think is right." It says that if the classifications shown on the policy don't describe your actual exposures, then the insurance company " will assign proper classifications." This is an unambiguous promise by the insurance company that it will ultimately use the correct classification to determine your premiums, even if the classification used in the Information Page to develop estimated premium is something different.

Remember that the workers' compensation insurance policy is what the lawyers call a "contract of adhesion." It's a unilateral contract, drafted by insurance company. The only choice the employer gets is whether or not to accept the terms of this contract that was drafted by the other party, the insurance company. As the employer, you don't get to negotiate the terms of this policy; it's take it or leave it. This means that legally, any ambiguity is supposed to be resolved in favor of the employer. But there really isn't anything very ambiguous about this particular section of the policy. The insurance company contractually agrees that it will use the correct classification to determine the premiums for the policy.

Sometimes insurance companies need to be reminded about this contractual obligation, because in practice some of their people sometimes get a little sloppy about using correct classifications. As the policyholder, you have the right to insist that the insurance company live up to the terms of the contract that it drafted.

But how does one know what the "correct classification" really is for a particular employer? That's actually addressed in the preceding section of Part Five-Premiums, Section A, "Our Manuals," which reads:

> All premium for this policy will be determined by our manuals of rules, rates, rating plans and classifications. We may change our manuals and apply the changes to this policy if authorized by law or a governmental agency regulating this insurance.

Now, this might appear to give the insurance company carte blanche to write its own rules. But this isn't quite so. Because even though an insurance company could theoretically write its own manual of rules about all of these things, in actual practice they don't.

The manuals of rules, rates, rating plans, and classifications that are referred to here are actually the manuals written by NCCI or other rating bureaus. Insurance companies don't want to take the time and effort to create their own manuals of rules. They use the manuals created by NCCI (or other rating bureaus in the non-NCCI states) because those manuals are well understood and familiar by insurance company personnel and are submitted to and approved by state insurance regulators. So this section of the policy commits the insurance company to following the manuals of rules and regulations that have been approved by state regulators for workers' compensation insurance.

That means that "proper classifications" are defined by the manuals of rules written by NCCI or other rating bureaus, as approved by state regulators. So the insurance company is required, by the terms of the contract, to use the proper classification and other rating elements for your business according to the detailed manuals of rules filed with regulators. The company can't just make it up as it goes, much as it might like to sometimes. There are detailed manuals of rules that govern the details of how the insurance company is supposed to compute the premium for worker's compensation insurance.

NCCI produces the following manuals that set out in excruciating detail different aspects of how premiums are to be calculated. These are:

The Basic Manual for Workers' Compensation and Employers' Liability Insurance. This manual lays out the general rules for premium computation, coverage, classifications, payroll, rates, cancellation, endorsements, and many other aspects of the Workers Compensation policy.

The Scopes® of Basic Manual Classifications. This manual gives the details of what is intended to be covered by each of its NCCI classification codes (including state special classification).

The Experience Rating Plan Manual. This gives the detailed rules on how experience modification factors are to be computed and applied to policies.

The Retrospective Rating Plan Manual for Workers' Compensation and Employers' Liability Insurance. This manual contains the detailed rules that govern retrospective rating plans (a particular kind of loss-sensitive plan) in NCCI states.

Remember that in states that don't use the NCCI system, the independent rating bureaus for those states produce their own sets of manuals that govern policies covering those states.

This same policy section means that the insurance company has to follow the manual rules about things like experience modification factors and other credits and adjustments to the policy.

There is another important section on page 5 of the policy. Take a look at Section G-Audit. This policy provision states:

> You will let us examine and audit all your records that relate to this policy. These records include ledgers, journals, registers, vouchers, contracts, tax reports, payroll, and disbursement records, and programs for storing and retrieving data.

"All your records that relate to your policy"—That's a pretty broad description and it covers a lot of territory. The specific documents named in the following sentence do not limit the insurance company to just "ledgers, journals, registers…," but rather, these are just offered as examples. The insurance company, per the terms of the contract, has the right to examine "all your records that relate" to your policy. This question often comes up when the employer is in the middle of an audit, particularly an extreme audit, when the records demands of an insurer may seem a bit onerous. So keep in mind that, when push comes to shove, the policy gives the insurance company the right to examine any record of yours that relate to the policy. So any record that relates to anything affecting the coverage or premium computation is fair game.

Another important part of this contract is found at the end of page 4 and spills over to the start of page 5. It is headed Part 4, "Your Duties If Injury Occurs" and reads:

> Tell us at once if injury occurs that may be covered by this policy. Your other duties are listed here.
> Provide for immediate medical care and other services required by the workers' compensation law.
> Give us or our agent the names and addresses of the injured persons and of witnesses, and other information we may need.
> Promptly give us all notices, demands, and legal papers related to the injury, claim proceeding or suit.
> Cooperate with us and assist us, as we may request, in the investigation, settlement, or defense of any claim, proceeding, or suit.
> Do nothing after an injury occurs that would interfere with our right to recover from others.
> Do nothing voluntarily make payments, assume obligations, or incur expenses, except at your own cost.

Pay particular attention to the part that says the employer must tell the insurance company at once if an injury occurs that may be covered by this policy. If the employer fails to notify the insurance company in a timely manner about an injury, the insurance company can decline coverage. So anytime an employer attempts to handle some apparently minor injury on its own (to hold down the costs that will be used to figure future premiums), the employer runs the risk of the insurance company being able to deny coverage if that claim develops into something more serious and expensive.

And make no mistake about it, sometimes injuries that seem to be minor later turn out to have complications that cost a lot of money. Or maybe someone just alleges that it had expensive complications—which from your point of view, can be just as serious. Investigating such allegations and defending yourself against even spurious allegations like this can be very expensive. If you report them promptly to your insurance company, all those expenses become someone else's headache. And that's what you're paying all that premium for—to make these matters someone else's responsibility.

There's another section of the standard policy that has occasionally figured into some cases we've worked on, so I recommend that all employers be aware of it. This provision is right at the beginning of the policy, right at the top of page 1, in the "General Section," headed "The Policy" and it reads as follows:

This policy includes at its effective date the Information Page and all endorsements and schedules listed here. It is a contract of insurance between you (the employer named in Item 1 of the Information Page) and us (the insurer named on the Information Page). *The only agreements relating to this insurance are stated in this policy. The terms of this policy may not be changed or waived except by endorsement issued by us to be part of this policy.*

I've placed the last two sentences of this provision in italics (even though the policy itself does not) because these sentences actually set forth a part of this contract that is very important, something sometimes deliberately contravened by insurance companies. In the section of this book about loss-sensitive rating plans, we reviewed how some insurance companies have issued separate side agreements that change the way the premium is computed.

If these side agreements contain provisions that change what the policy itself says about the computation of premiums, and if those side agreements are not actually endorsed onto the policy itself, then the insurance company has violated this provision of the policy.

If the terms of the side agreement produce higher premiums than those called for under the terms of the policy itself, and if such a side agreement is not actually endorsed onto the policy, you as the policyholder have the right to insist that the insurance company compute your premiums per the terms of the policy itself. Of course, your insurance company may well not be too happy about such an insistence, so you may need to reserve such insistence only for circumstances when you are prepared to end your relationship with that insurer. In the end, you may need to file a complaint with your state insurance regulator or even go to court, to insist that your premium be computed per the terms of the policy.

The insurance company will, in all likelihood, assert that you entered into a separate contract (the side agreement) that they have the right to enforce. So this isn't an arguments that you want to get into lightly. To avoid such disputes, you may want to make sure that any separate agreement that your insurance company wants you to sign is in fact consistent with the terms of the policy and is endorsed onto the policy itself. If your insurer is not willing to comply, it may well be a warning sign that your insurance company is trying to sell you a rating plan that has not actually been authorized by regulators.

These aren't the only important sections of the workers' compensation policy, of course. Each and every provision of the policy can be important. But the sections annotated above are those that are often the subject of questions by employers or disputes between employers and insurers. The entire standard workers' compensation insurance policy is reproduced on the following pages, for your review and reference.

WORKERS' COMPENSATION AND EMPLOYER'S LIABILITY INSURANCE POLICY

In return for the payment of the premium and subject to all terms of this policy, we agree with you as follows:

GENERAL SECTION

A. The Policy

This policy includes at its effective date the Information Page and all endorsements and schedules listed there. It is a contract of insurance between you (the employer named in Item I of the Information Page) and us (the insurer named on the Information page). The only agreements relating to this insurance are stated in this policy. The terms of this policy may not be changed or waived except by endorsement issued by us to be part of this policy.

B. WHO IS INSURED

You are insured if you are an employer named in Item 1 of the Information page. If that employer is a partnership, and if you are one of its partners, you are insured, but only in your capacity as an employer of the partnership's employees.

C. Workers Compensation Law

Workers' Compensation Law means the workers or workmen's compensation law and occupational disease law of each state or territory named in Item 3.A of the Information Page. It includes any amendments to that law which are in effect during the policy period. It does not include any federal occupational disease law or the provisions of any law that provide nonoccupational disability benefits.

D. State

State means any state of the United States of America, and the District of Columbia.

E. Locations

This policy covers all of your workplaces listed in Items 1 or 4 of the Information Page; and it covers all other workplaces in Item 3.A. states unless you have other insurance or are self-insured for such workplaces.

PART ONE
WORKERS COMPENSATION INSURANCE

A. How This Insurance Applies

This workers compensation insurance applies to bodily injury by accident or bodily injury by disease. Bodily injury includes resulting death.

1. Bodily Injury by accident must occur during the policy period.
2. Bodily injury by disease must be caused or aggravated by the conditions of your employment. The employee's last day of last exposure to the conditions causing or aggravating such bodily injury by disease must occur during the policy period.

B. We Will Pay

We will pay promptly when due the benefits required of you by the workers' compensation law.

C. We Will Defend

We have the right and duty to defend at our expense any claim, proceeding or Suit against you for benefits payable by this insurance. We have the right to investigate and settle these claims, proceedings or suits.

We have no duty to defend a claim, proceeding or suit that is not covered by this insurance.

D. We Will Also Pay

We will also pay these costs, in addition to other amounts payable under this insurance, as part of any claim, proceeding or suit we defend:

1. Reasonable expenses incurred at our request, but not loss of earnings;
2. Premiums for bonds to release attachments and for appeal bonds in bond amounts up to the amount payable under this insurance;
3. Litigation costs taxed against you;
4. Interest on a judgment as required by law until we offer the amount due under this insurance; and
5. Expenses we incur.

E. Other Insurance

We will not pay more than our share of benefits and costs covered by this insurance and other insurance or self-insurance. Subject to any limits of liability that may apply, all shares will be equal until the loss is paid. If any insurance or self-insurance is exhausted, the shares of all remaining insurance will be equal until the loss is paid.

F. Payments You Must Make

You are responsible for any payments in excess of the benefits regularly provided by the workers' compensation law including those required because:

1. Of your serious and willful misconduct;
2. You knowingly employ an employee in violation of law;
3. You fail to comply with a health or safety law or regulation; or
4. You discharge, coerce or otherwise discriminate against any employee in violation of the workers compensation law.

If we make any payments in excess of the benefits regularly provided by the workers' compensation law on your behalf, you will reimburse us promptly.

G. Recovery From Others

We have your rights, and the rights of persons entitled to the benefits of this insurance, to recover our payments from anyone liable for the injury. You will do everything necessary to protect those rights for us and to help us enforce them.

H. Statutory Provisions

These statements apply where they are required by law.

1. As between an injured worker and us, we have notice of the injury when you have notice.
2. Your default or the bankruptcy or insolvency of you, or your estate will not relieve us of our duties under this insurance after an injury occurs.
3. We are directly and primarily liable to any person entitled to the benefits payable by this insurance. Those persons may enforce our duties; so may an agency authorized by law. Enforcement may be against us or against you and us.

4. Jurisdiction over you is jurisdiction over us for purposes of the workers' compensation law. We are bound by decisions against you under that law, subject to the provisions of this policy that are not in conflict with that law.
5. This insurance conforms to the parts of the workers compensation law that apply to:
   a. Benefits payable by this insurance;
   b. Special taxes, payments into security or other special funds, and assessments payable by us under that law.
6. Terms of this insurance that conflict with the workers' compensation law are changed by this statement to conform to that law.

Nothing in these paragraphs relieves you of your duties under this policy.

PART TWO
EMPLOYERS' LIABILITY INSURANCE

A. How This Insurance Applies
This employers' liability insurance applies to bodily injury by accident or bodily injury by disease. Bodily injury includes resulting death.
1. The bodily injury must arise out of and in the course of the injured employee's employment by you.
2. The employment must be necessary or incidental to your work in a state or territory listed in Item 3.A of the Information page.
3. Bodily Injury by accident must occur during the policy period.
4. Bodily injury by disease must be caused or aggravated by the conditions of your employment. The employee's last day of last exposure to the conditions causing or aggravating such bodily injury by disease must occur during the policy period.
5. If you are sued, the original suit and any related legal actions for damages for bodily injury by accident or by disease must be brought in the United States of America, its territories or possessions or Canada.

B. We Will Pay

We will pay all sums you legally must pay as damages because of bodily injury to your employees, provided the bodily injury is covered by this Employer's Liability Insurance.

The damages we will pay, where recovery is permitted by law, include damages:

1. For which you are liable to a third party by reason of a claim or suit against you by that third party to recover the damages claimed against such third party as a result of injury to your employee;
2. For care and loss of services; and
3. For consequential bodily injury to a spouse, child, parent, brother or sister of the injured employee; provided that these damages are the direct result of bodily injury that arises out of and in the course of the injured employee's employment by you; and
4. Because of bodily injury to your employee that arises out of and in the course of employment, claimed against you in a capacity other than as employer.

C. Exclusions

This insurance does not cover:

1. Liability assumed under a contract. This exclusion does not apply to a warranty that your work will be done in a workmanlike manner;
2. Punitive or exemplary damages because of bodily injury to an employee employed in violation of law;
3. Bodily injury to an employee while employed in violation of law with your actual knowledge or the actual knowledge of any of your executive officers;
4. Any obligation imposed by a workers' compensation , occupational disease, unemployment compensation, or disability benefits law, or any similar law;
5. Bodily injury intentionally caused or aggravated by you;
6. Bodily injury occurring outside the United States of America, its territories or possessions, and Canada. This exclusion does not apply to bodily injury to a citizen or resident of the United States of America or Canada who is temporarily outside these countries;
7. Damages arising out of coercion, criticism, demotion, evaluation, reassignment, discipline, defamation,

harassment, humiliation, discrimination against or termination of any employee, or any personnel practices, policies, acts or omissions;

8. Bodily injury to any person in work subject to the Longshore and Harbor Workers' Compensation Act 933 USC Sections 901-950), the Nonappropriated Fund Instrumentalities Act (5 USC Sections 8171-8173), the Outer Continental Shelf Lands Act (43 USC Sections 1331-1356) the Defense Base Act 942 USC Sections 1651-1654), the Federal Coal Mine Health and Safety Act of 1969 (30 USC Sections 901-942), any other federal workers' or workmen's compensation law or other federal occupational disease law, or any amendment to these laws;

9. Bodily injury to any person in work subject to the Federal Employers' Liability Act (45 USC Sections 51-60), any other federal laws obligating an employer to pay damages to an employee due to bodily injury arising out of or in the course of employment, or any amendments to those laws;

10. Bodily injury to a master or member of the crew of any vessel;

11. Fines or penalties imposed for violation of federal or state law;

12. Damages payable under the Migrant and Seasonal Agricultural Worker Protection Act (29 USC Sections 1801-1872) and under any other federal law awarding damages for violation of those laws or regulations issued thereunder, and any amendments to those laws.

D. We Will Defend

We have the right and duty to defend, at our expense, any claim, proceeding or suit against for damages payable by this insurance. We have the right to investigate and settle these claims, proceedings and suits.

We have no duty to defend a claim, proceeding or suit that is not covered by this insurance. We have no duty to defend or continue defending after we have paid our applicable limit of liability under this insurance.

E. We Will Also Pay

We will also pay these costs, in addition to other amounts payable under this insurance, as part of any claim, proceeding or suit we defend:

1. Reasonable expenses incurred at our request, but not loss of earnings;
2. Premiums for bonds to release attachments and for appeal bonds in bond amounts up to the limit of our liability under this insurance;
3. Litigation costs taxed against you;
4. Interest on a judgment as required by law until we offer the amount due under this insurance; and
5. Expenses we incur.

F. Other Insurance

We will not pay more than our share of damages and costs covered by this insurance and other insurance or self-insurance. Subject to any limits of liability that apply, all shares will be equal until the loss is paid. If any insurance or self-insurance is exhausted, the shares of all remaining insurance and self-insurance will be equal until the loss is paid.

G. Limits of Liability

Our liability to pay for damages is limited. Our limits of liability are shown in Item 3.B. of the Information page. They apply as explained below.

1. Bodily Injury by Accident. The limit shown for "bodily injury by accident-each accident" is the most we will pay for all damages covered by this insurance because of bodily injury to one or more employees in any one accident. A disease is not bodily injury by accident unless it results directly from bodily injury by accident.
2. Bodily Injury by Disease. The limit shown for "bodily injury by disease-policy limit" is the most we will pay for all damages covered by this insurance and arising out of bodily injury by disease, regardless of the number of employees who sustain bodily injury by disease. The limit shown for "bodily injury by disease-each employee" is the most we will pay for all damages because of bodily injury by disease to any one employee. Bodily injury by disease does not include disease that results directly from a bodily injury by accident.

3. We will not pay any claims for damages after we have paid the applicable limit of our liability under this insurance.

H. Recovery From Others

We have your rights, and the rights of persons entitled to the benefits of this insurance, to recover our payments from anyone liable for the injury. You will do everything necessary to protect those rights for us and to help us enforce them.

I. Actions Against Us

There will be no right of action against us under this insurance unless:

1. You have complied with all the terms of this policy; and
2. The amount you owe has been determined with our consent or by actual trial and final judgment.

Part Three
Other States Insurance

A. How This Insurance Applies

1. This other states insurance applies only if one or more states are shown in Item 3.0 of the Information Page.
2. If you begin work in any one of those states after the effective date of this policy and are not insured or are not self-insured for such work, all provisions of the policy will apply as though that state were listed in Item 3.A of the Information page.
3. We will reimburse you for the benefits required by the workers compensation law of that state if we are not permitted to pay the benefits directly to persons entitled to them.
4. If you have work on the effective date of this policy in any state not listed in Item 3.A of the Information Page, coverage will not be afforded for that state unless we are notified within thirty days.

B. Notice

Tell us at once if you begin work in any state listed in Item 3.C of the Information Page.

Part Four
Your Duties if Injury Occurs

Tell us at once if injury occurs that may be covered by this policy. Your duties are listed here.

1. Provide for immediate medical and other services required by the workers' compensation law.
2. Give us or our agent the names and addresses of the injured persons and of witnesses, and other information we may need.
3. Promptly give us all notices, demands and legal papers related to the injury, claim proceeding or suit.
4. Cooperate with us and assist us, as we may request in the investigation, settlement, or defense of any claim, proceeding or suit.
5. Do nothing after an injury occurs that would interfere with our right to recover from others.
6. Do not voluntarily make payments, assume obligations or incur expenses, except at your own cost.

Part Five-Premium

A. Our Manuals

All premium for this policy will be determined by our manuals of rules, rates, rating plans and classifications. We may change our manuals and apply the changes to this policy if authorized by law or a governmental agency regulating this insurance.

B. Classifications

Item 4 of the Information page shows the rate and premium basis for certain business or work classifications. These classifications were assigned based on an estimate of the exposures you would have during the policy period. If your actual exposures are not properly described by those classifications, we will assign proper classifications, rates and premium basis by endorsement to this policy.

C. Remuneration

Premium for each work classification is determined by multiplying a rate times a premium basis. Remuneration is the most common premium basis. The premium basis includes payroll and all other remuneration paid or payable during the policy period for the services of:

1. All your officers and employees engaged in work covered by this policy; and

2. All other persons engaged in work that could make us liable under part One (workers' compensation insurance) of this policy. If you do not have payroll records for these persons, the contract price for their services and materials may be used as the premium basis. This paragraph 2 will not apply if you give us proof that the employers of these persons lawfully secured their workers' compensation obligations.

D. Premium Payments

You will pay all premium when due. You will pay the premium even if part or all of a workers' compensation law is not valid.

E. Final Premium

The premium shown on the Information Page, schedules, and endorsements is an estimate. The final premium will be determined after this policy ends by using the actual, not the estimated, premium basis and the proper classifications and rates that lawfully apply to the business and work covered by this policy. If the final premium is more than the premium you paid to us, you must pay us the balance. If it is less, we will refund the balance to you. The final premium will not be less than the highest minimum premium for the classifications covered by this policy.

If this policy is canceled, final premium will be determined in the following way unless our manuals provide otherwise:
1. If we cancel, final premium will be calculated pro rata based on the time this policy was in force. Final premium will not be less than the pro rata share of the minimum premium.
2. If you cancel, final premium will be more than pro rata; it will be based on the time this policy was in force, and increased by our short-rate cancelation table and procedure. Final premium will not be less than the minimum premium.

F. Records

You will keep records of information needed to compute premium. You will provide us with copies of those records when we ask for them.

G. Audit

You will let us examine and audit all your records that relate to this policy. These records include ledgers, journals, registers, vouchers, contracts, tax reports, payroll and disbursement records, and programs for storing and retrieving data. We may conduct the audits during regular business hours during the policy period and within three years after the policy period ends. Information developed by audit will be used to determine final premium. Insurance rate service organizations have the same rights we have under this provision.

Part Six-Conditions
A. Inspections

We have the right, but are not obliged to inspect your workplaces at any time. Our inspections are not safety inspections. They relate only to the insurability of the workplaces and the premiums to be charged. We may give you reports on the conditions we find. We may also recommend changes. While they may help reduce losses, we do not undertake to perform the duty of any person to provide for the health or safety of your employees or the public. We do not warrant that your workplaces are safe or healthful or that they comply with laws, regulations, codes or standards. Insurance rate service organizations have the same rights we have under this provision.

B. Long-Term Policy

If the policy period is longer than one year and sixteen days, all provisions of this policy will apply as though a new policy were issued on each annual anniversary that this policy is in force.

C. Transfer of Your Rights and Duties

Your rights or duties under this policy may not be transferred without our written consent.

If you die and we receive notice within thirty days after your death, we will cover your legal representative as insured.

D. Cancelation

1. You may cancel this policy. You must mail or deliver advance written notice to us stating when the cancelation is to take effect.

2. We may cancel this policy. We must mail or deliver to you not less than ten days' advance written notice when stating when the cancelation is to take effect. Mailing that notice to you at your mailing address shown in Item 1. Of the Information Page will be sufficient to prove notice.
3. The policy period will end on the day and hour stated in the cancelation notice.
4. Any of these provisions that conflict with a law that controls the cancelation of the insurance in this policy is changed by this statement to comply with that law.

E. Sole Representative

The insured first named in Item 1 of the Information page will act on behalf of all insureds to change this policy, receive return premium, and give or receive notice of cancelation.

APPENDIX E

DEALING WITH INSURANCE COMPANIES

If and when you identify some error in computing your Workers Compensation insurance charges, you'll need to work with your insurance company to get it corrected. This can be a process somewhat analogous to Alexander the Great and the Gordian Knot. You may be tempted to consider Alexander's solution to the problem, which was just to slash the knot with his sword, but you will probably find that insurance disputes can often be resolved without resort to cutlery. Here are some tactical suggestions, gleaned from years of experience in dealing with insurance companies on behalf of clients.

Document Everything
Put as much of your communication with the insurer in writing as possible. Keep everything in one single file where you can keep it all together, separate from other insurance documents. If you communicate by e-mail, print out all such electronic communications and keep these hard copies in the file. If you have phone conversations with insurance company personnel, document these in detail by noting whom you spoke with, when, and what was said. Make sure you get the full names of everyone you speak with and note it in the file.

Pay Undisputed Premium
If you feel an error in computation has increased the premium improperly and you haven't yet paid the bill, make sure you pay the undisputed portion of any additional premium owed (if any). So if the insurance company has figured the total audited premium at $125,000, and you already paid $75,000 in during the term of the policy, the insurer will be billing you for $50,000 in additional premium. But if you find once the error is corrected you would only

owe a total of $100,000, pay the undisputed $25,000 portion of the additional premium and explain in writing why you have not paid the remaining $25,000.

Paying the undisputed portion of any additional premium puts in a much stronger position if you have to turn to state insurance regulators for assistance, and preserves your rights under NCCI rules to prevent cancellation of your subsequent policy while an appeal is pursued.

Keep the Agent/Broker in the Loop

Assuming that the agent or broker for the disputed policy is still your agent, you want to keep him or her informed of everything you do. The insurance producer may want you to leave everything to him or her, and this can be useful to a point. But if the producer cannot get the insurance company to revise the audit, and you still feel you are correct, don't just accept the producer's assurances that he or she has done everything that can be done. You have the right to deal directly with the insurance company's audit personnel if you have need. But make sure to keep all communications with auditors and other insurance company personnel professional, no matter how tempting it may be to get upset and level accusations at them of wrongdoing or incompetence. Such accusations are counter-productive, in my experience.

Sometimes Alexander's Approach Can Work

If patient and professional discussion and communication just don't make any difference to your insurance company, yet you're convinced you're right, it may be time to stop trying to unravel the knot and pull out your sword. You can do this by filing a complaint with your state insurance regulators. Every state insurance regulatory agency (or monopolistic state fund) has a way for consumers to file formal complaints against an insurer. Take a look at the web site for your state insurance regulators to see what procedure they have in place for this. If you can't get satisfaction there, but are still convinced your insurance company is wrong, you may want to contact an independent consultant specializing in handling such matters. You may also want to consult an attorney (particularly if there are significant sums at stake).

NCCI Appeals Boards

States that use the manual rules of NCCI have all set up appeals boards to hear disputes over classifications, experience modifiers, and payroll audits. These are relatively informal hearings, but can often provide relief from insurance company errors. To find out about your state's appeal process, contact your state insurance regulators.

If a Collection Agency Gets Involved

Often, the staff of an insurance company will forward disputed audits to outside collection agencies once they perceive that they're not being paid what they think they're owed in a reasonable time frame. And collection agencies get paid for being fairly tough in handling collections. But in my experience, even tough collection agencies respect legitimate audit disputes, if you send documentation to them that the matter has been sent for review to a legitimate third party such as an insurance regulator or appeal board. So if your account gets turned over to a collection agency, send the agency copies of all correspondence with the insurer and with the third parties, and ask them to suspect collection efforts until the dispute is resolved. In my experience, collection agencies will respect such requests.

Pursue Appeals

As you may have observed from reading some of the case histories in this book, it can sometimes take a very persistent effort to finally resolve a premium dispute successfully. Often, we've seen clients who were turned down initially, only to ultimately prevail by continuing to pursue the matter higher up the regulatory food chain. So just because an NCCI inspection doesn't yield the desired results, don't necessarily roll over and pay the bill. Do your homework and gather your documentation, if needed. If you're still sure you're correct then spend the time and effort to take the matter to the next level. Often, such efforts pay off.

APPENDIX F

REPORTING CHANGES IN OWNERSHIP

Under the rules developed by the National Council on Compensation Insurance, Inc. ("NCCI") and most other rating bureaus, separate business entities that share a sufficient degree of common ownership are supposed to be combined together for computing an experience modification factor. (Pennsylvania is a notable exception to this—their rules give employers a choice about combining entities with common ownership.)

Employers need to be careful about this point, because the insurance system often doesn't catch changes in ownership very well on its own. The NCCI rules impose responsibility on the policyholder (that is, the employer) to inform them of changes in ownership. To avoid accusations of impropriety, make sure you report changes in ownership promptly. Your insurance agency can help you to fill out the appropriate NCCI form, the ERM-14. (It's called an ERM form because it's part of the *Experience Rating Manual* created by NCCI.)

Employers need to be aware of how ownership can affect experience modifiers, because if the information used to calculate your modifier is out of date you might end up with a modifier higher than it really should be and, thus, end up paying premiums higher than you should.

An employer could also leave himself open to charges of fraud if he fails to report changes in ownership. If your failure to report accurate ownership information produces a modifier lower than it really should be, this could be viewed as a deliberate insurance fraud, a felony in many states. And as we discussed earlier, many prosecutors are making such prosecutions a higher priority than ever before. Insurance companies are well aware of this trend, and are often eager to encourage prosecutors to look at filing criminal charges when the insurance company feels an employer has not exhibited good faith.

But keep in mind that reporting accurate ownership information can cut the other way also—it often lowers experience modifiers.

Because the insurance system relies on employers to report changes in ownership, and many employers are unaware of this obligation or how ownership impacts experience modifiers, mistakes in this area are not uncommon.

NCCI rules regarding combination of entities are as follows.
Business entities are supposed to be combined for experience rating if they have more than 50 percent common ownership. That is, if the same person, group of people, or corporation owns more than 50 percent of each of the business entities in question, then those entities are required to have their experience modifier calculated on a combined basis.

Entities are also required to be combined if one entity owns more than 50 percent of another entity that in turn owns more than 50 percent of another entity. In such a case, all of these business entities would be combined.

A number of years ago, NCCI rules were different. Then, when ownership changed, the experience modifier of a company would re-set back to 1.00. Loss and payroll data from policies under the new ownership would then be used to calculate an experience modifier for the company, but data from policies under old ownership would not be used. But this rule changed long ago, although some business managers (and even insurance producers of a certain age) sometimes aren't aware of the change in rules.

Under current NCCI rules, an experience modifier re-sets to 1.00 only if a change in ownership is accompanied by a change in operations sufficient to qualify the company for a different governing classification. This is relatively rare.

But keep in mind that when one company acquires another company that already has its own modifier, a new modifier is supposed to be calculated on a combined basis. So acquiring an existing company can change the modifier that applies to both operations.

For example, if Midwest Masonry has an experience modifier of 1.04, but gets purchased by a larger company known as Aggregate Construction Enterprises, that has a modifier of .93, then under the rules, a new modifier should be calculated that would apply to both Midwest and Aggregate, even if they are on separate policies with different insurance companies.

This new combined modifier would be calculated based on the combined past loss and payroll data of the two companies, so it might come out to something like a .94. It depends to a great degree on the relative size of the two companies. If Aggregate is a lot larger than Midwest, the loss and payroll data for the former will predominate in the calculation because of their larger payrolls. So in such a case the relatively poor loss history of Midwest (with a 1.04 modifier) would now be part of a much larger calculation, so the impact on the modifier would be diluted.

Most, but not all, entities that have common ownership get combined for experience rating. A joint venture, for instance, doesn't impact the modifiers of the members of the joint venture. A separate modifier is calculated for the joint venture based on the modifiers of the members. So if Midwest Masonry and Aggregate Construction Enterprises formed a joint venture called Builders Two, the modifier used on the policy for Builders Two would be an amalgam of the modifiers for Midwest and Aggregate. But Midwest and Aggregate would keep their own separate modifiers on their own policies, and the losses that happen under the separate Builders Two policy would not be used on future modifiers of Midwest or Aggregate.

Also, keep mind that a few states don't integrate rating data for experience modifiers. California, Delaware, Michigan, New Jersey, and Pennsylvania calculate "stand alone" modifiers for companies that work within their borders. Same applies for monopoly state funds.

So if Midwest Masonry got acquired by Aggregate Construction Enterprises, but Midwest works only in Michigan while Aggregate works in California, Arizona, Washington (state), New York, and Illinois, then Midwest would continue to have its own separate Michigan modifier calculated by the Michigan rating bureau. This would be based only on Michigan loss and payroll data.

Aggregate would have a separate California modifier for its operations there, and a separate interstate modifier calculated by NCCI for Aggregate's operations in NCCI states. Arizona and Illinois and NCCI states, while New York, though using an independent rating bureau, integrates rating data with NCCI.

Because Washington state is a monopoly fund, loss and payroll from there would also be segregated and only applied in a Washington-only modifier.

To complicate matters even further, sometimes NCCI will combine entities that don't strictly meet the common ownership definitions in the manual. That's because NCCI rules also allow for combination of entities that share common "physical assets," although these aren't spelled out. So sometimes disputes arise over whether or not entities should be properly combined. NCCI in the past has tended to make these decisions unilaterally, defining 'assets" rather broadly to include customers and employees. These can often be successfully disputed using appeals board mechanisms or through hearings at state insurance regulators.

APPENDIX G

CAPTIVES AND RENT-A CAPTIVES

Companies that pay $500,000 or more per year for Workers Compensation have likely received proposals that involve use of a "captive" insurance company. Once captives were the exclusive province of very large corporations, but newer developments in this field mean that much smaller employers may now also be offered Workers Compensation programs that utilize a captive.

Simply put, a captive insurance company is one that is owned by the insured. Captives are often established, or domiciled, outside the U.S. But some states such as Vermont have also passed statutes and regulations to facilitate captives being domiciled within their jurisdictions.

Here are the locations that domicile the most captives, per 2007 figures.

Domicile Number of Captives
Bermuda 987
Cayman Islands 733
Vermont 542
British Virgin Islands 380
Guernsey 378
Barbados 300
Luxembourg 210
Dublin 208
Turks & Caicos 165
Isle of Man 160

Setting up your own captive insurer can be a fairly complex task, suitable only for very large employers. But recent years have seen significant growth in some versions of captives that are viable alternatives for some other companies that would not be in a position to consider a traditional captive.

Rather than one single employer establishing its own captive, an association of businesses may create a captive insurance company that is available to members of the association. Or a group of companies in the same or similar fields may band together to form a captive.

Another variant is an "agency captive" where a particular insurance agency establishes a captive that it can then make available to its clients. And a more recent development has been that of "rent-a-captives" wherein a captive is created by a sponsor and made available to various qualifying employers. These multiple employers typically would not find the creation of their own captive a viable option, but by participating in the rent-a-captive they can obtain many of the benefits of a captive while avoiding the expense and difficulties involved in creating their own.

Because states only allow insurance companies that meet specific criteria to write Workers Compensation insurance, captives often have to resort to fronting arrangements. A fronting company would be an insurer that is approved to write Workers Compensation insurance in various states. The fronting company would agree to issue polices to owners of the captive, and then obtain reinsurance from the captive for all claims. The fronting company earns a fee, and the captive gets to provide valid Workers Compensation insurance via the front.

Benefits of a Captive

The essential benefit of a captive insurer is that it allows the owner/policyholder to obtain many of the benefits other insurers utilize, such as reinsurance markets and investment income. A captive can also provide coverage that is difficult or prohibitively expensive in traditional markets for certain kinds of employers. Captive arrangements can also smooth out the swings in insurance pricing that are a feature of commercial insurance markets. Plus, the owners of a captive get to participate in the capital growth that can accrue to a well-run insurance company.

The deductibility of insurance premiums paid to captives has been an area of some controversy. IRS rulings on the subject have changed over time, sometimes dramatically, and court decisions have also served to alter the deductibility of captive insurance premiums. As of this writing, it appears that premiums paid to captives are usually deductible, but this should not be taken as a hard and fast rule. The best advice is to consult a tax professional on issues pertaining to current rules on this subject.

Captive insurance programs can be a valuable tool for some employers, but the complexity of the issue demands that employers do their homework before entering into such an arrangement. Captive insurance programs normally make sense only when utilized over the long term.

APPENDIX H

WHEN AN INJURY HAPPENS

Make sure your supervisory people know what needs to be done when a workplace injury is reported to them.

- Provide aid to the injured party. If the injury is serious, get medical help as quickly as possible. Call an ambulance if necessary. Make sure your people know what medical care providers are closest for emergency response. For less urgent situations, work with your insurer to identify preferred local providers of medical care and make sure your people have this information.
- Accompany the injured worker to medical facilities.
- Notify family of the injured worker if the injury is serious.
- Report the incident to appropriate parties at your company.
- Assign a responsible person within your company to follow up on the claim.
- Reassure the injured worker and family that proper insurance coverage is in place and that your firm will make sure that the insurance company responds appropriately.
- Let the employee and family know whom they should contact at your firm if there are any problems dealing with the insurance company.
- Take written statements from any witnesses to the injury and establish a file to maintain this documentation for later use by your insurer.
- Determine if any other workers may have been exposed to blood or other bodily fluids due to workplace injury

of another. Document this at time of occurrence and determine what state laws may apply regarding this workplace exposure and comply with any notification or testing requirements for those exposed workers. Make sure appropriate testing is done on a timely basis.

- Communicate closely with the insurer to maximize positive outcome for worker and minimize possible negative treatment of worker by insurer.
- Make sure initial benefits are paid on a timely basis by insurer.
- Communicate closely with the worker to identify any potential problems with the way the insurer is handling the matter and let the workers know about your efforts to address any problems.
- Consider obtaining an independent medical evaluation if needed.
- Work with the insurer to develop a return to work plan and/or light duty that may be available and appropriate for injured worker.
- Review the cause of injury with safety personnel (both in-house and from insurer) to learn from the occurrence and make changes as appropriate to reduce future exposures.

After proper care is provided to an injured worker, it is important to have procedures in place to gather the information that will be important in making sure the claim is handled properly. Here is the kind of information that needs to be gathered.

About the Worker:
- Name—including nicknames, maiden name if female, and previous names
- Address—current and previous (including how long at each address)
- Phone numbers—home and cell
- Social security and drivers license numbers
- Gender

- Date of birth
- Marital status
- Dependents and immediate family contact
- Non-relative contact
- Date of hire (and state hired in, if applicable)
- Job classification, if applicable (insurance classification or company classification)
- Vehicle information—make, model, year
- Interests and hobbies (these might have a bearing on some injuries that might be claimed as work related, but are really caused by leisure activities)
- How long a resident in the state

About the Injury
- Date, time, location, and where at workplace injury occurred
- Date of death (if applicable)
- State of injury
- Nature of injury (sprain, fracture, etc.)
- Body parts affected; any previous injury to the affected body parts
- Source of injury (machines, hand tools, buildings, etc.)
- Type of injury (fall, struck by object or vehicle, overexertion, repetitive motion trauma)
- Witness information
- Work process involved (lifting, carrying, etc.)
- To whom the injury was reported
- Who filled out the first report of injury
- When the injury was first reported

About the Claim
- Date notification was given to employer
- Who was notified, by whom
- Date the insurance was company notified
- Date the state agency was notified
- State case number
- Average weekly wage

- Benefit rate
- Healthcare givers providing services
- Costs of medical care provided
- Other benefits lost (did employer stop paying vacation, health benefits, etc.)
- Other benefits received
- Offset for other benefits
- Date disability started
- Date of first payment
- Projected return to work date
- Date case closed
- Date of maximum medical improvement
- Impairment rating
- Lost days
- Total benefits paid
- Reserves set by insurer
- Vocational rehabilitation activity
- Possibility of subrogation (is some third party responsible)
- Second injury fund potential

Oral Statement from Injured Worker

- Make sure all interviews with workers are done in a non-confrontational, non-adversarial manner.
- Make sure interviewer demonstrates concern and empathy with the worker.
- Allow the worker to talk, and make sure to listen.
- Reenact the accident with the worker.
- Check for any photos and/or a video of the accident that may exist.

Written Statement From Worker

- Note the location where the statement is taken.
- Let the employee write the statement himself when possible.
- The statement should be written in ink.
- Record the statement as soon as possible after the injury occurs.

- Make sure to note the workers pre-injury and post-injury actions.
- Get signatures of worker and any witnesses on the statement, if possible.
- Make sure the employee initials any changes made on the statement.
- Leave a copy of the statement with worker.
- Make sure the statement contains the date and time it was taken.

Oral Statement From Witnesses
- Note witnesses location at the time of injury.
- Record witnesses relationship to the injured worker.
- Interview witnesses individually.
- Make sure the statement is unrehearsed.

Written Statement From Witnesses
- Make sure the witness statement is recorded in ink.
- Record the witness statement as soon as possible after injury.
- Make sure the witness statement describes witness actions before, during, and after the injury.
- Make sure the witness signs the statement and initials any changes.
- Make sure the witness statement includes date and time it was created.
- Leave a copy of the statement with the witness.

If Litigation Occurs
- Note the defense attorney and law firm used by insurer.
- Note claimant attorney and law firm retained by worker.
- Document carefully the history of the dispute.
- Keep informed of any settlement discussions; make sure the insurer does not settle disputed claims too readily, to your detriment.